Borders & Boundaries

Borders & Boundaries
WOMEN IN INDIA'S PARTITION

Ritu Menon
&
Kamla Bhasin

Borders & Boundaries: Women in India's Partition
was first published in 1998 by
Kali for Women

This edition published by
Women Unlimited
(an associate of Kali for Women)
7/10, FF, Sarvapriya Vihar
New Delhi - 110016

www.womenunlimited.in

First paperback edition, 2000
Reprinted, 2004
Reprinted, 2007
Reprinted, 2011
Reprinted, 2017
Reprinted, 2018
Reprinted, 2022

ISBN: 978-81-86706-35-0

Cover design: Neelima Rao
Cover: Detail from Nilima Sheikh's *Traveller* (1998),
'Postcards from Umbria' series, 18 x 15 cm,
mixed tempera on vasli paper

Printed at Chaman Offset, New Delhi - 110002

To all those women
who survived Partition
and lived to tell the tale

Acknowledgements

This book was initially conceived of as a three country oral history of how women in Pakistan, India and erstwhile East Pakistan (Bangladesh) experienced the partition of India in 1947. We thought then, that this might be one way of crossing new borders and old boundaries, but for a variety of reasons (mainly to do with scope and scale) this plan had to be modified.

We would like, first of all, to acknowledge and thank all the women with whom we discussed this project even before it became one. Niru Dutt, who told us about the lady from Campbellpur, in 1984; Baljeet Mehra, who spoke with psychoanalytical insight about the trauma of dislocation among women, and of her experience of working with refugees at the Kingsway Camp in 1947; Nighat Said Khan, with whom we talked endlessly about how divisions of all kinds take place, and who agreed so readily to research the experience of Pakistani women in West Punjab and Sind—she has been a fellow traveller on this journey in more ways than one; Anis Haroon, whose own journey from Hyderabad in India to Karachi in Sind informed her understanding of Partition in special ways; Veena Das, who encouraged and supported the project from the very beginning; and Salma Sobhan, who would have collaborated on research in Bangladesh had we carried out the study as originally planned.

Amrita Chhachhi, Radhika Coomaraswamy, Malathi de Alwis, Kumari Jayawardena and Shahnaz Rouse, as activists who have been involved with the women's movement in South Asia and with whom we have, over the years, shared our common concerns regarding identity politics, ethnicity and the increasing chauvinism in our countries.

So many people helped in many ways and made our work

so satisfyiṅg that it just went on and on! First among them are the women who form the backbone of this book who welcomed us into their homes, were so generous with their time and memories and so obliging with our requests for more. Above all, however, it was the courage and dignity with which they lived that made the deepest impression on us. We cannot thank them enough for allowing us to enter their lives. In a way, this is their work as much as it is ours without, of course, the shortcomings. For those only we are responsible.

Among the wider circle of people we consulted whose advice and suggestions helped considerably, we would like to thank Gouri and Partha Chatterjee for helping us locate Pather Shesh, the last of the refugee colonies in Calcutta; Chitra Joshi for transcribing and translating one of our interviews; Kamini Karlekar for research assistance; Nayana Kathpalia for introducing us to Kamla Patel's writings and to Kammoben herself; Manoj Panjani for his help in archival research; Harish Puri for his help and generosity in Amritsar; and Ramesh and Arati Sharma for providing us with very useful information on, and contacts in, Karnal.

To a large number of friends and colleagues who helped us refine, revise, amend and modify the research as we went along, our sincere appreciation and gratitude; but especially to the following who read and re-read the many drafts and versions of our work, and made the kind of perceptive and thoughtful comments that are an author's lifeline. Paola Bacchetta, Amrita Basu, Patricia Jeffery and Kalpana Ram painstakingly read different sections of the manuscript and helped enormously in clarifying our presentation and analysis; Bina Agarwal, Zoya Hasan and Kumkum Sangari gave valuable suggestions on organizing the interviews and accompanying text. Thanks are due to the Nanditas (Gandhi and Shah), Malavika Karlekar and Pogey Menon for their close and careful reading of *Speaking for Themselves*; to Ratna, for being so meticulous; to Anu and Kamal for their enthusiasm, and to Mushir for his faith.

To O.P. for Anandgram and Baljit for Red Coombe, perfect writing environments. And to Anjali Sen, Director, National Gallery of Modern Art for all her help with "Mataji".

Finally, if it hadn't been for NORAD (the Norwegian Agency for Development Cooperation) which partially funded our research; Juhi Jain who keyed in and corrected tirelessly; and Gopalakrishnan who typeset, and noticed every slip-up there may have been neither beginning nor end to this project. Thanks and more are due to them all.

Contents

Preface

Partition.

For a long time, and certainly all the time that we were children, it was a word we heard every now and again uttered by some adult in conversation, sometimes in anger, sometimes bitterly, but mostly with sorrow, voice trailing off, a resigned shake of the head, a despairing flutter of the hands. All recollections were punctuated with "before Partition" or "after Partition", marking the chronology of our family history.

We learnt to recognize this in many ways, but always with a curious sense of detachment on our part. The determined set of my grandmother's mouth as she remembered walking out of our house in Lahore, without so much as a backward glance; her unwavering bias against "Mussalmans" and her extreme and vocal disapproval of my Muslim friends in college; the sweet nostalgia in my uncle's voice and eyes as he recalled Faiz and Firaq and Government College, and recoiled at the soulless Hindi that had displaced the supple and mellifluous Urdu of his romantic youth; the endless recreation by my mother and aunts of Anarkali and the Mall and Kinnaird and Lawrence Gardens and. . . Impatiently we would wander off, at ease and quite at home in an India-that-was-not-Lahore, unconcerned by how we came to be here at all. Just as we hadn't known British Rule so, too, we didn't know Partition—and Pakistan was another country, anyway. What did we really have to do with it?

How effortlessly does history sometimes manage to conceal our past from us. Growing up in independent India, glorying in a freedom gained through non-violence, our gift to liberation struggles everywhere, everything that happened pre-1947 was safely between the covers of our history books. Comfortably distant, undeniably laid to rest. Swiftly we drew the outlines of our maps—India, West Pakistan, East Pakistan, the Himalayas, Kash-

mir (the line wavered a bit there), Nepal. . . Then the rivers, c:ties, smaller towns. If we were required to, the climatic zones, the crops, the rainfall, everything in its place, each country neatly labelled. So, too, the litany of historic events and dates, the rise and fall of dynasties and destinies, culture, civilization, heroes and villains, martyrs and traitors. The rich tapestry unfurled to end at our tryst with destiny.

1984 changed all that. The ferocity with which Sikhs were killed in city after city in north India in the wake of Indira Gandhi's assassination, the confusion and shock that stunned us into disbelief and then into a terrible realization of what had happened, dispelled forever that false sense of security. Those who experienced the brutality and orchestrated fury of the attacks recalled that other cataclysmic moment in the country's recent past—a past they believed had been left behind. But here was Partition once more in our midst, terrifying for those who had passed through it in 1947. . . Yet this was our own country, our own people, our own home-grown violence. Who could we blame now?

It seemed during those days and weeks and months of trying to come to terms with what had happened, that it was no longer possible to think of Partition as something that had occurred in another country, that belonged to time past. Indeed, it seemed that we could hardly comprehend what was in our midst now without going back to what had transpired then, without excavating memory, ransacking history.

How do we know Partition except through the many ways in which it is transmitted to us, in its many representations: political, social, historical, testimonial, literary, documentary, even communal. We know it through national and family mythologies, through collective and individual memory. Partition, almost uniquely, is the one event in our recent history in which familial recall and its encoding are a significant factor in any general reconstruction of it. In a sense, it is the collective memory of thousands of displaced families on both sides of the border that have imbued a rather innocuous word—partition— with its dreadful meaning: a people violently displaced, a country divided. Partition: a metaphor for irreparable loss.

As we travelled from place to place speaking to men and women, *we carried with us not only their individual memories but, in an unexpected twist, a "memory" of undivided India. In Amritsar we felt a kind of so-near-and-yet-so-far-ness about not being able to cross over to Lahore. Or, in Lahore, not being able to visit Sheikhupura or Mianwali, so vivid now from so many memories, not our own. This was only partly a result of listening to stories about old, old friendships and, yes, old enmities and prejudices, too. It was also a kind of rekindling of personal memory which made me locate my grandparents' home on Nisbet Road in Lahore where I, alone of all my siblings, had not been born. The impatience with memory that had marked my childhood and adolescence was replaced by something so complex that it is difficult to unravel. In Lahore, forty years after Partition, I experienced such a shock of recognition that it unsettled me. These were not places I had known or streets I had walked, they were not the stuff of "my" memories. I resisted going to Sacred Heart Convent, to Kinnaird, Anarkali, Mayo Gardens, in an attempt to dispel memory. It came flooding in.*

At night, till two or three or four in the morning I would talk with friends whose families had come (gone?) to Pakistan from Rampur, Delhi, Aligarh, Hyderabad, Lucknow. As we talked we resurrected so many memories that we found ourselves interrupting each other, often anticipating what was about to be said so that the outlines became blurred again. We had to remind ourselves that we "belonged" to two different countries now. Yet, what were we remembering? None of us was old enough to have experienced Partition at first hand or to have grown up in anything other than two separate nations. So it wasn't nostalgia. And no one wanted to return to the past. But remembering enabled us to approach the fact of Partition together, yet separately, to talk about our families, our countries, our histories and, slowly, our identities. Carefully, warily even, we spoke about religion and conflict, about prejudice and, remembering, found we had to consciously recall the parting of ways in order not to misunderstand it. To forget for a while, our family and national mythologies.

Through those seemingly endless conversations that resumed at odd times—walking through Anarkali; in the middle of Tariq Ali's film on Partition; late at night, almost asleep, feeling sud-

denly "homesick" for places we had left behind—we learnt to accept the complicated legacy of division and creation on either side of the border. There have been many breaks in the conversation since then, many silences; some things we understand better, others we mistrust more deeply. Yet, years later, it seems to me that this is one conversation that can have no closure, one memory that refuses to go away.

R.M.

Speaking for Themselves

Partition History, Women's Histories

I

As an event of shattering consequence, Partition retains its pre-eminence even today, despite two wars on our borders and wave after wave of communal violence. It marks a watershed as much in people's consciousness as in the lives of those who were uprooted and had to find themselves again, elsewhere; indeed it sometimes seems as if two quite distinct, rather than concurrent, events took place at independence, and that Partition and its effects are what have lingered in collective memory. Each new eruption of hostility or expression of difference swiftly recalls that bitter and divisive erosion of social relations between Hindus, Muslims and Sikhs, and each episode of brutality is measured against what was experienced then. The rending of the social and emotional fabric that took place in 1947 is still far from mended.

There is no dearth of written material on the Partition of India: official records, documents, private papers, agreements and treaties, political histories, analyses, a few reminiscences. A vast amount of newspaper reportage and reams of government information exist on the resettlement and rehabilitation of refugees from Punjab and Bengal; on negotiations between India and Pakistan, on the transfer of power and the division of assets; and there are hundreds of pages of Parliamentary debates on the myriad issues confronting both countries and both governments. Nationalist historiography has generally seen Partition as the unfortunate outcome of sectarian and separatist politics, and as a tragic accompaniment to the exhilaration and promise of a freedom fought for with courage and valour. Historical analyses over the last three or four decades, however, have uncovered the processes and strategies that led to the successful manipulation of Muslim perception in favour of a separate homeland, based on ineluctable differences between Hindus and Muslims. Although, as Mushirul Hasan has argued, the two-nation theory ". . . hardly reflected the consciousness of a community,"[1] it is one of the abiding conundrums of Indian independence that a partition that seemed impossible and remote as late as 1946 was, one year later, presented as the "logical" resolution of the incompatibility of Muslim political destiny with Hindu majority power. A partition that was striking for its failure "to satisfy the interests of the very Muslims who are supposed to have demanded it,"[2] a division that was remarkable for having been decided almost in the blink of an eye.

As Partition historians have unravelled the complexity of the movement which culminated in the violent, fratricidal sundering of a country, earlier nationalist and separatist justifications of it have given way to more considered and careful analyses of how exactly religion became the determinant of nationality. When India was partitioned, some sixty million of her ninety-five million Muslims (one in four Indians) became Pakistanis; some thirty-five million stayed back in India, the largest number of Muslims in a non-Muslim state.

It is not our purpose here to review the wealth of historical writing on Partition,[3] but it may be worth recapitulating some key concerns raised by political historians, recently. It is evident that a combination of social, historical and political factors were responsible for the simultaneous division of India and creation of Pakistan. The two-nation theory, it is generally agreed, was put forward as an ideological counterweight to secular nationalism, and derived a large part of its emotional appeal from a fear of political oblivion for Muslims once the British quit India. In the 1930s, however, and till the Second World War in fact, Chaudhry Rehmat Ali's scheme for a separate country was given short shrift, certainly by the All India Muslim League, and even by those like Mohammad Iqbal who made a case for provincial autonomy "within the body politic of India".[4] The slow process of mobilisation through the 1930s, characterised by a series of political negotiations via the Cripps Mission and the declaration of separate electorates for Hindus and Muslims, made of Jinnah's 1940 Lahore Resolution an even more dramatic declaration than it was:

> It is a dream that Hindus and Muslims can ever evolve a common nationality, and this misconception of one Indian nation has gone far beyond the limits. . . it will lead India to destruction if we fail to revise our notions in time. . . .
>
> Musalmans are a nation, according to any definition of a nation, and they must have their homeland, their territory and their state. We wish to live in peace and harmony with our neighbours as a free and independent people. We wish our people to develop to the fullest our spiritual, cultural, economic, social and political life in a way that we think best and in consonance with our own ideals. . . Ladies and Gentlemen, come forward as servants of Islam, organise the people economically, socially, educationally and politically and I am sure that you will be a power that will be accepted by everybody.[5]

Various accounts have highlighted the importance of Muslim mobilisation in the provinces to draw attention away from the high politics of League vs. Congress, with the British as dividers and rulers.[6] Others, notably Ayesha Jalal, have emphasized the crucial and decisive role of Jinnah, sole spokesman for a Muslim Homeland, in refusing to clarify the terms of, or elaborate upon, the Lahore Resolution, thus retaining a political advantage over the Congress. In her reading, it was this masterly understanding of *real politik* that pulled the carpet from under the feet of all other political players in favour of the AIML, despite its modest electoral performance. Others are more inclined to note the gradual crystallization of "Muslimness" among Indian Muslims, particularly in the 1930s and 1940s. Farzana Sheikh, for example, has argued that the evolution of "Muslim politics" was the culmination of a history of ideas that believed Muslims and Muslimness were fundamentally different from other political sensibilities, leading to the conviction that "Muslims ought to live under Muslim governments". "It is neither insignificant nor coincidental," she says, "that the manner in which Indian Muslims expressed their opposition to Western representation conformed closely to the political norms of Islam."[7] Francis Robinson carries this further by saying that there is indeed, a "fundamental connection" between Islamic traditions and political separation;[8] the logical outcome of this is two nations, based on religious difference, requiring physical separation (as opposed to federal autonomy) in order to realize their political and cultural aspirations.

This view runs counter to those who reject the notion of any objective differences between Hindus and Muslims *as Hindus and Muslims*; they look instead at the complex interplay of historical and political forces, class compulsions, the politics of power (both in the provinces and at the centre), and the pressure on the British to arrive at a negotiated settlement, that led to the rapid consolidation of strength by the Muslim League.[9] Though they are wary of the essential difference thesis, they do not wholly endorse the nationalist view either. The latter gives primacy to the composite nationality concept (its cruder articulation being "unity in diversity"), arguing for the cultural assimilation and social intermingling of Hindus and Muslims, but failing to recognize or pay enough attention to the genuine fears and cleavages among both. Mushirul Hasan, in his considerable and impressive oeuvre on the Partition, has meticulously delineated the progression of these prevailing and countervailing forces up until the elections of 1946 and Direct Action Day, after which, as he says, "the creation of Pakistan could not be denied".[10]

The abundance of political histories on Partition is almost equalled by the paucity of social histories of it. This is a curious and somewhat inexplicable circumstance: how is it that an event of such tremendous societal impact and importance has been passed over virtually in silence by the other social sciences? Why has there been such an absence of enquiry into its cultural, psychological and social ramifications? There can be no one answer to this question, but what seems to have stepped in, at least partly, to record the full horror of Partition is literature, the greater part of which was written in the period immediately following the division of the country. In one sense, it can be considered a kind of social history not only because it so approximates reality (what Alok Rai calls "a hypnotic, fascinated but also slavish imitation of reality"[11]) but because it is the only significant non-official *contemporary* record we have of the time, apart from reportage.

Popular sentiment and perception, at least as reflected in Partition literature particularly in Hindi, Urdu and Punjabi,[12] almost without exception registered the fact of Partition with despair or anger and profound unhappiness. "How many Pakistans?" asks one writer, while another says she felt as if a limb had been cut off. "Who killed India?" cries a third; "the Ganges in mourning", echoes a fourth. The futility and tragedy of demarcating boundaries, and the impossibility of dividing homes and hearts are the theme of story after story, as is the terrible violence that accompanied forced migration. Nowhere in the thousands of pages of fiction and poetry do we find even a glimmer of endorsement for the price paid for freedom, or admission that this "qurbani" (sacrifice) was necessary for the birth of two nations.[13] Rather, a requiem for lost humanity, for the love between communities, for shared joys and sorrows, a shared past. In the annals of Indian history, Partition is unique for the literary outpouring that it occasioned; Jason Francisco, reviewing recent anthologies of Partition writing—fiction, memoirs, poetry, testimonies, diaries, fragments—identifies three thematic concerns in these texts: rupture, protest and repair. These three motifs, he says, "form a natural response to Partition, a continuum from pain to healing"[14] and, via stories of repair, to the "healing power of memory". He is right in underlining the difficulty experienced in assimilating the barbarity and viciousness of Partition into normal life, and the essential problem of writing Partition as the human experience it was—namely that the overwhelming majority of its events went unrecorded, unverbalised; historical fiction, thus, "validates historical truth precisely in its power to represent".[15]

The importance of literary, autobiographical, oral historical and fragmentary material for an understanding of Partition has now been acknowledged by historians and others, concerned especially with the study of ethnic conflict
and violence[16] and, by extension, for the writing of history
itself. Official memory, after all, is only one of many memories. Different sorts of telling reveal different truths, and the
"fragment" is significant precisely because it is marginal
rather than mainstream, particular (even individual) rather
than general, and because it presents history from below.
The perspective such materials offer us can make for insights
into how histories are made and what gets inscribed, as well
as direct us to an alternative reading of the master narrative. At their most subversive, they may counter the rhetoric of nationalism itself; may even enable us to rewrite this
narrative as what Gyan Pandey calls "histories of confused
struggle and violence, sacrifice and loss, the tentative forging of new identities and loyalties".[17] Their recuperation is
important for yet another reason: without them, the myriad
individual and collective histories that simultaneously run
parallel to official accounts of historic events and are their
sequel, almost inevitably get submerged; with them may also
be submerged the countering of accepted—and acceptable—
versions, to be buried eventually in the rubble of history.

II

*"Itihas mein sirf naam aur tarikh sahi hoti hai,
baaqi nahin."**

— Gulab Pandit, social worker

To the best of our knowledge there has been no
feminist historiography of the partition of India, not even of
the compensatory variety.[18] Women historians have written on
this cataclysmic event but from within the parameters of the
discipline, and still well within the political frame. Even
accounts of women's contribution to the freedom movement

* "In history books, only the names and dates are correct, not the rest."

have tended to be male-centred—women do figure, but as members of prominent political families (Sarojini Naidu, Aruna Asaf Ali, Kamladevi Chattopadhyay, Ammu Swaminadhan, Kasturba Gandhi, the Nehru women, and so on), or as the thousands who came out in response to Gandhi's call for *satyagraha*. They have been seen as supplementary to male action, rather than as actors in their own right, contributing to something that existed independent of them. Consequently, the importance of such a historic time has been evaluated not with specific reference to them, but with reference to the movement in question.[19] Yet the story of 1947, while being one of the successful attainment of independence, is also a gendered narrative of displacement and dispossession, of large-scale and widespread communal violence, and of the realignment of family, community and national identities as a people were forced to accommodate the dramatically altered reality that now prevailed.

Women's history, in Joan Kelly's famous formulation, has a dual goal: to restore women to history and to restore our history to women.[20] The aim of the enterprise is to "make women a focus of enquiry, a subject of the story, an agent of the narrative";[21] in other words, to construct women as a historical subject and through this construction, "disabuse us of the notion that the history of women is the same as the history of men, that significant turning points in history have the same impact for one sex as for the other".[22] This is not to say that the history of women cannot, in any circumstance, ever be the same as that of men, simply that it cannot be subsumed in the history of mankind. Women's experience of it has implications for historical study in general, and women's history has revitalised theory by problematising at least three of the basic concerns of historical thought: periodisation; the categories of social analysis; and theories of social change.[23]

Because the traditional time-frame of history has been derived from political history, the absence of women in historical accounts is most unsurprising. Women have been excluded from making war, wealth, laws, governments, arts

and science; and men, "functioning in their capacity as historians, considered exactly those activities constitutive of
civilization: hence, diplomatic history, economic history,
constitutional history, political history," and so on.[24] Feminist historiography has focused attention on the necessity
of restoring women to history not only to challenge conventional history-writing, but to emphasize that a representative history can only be written if the experience and
status of one half of humankind is an integral part of the
story. Rejecting the women-as-a-separate-chapter syndrome,
Hélène Cixous insists that "we insinuate ourselves into the
text, as it were".

The task of restoration has only just begun, and it has not
been easy, primarily because the historical archive has little
to offer for such a reconstruction. For example, feminist historians have had to tease information out of census data
and interpret demographic changes, to arrive at an understanding of how and when critical shifts in women's status
with regard to fertility and mortality took place.[25] They have
also had to examine other sources—women's letters, diaries, autobiographies and testimonies—in order to first,
locate them in history, and then reinterpret and challenge
the historical record. The progression from "compensatory"
to "contributory" history, and finally to a reconcept-
ualisation of it is a long and arduous one, methodologically
as well as otherwise.[26] At each stage of the endeavour, searching questions have to be asked not only of historical enquiry
as we have known it, but of the inadequacy of our own conceptual tools and methodological techniques. The task is further complicated by the fact that women can neither be considered a minority or subgroup, nor a race or class apart;[27]
for as both Gerda Lerner and Joan Kelly have shown, they
are the "social opposite not of a class, a caste or of a majority (since we are a majority) but of a sex: men".[28] Sensitive
feminist historiography therefore requires not only the addition of other categories to inform our understanding of
historical processes,[29] but a history of the dialectical relations between men and women *in history*. The attempt, in

Joan Scott's words, throws light "not only on women's experience but on social and political practice . . . and per-
mits historians to raise critical questions regarding the rewriting of history".[30]

In the light of the above, how do we embark on a feminist reading of Partition? What sorts of questions do we raise
and where do we find our sources? How do we disentangle
women's experiences from those of other political non-actors to enable us to problematise the general experience of
violence, dislocation and displacement from a gender perspective? How do we approach the question of identity,
country and religion, of the intersection of community, state
and gender? How do we evaluate the state's responsibility
to refugees in general and women refugees in particular, as
articulated in the policies and programmes of the government? How do we, as feminists concerned with issues of
identity politics, unravel the complex relationship of a post-
colonial state with religious communities in the aftermath
of convulsive communal conflict?

Where, in short, do we begin?

The historical archive, for reasons outlined above, is un-
likely to yield the kind of information we are looking for.[31]
It is not that women are *altogether* absent from Partition histories or even from official records; it is just that they figure
in the same way as they have always figured in history: as
objects of study, rather than as subjects. They are present in
some reports and policy documents, and no account of Partition violence for instance, is complete without the numb-
ing details of violence against women. Yet they are invis-
ible. Furthermore, their experience of this historic event has
neither been properly examined nor assigned historical
value. This is not to valorise experience over other equally
important considerations, rather to recognize that it adds a
critical dimension to any analysis of the impact of such an
event on men and women, on relations between them, and
between gender and social and historical processes.

Partition fiction has been a far richer source both because
it provides popular and astringent commentary on the poli-

tics of Partition and because, here and there, we find women's voices, speaking for themselves.[32] But the most useful material for our purpose has been the very few first-hand accounts and memoirs by women social workers who were involved in the rehabilitation of women, and the oral testimonies we set out to obtain from them and other women in ashrams and refuges in Punjab and Haryana, the field of this research.

We began, though, with the women in our own families and, gradually, the blurred outlines of their earlier geography began to get filled in. From them, and later from all the people we spoke to, we learnt of their life in undivided India, of social and personal relationships between Hindus and Muslims, and the composite culture of the Punjab. The loss of homes was almost less painful, more bearable, than the loss of friendships and of what they had assumed were shared destinies. Listening to them, in retrospect, it was easy to forget that along with deep affection and amity had been equally deep-seated prejudices and taboos; as one of the Hindu women we interviewed said to us, *"roti-beti ka rishta nahin rakhte the, baki sab theek tha"*. (We neither broke bread with them, nor inter-married, but the rest was fine.) From men in the family we heard something of the growing politics of separation and the Pakistan Movement, the almost imperceptible shift towards accepting the notion of two nations.

But this was only a very casual, most cursory introduction to what we were seeking because neither of our families experienced the kind of violence and destitution that millions of others did, even though they had been forced to leave. We realized we would have to simultaneously widen our horizon and narrow our focus. The choice of Punjab was obvious for personal and historical reasons both, and because it had been the site of maximum relocation and rehabilitation.[33] The most comprehensive resettlement scheme in the country, rural as well as urban, had been implemented in Punjab and, of course, it had also witnessed the greatest violence and killings in the course of the migrations. Here, too, were the numerous ashrams and homes to which destituted women were brought and given shelter and employment: Jalandhar, Amritsar, Karnal, Rajpura, Hoshiarpur . . . right up to Rohtak.

Forty years after Partition, there were no "communities" of women we could identify whom we might find, waiting to be found. Families had dispersed, resettled, moved many times over and, initially at least, we were not looking for women in families. We were looking for those who had been left quite alone. People we spoke to said, "Partition? What do you want to talk about that for? Anyway, it's too late—they're all dead." This was true; many were undoubtedly dead, but we persisted. "Speak to so-and-so," people said, "she'll know." Sometimes she did, sometimes she didn't, and sometimes she'd say, "I'm not the person you want, but ask—." Eventually we found that there *did* exist communities of sorts of women, in ashrams or homes, set up where the first of the refugee camps had been established in erstwhile East Punjab.

But this wasn't enough. We needed to know what the women couldn't tell us, the how and why of the ashrams and of rehabilitation, of what happened to the widowed women, to those whose husbands were missing, whose families couldn't be traced. "Speak to—" the women told us, "she was the warden here for twenty years." We travelled to different cities to meet them; we lived with them, we went back to them, sometimes once or twice, sometimes more often. They became friends, occasionally they would write and ask what we were doing with all this material, that they had remembered something else, and had we been able to contact—yet? We moved from person to person, place to place, but without a fixed plan or design. Our journeys took us to Jammu, Amritsar, Bombay, Jodhpur, Lucknow, Kota. We spoke mainly to women, but also to men, to Hindus, Muslims and Sikhs. We talked to senior government and police officers, politicians, doctors, social workers.

We went back to the records to find what we could of the women's stories there, as disaggregated data, memoranda, reports, official statements, government documents. We did this not because we wanted to corroborate what they said, but because it was important to locate their stories in a po-

litical and social context, to juxtapose the official version
with the unofficial ones.

III

      Hardly ever, and hardly anywhere, have
women "written history". They have left few accounts, personal or otherwise, and have committed much less to writing than men. Women historians have noted this absence[34]
and emphasized the importance of retrieving women's history though oral sources. Because women have used speech
much more widely than the written word, oral history practitioners have found in interviews and testimonies a rich
vein to mine and to surface what, so far, has been hidden
from history.

      "The real value of these oral testimonies," say the women
of Stree Shakti Sanghatana who presented a remarkable account of women in the Telengana movement, "lies in their
ability to capture the *quality* of women's lives. . . . We are
able to document experiences that traditional history would
have ignored or even dismissed, to appreciate the issues as
they appeared to the actors at the time, and set their responses. . . against the backdrop of that understanding."[35]

      For feminists, oral history holds the very real promise of
exploring the social experience of women and retrieving it
as both "compensatory" and "supplementary" women's
history. While welcoming its extraordinary potential, however, we must be equally attentive to its complexities. Early
on, feminist oral historians realized that traditional oral history methodology was still grappling with the separation
of subject and object, interviewer and interviewee, thought
and feeling, the political and the personal.[36] Most feminists
advocate empathy and mutuality, rejecting all the hierarchies inherent in the formal, impersonal, falsely neutral "interview". At the same time they raise important questions
regarding the ethical problems of personal narrative. They
are concerned about the uncomfortable fact of class privilege in almost all interviewing situations; the matter of ma-

terial inequality between the researcher and her subject; and the ethical and moral implications of collecting personal narratives in the first place and utilizing them for research.[37] Our own research posed similar problems at almost every stage; particularly troubling was our complete inability to deal with the reversal of roles, when questions were posed *by* the women *to* us: "What is the use of asking all this now? It's too late—you can't change anything." Our response rang hollow even to our own ears: we want to communicate an experience of Partition hitherto ignored and, in fact, unsought; to set the record a little straighter, to make women visible, to better understand historical process. The women, unfailingly gracious and generous in their sharing, accepted our explanation, unsatisfactory as it must have been to them—for no matter how "honest" or candid we might be about our project, it was they who were laying bare their lives, not we, ours.

Then, there are related problems of accuracy and fidelity to the letter and spirit of the narrative; of interpretation, evaluation, selection and representation; the troubling issue of "authorship" and the fact that, in the end, it is the researcher who controls the material, however participatory the research may have been. The responsibility for the distortions or limitations of our studies rests squarely with feminist oral historians as does the dilemma of how much to tell. When confidentiality is enjoined, are we justified in presenting a life story in the interests of advancing historical understanding, especially when that story is deeply personal or traumatic?[38]

The assumption of most feminist research is that it is committed to social transformation, and to women. By highlighting the contradiction between feminist principles and fieldwork practice, feminist oral historians insist that we be mindful of the exploitation that ethnographic method exposes subjects to, and remind us exactly how ambivalent the relationship between feminism and ethnography can be. In Daphne Patai's view, all those who claim that by allowing their subjects to speak they have "empowered" them, need to ask themselves: "Is this empowerment or appropriation? And what does it mean. . . for researchers to claim the right to validate the experience of others"?[39] Since we are almost always in a situation where "other" people are the subject of "our" research, the old hierarchies and inequalities tend to get reproduced all over again. Feminists and other practitioners of participatory research have tried to redress this imbalance somewhat by "returning" the research to their subjects or initiating some form of action that maintains continuity with them. At best, such attempts only demonstrate a sincerity of purpose and sensitivity to the larger question of power and control; they do little, in the end, to resolve the ethical issue bedevilling us because of the very nature of oral history and of what lies at its heart: individual testimony.

Our own attempt has been to present the women's stories in their own words and at some length, in dialogue with ourselves, and severally, with other voices but in a privileged position; the women are always at the centre. Our narrative is determined by their stories, and our analysis made possible by juxtaposing their versions of particular experiences with other versions, official or otherwise, and with available historical records.

IV

All life lines are broken at some point or another. Personal tragedy, an irreparable loss, a natural disaster or cataclysmic historical moment shape lives in ways that are forever marked by that event. Our concern in speaking to women about how they experienced the Partition of India was two-fold: first, to see how the lives of those who are non-actors in the political realm are shaped by an epochal event, and how their experience of it enables a critique of political history and the means of writing it differently. Second, to study a time marked by massive disruption and crisis through life-stories that would, both, bear witness and allow us to attempt a gendered social history.

Yet, how were we to link the stories of women's lives with the story of the nation, the history that we had been told? Of what significance were these fragments in the grand mosaic of freedom? How were we to present the history of that time from the perspective of those who knew anything could happen but had no way of forestalling it? Should we simply reproduce what they said in their own words, with the full power and evocation of the original? Somehow we felt that without context or commentary, such a presentation might leave their testimonies as defenceless as the women themselves, open to scepticism, dismissal, disbelief; to charges of exaggeration and nostalgia, not to be trusted. Or we could write a narrative account, weaving their stories in and out of it in the third person, referring to them to substantiate an argument, corroborate a hypothesis. We could attempt a sociological reconstruction with data on households, occupations, social and economic status, how and where relocated, and so on; or we could concentrate on a particular village or town that had been affected and follow the path of its refugees and its women, in all the rich and unhappy detail that this kind of treatment allows. But that might shift the focus away from the women. In the end we decided to use a combination of commentary and analysis, narrative and testimony, to enable us to counterpoint documented history with personal testimony; to present different versions constructed from a variety of source material: in-depth interviews, government reports and records; private papers, memoirs, autobiographies; letters, diaries, audio-tapes; parliamentary debates; and legal documents. This would allow the women, speaking for themselves, to be heard—sometimes challenging, sometimes agreeing with, sometimes probing historical "facts", insinuating themselves into the text and thereby compelling a different reading of it. The juxtaposition of documented history and personal history forces a re-examination of what James Young calls the "activity of telling history itself," and of recognizing that the "legitimacy of historical sources cannot rest solely on their factual element". The kind of knowledge that the "activity of witness" brings us is not purely historical;[40] rather it is imbued with an experience of historical events and with the profound understanding that their meaning can never be settled.

None of the life-stories presented here is complete. Impossible and undesirable, both, to compress lives between the covers of a book; besides, in what way could we mark the "beginning" or "end" of the women's stories? Fragments of memory, shards of a past, remembrances bitter and sweet are strung together in a sequence that often has no chronology. Indeed a lack of sequence marked all the interviews, and the ordering of events was generally erratic. We learnt to recognize this as a feature of recalling traumatic experience: recollection makes for a reliving of time past even as time present interrupts memory. Everyday time and life-time overlap, and each woman's story reveals how she has arranged her present within the specific horizons of her past and her future.[41] So the telling breaks off, we leave and return and sometimes the story resumes where it left off, at others not. Sometimes it contradicts itself because, each day, we remake ourselves, each telling presents us in another dimension, and each time we remember, we remember differently. Occasionally, we will reach a point in the story where memory refuses to enter speech. Some memories are elaborated, some elided, some never summoned up at all; thus it is that from the totality of a life only a fragment is offered here, some part of the broken line. Yet, in representing the women's stories, albeit in their own words, the "essential provisionality" of their accounts is made fixed and immutable; it begins and ends, it appears to be a seamless whole.

For most of the women remembering was important, but as important was *remembering to others*, having someone listen to their stories and feel that their experience was of value. We realized, once the floodgates were opened, that we could not always determine the flow. Sometimes murky, sometimes clear, often we simply just sat by the stream grateful that it was flowing. It is true that not every woman spoke without demur or hesitation. More than once we heard the cry, "Why rake up the past again?" but almost the next breath would bring forth an incident, an encounter, a tragedy recalled, a past resurrected. Once begun, the "interviews" became like conversations, our questions more like interjections that sometimes received a direct response, but more often, an extended reminiscence that might refer to the question only tangentially. Much further into the telling we might suddenly find it being addressed in another context, opening up yet another vista. Where we encountered genuine reluctance or an unwillingness to disclose, we simply did not press the issue.

Not all the stories we heard were intrinsically different: what is different is how events have been grasped, how remembered; how they have been understood or misunderstood; how each woman assimilated her experience. All are part of the narration, and part of an unfolding history. Some women never recovered from Partition, others saw in this rupture a moment of unexpected liberation for themselves *as women*. Any number were resettled or rehabilitated in some manner and echoes of their stories are to be found even in the handful presented here. Others form the bedrock from which our narrative proceeds, a narrative that contextualises them and highlights the gendered nature of historical experience and its recording. The stories that we have selected are a mix of women destituted as a result of Partition; women unalterably affected but not devastated by it; social workers whose own lives changed dramatically in the course of their work; and one woman who, as she said, "spread her wings" after she left Karachi. The stories might supplement each other, or sometimes serve as counterpoints, but each is distinct and dwells on those experiences that relate most directly to the themes which emerged with sharp clarity from the accounts: violence; abduction and recovery; widowhood; women's rehabilitation; rebuilding; and belonging.

These form the six thematic clusters. Each cluster, in turn, tries to unravel the tangled skein of relationships between women, religious communities and the state, both within and across the two new nations; between women and their families, "real" and "acquired"; between women and their men, women and their country. It does so by bringing the normative to crisis: mass widowhood on an unprecedented scale, compelled the state to step in as rehabilitator and, in the process, made for a temporary suspension of the traditional inauspiciousness and taboos surrounding widows. At the same time as it released a very large number of women into the workforce, it also put the welfarist assumptions of the state to test. Forced migration was often accompanied by mass abduction and the conversion of women and children; families, communities, governments and political parties converged to "recover" these women with extraordinary zeal and restore them to where they "rightfully belonged". Women's sexuality, as it had been violated by abduction, transgressed by enforced conversion and marriage and exploited by impermissible cohabitation and reproduction was at the centre of debates around national duty, honour, identity and citizenship in a secular and democratic India. The figure of the abducted woman became symbolic of crossing borders, of violating social, cultural and political boundaries. The extent and nature of violence that women were subjected to when communities conflagrated, highlights not only their particular vulnerability at such times, but an overarching patriarchal consensus that emerges on how to dispose of the troublesome question of women's sexuality. Together, the clusters lay bare the multiple patriarchies of community, family and state as experienced by women in their transition to freedom, and explore the deep complicities between them.

Country. Community. Religion. Freedom itself: a closer examination of what meaning they have for women has led feminists to ask searching questions about women's asymmetrical relationship to nationality and citizenship; and to appreciate the role assigned to them in any renegotiation of identities, whether ethnic, communal or national. Such an analysis of the experience of abducted women, for instance, sheds light not only on the Indian state and its articulation of its role and responsibilities vis-à-vis its female citizens, but also on its perception of its role vis-à-vis Pakistan, Hindu and Muslim communities, and displaced Hindu families. The issue of gendered identities is central to any discussion on the interplay of community, class and caste with wider political, economic and social forces. The adoption of a perspective that locates women at the intersection of these forces rather than at the periphery, casts an entirely new light on the apparent fixity of defining features of identity; indeed, the presence, absence and precise location of women turns out to be one of the crucial elements that throws these "fixed" identities into disarray and confusion. Thus, are we made to look anew at those age-old borders and boundaries: nation, religion, community, gender; those ancient myths about shame and honour, blood and belonging. And thus, do the women's "histories" interrogate not only the history we know, but how we know it.

The Partition of India in 1947 was an undeclared civil war, and since then we have had disputed borders in every country of South Asia. The religion-based division of the country anticipated many of the questions that trouble us now across the subcontinent: ethnicity, communalism, the rise of religious fundamentalism and cultural nationalism. Sharply, but poignantly, Partition posed the question of "belonging" in a way that polarized choice and allegiance, aggravating old, and new, antagonisms. Subsequent contestations have revived and rephrased the question in ever more complex ways, and how it is answered has far-reaching implications for women.

Notes

[1] Mushirul Hasan (ed.), *India's Partition: Process, Strategy and Mobilization* (Delhi: Oxford University Press, 1993). p. 1. Hasan's elegant and concise Introduction presents us with an excellent summary of current concerns and debates in Partition historiography, as well as a clear-sighted analysis of the forces that led to the crystallizing of the demand for Pakistan.

[2] Ayesha Jalal, *The Sole Spokesman: Jinnah, the Muslim League and the Demand for Pakistan* (New York: Cambridge University Press, 1985), p. 2.

[3] For a range of recent historical accounts see, among others, Mushirul Hasan, *India's Partition,* op. cit.; Mushirul Hasan, *Legacy of a Divided Nation: India's Muslims Since Independence* (Delhi: Oxford University Press, 1997); *South Asia*, Journal of South Asian St.,dies, Special Issue, "North India: Partition and Independence", Vol. XVIII, 1995 (Melbourne: South Asian Studies Association); Amit Kumar Gupta (ed.), *Myth and Reality: The Struggle for Freedom in India 1945–47* (Delhi: Manohar, 1987); Dàvid Page: *Prelude to Partition: The Indian Muslims and the Imperial System of Control* 1920–1932 (Delhi: Oxford University Press, 1982).

[4] Mushirul Hasan (ed.), *India's Partition*, op.cit, p. 6.

[5] M.A. Jinnah: "An Extract from the Presidential Address—Lahore, March 1940", in Hasan (ed.), op. cit., p. 56.

[6] Mushirul Hasan (ed.), *India Partitioned: The Other Face of Freedom* (Delhi: Roli Books, 1995), Introduction.

[7] Farzana Sheikh, "Muslims and Political Representation in India: The Making of Pakistan" in Hasan (ed.), *India's Partition*, op. cit., p. 82.

[8] Quoted in Hasan, *India's Partition*, op.cit., p. 36.

[9] Ibid., pp. 15–26.

[10] Ibid., p. 38.

[11] Alok Rai, "The Trauma of Independence: Some Aspects of Progressive Hindi Literature 1945–47" in Amit Kumar Gupta (ed.), *Myth and Reality*, op. cit., p. 322

[12] Partition fiction (and some non-fiction) is almost the only social history we have of this time. We do not intend to engage in a debate on how "fictional" Partition fiction is, but the point does need to be made that it is in fiction, rather than any other genre, that we find an attempt to assimilate the full import of what Partition meant. For more on this see Jason Francisco, "In

the Heat of Fratricide: the Literature of India's Partition Burning Freshly (A Review Article)" in *The Annual of Urdu Studies,* No. 2, 1996 (Madison: University of Wisconsin, Center for South Asia); Alok Bhalla (ed.), *Stories About the Partition of India,* 3 vols. (Delhi: Indus/HarperCollins, 1994); S.S. Hans, "The Partition Novels of Nanak Singh," and N.K. Jain, "The Partition Theme in Indo-Anglian Novels," in Amit Kumar Gupta (ed.), *Myth and Reality,* op. cit.; Mushirul Hasan (ed.), *India Partitioned* op. cit.; Samina Rehman, "Birjees: The *'Dastaan Go'* in Nighat Said Khan, Rubina Saigol, Afiya Shehrbano Zia (eds.), *Locating the Self: Perspectives on Women and Multiple Identities* (Lahore: ASR Publications, 1994); Veena Das and Ashis Nandy, "Violence, Victimhood and the Language of Silence" in *Contributions to Indian Sociology* (n.s.), vol. 19, no. 1 (Delhi: Sage Publications, 1985); Alok Bhalla, "Memory, History and Fictional Representations of the Partition", paper presented at a conference, "Movement and Memory", Iowa, 1997.

[13] In an appeal to the Indian electorate on the eve of the first general election in 1952, the Congress put out a pamphlet which declared, "The price of freedom was Partition. The Congress and its leaders resisted the idea . . . till the last moment and they yielded only when they realized that the alternative was indefinite perpetuation of foreign rule or civil war, or both. . . . A strong and stable Central Government could be established by peaceful means only through Partition. . ." Quoted in Mushirul Hasan (ed.), *India's Partition,* op. cit., p. 32.

[14] Jason Francisco, "In the Heat of Fratricide", op.cit., pp. 227–50.

[15] Ibid., pp. 239–40.

[16] Accounts of ethnic violence in the South Asian region, in particular, have used more of such material over the last two decades or so, to further an understanding of how such violence occurs, is experienced and dispersed in public consciousness. The testimony of the survivor is especially important in such considerations, "permitting the historian", in Amrit Srinivasan's words, "to smuggle the social structure into his studies". See Amrit Srinivasan, "The Survivor in the Study of Violence" in Veena Das, *Mirrors of Violence: Communities, Riots and Survivors in South Asia* (Delhi: Oxford University Press, 1990), pp. 305–20. In the same volume, see also essays by Veena Das, "Our Work to Cry: Your Work to Listen", and Valli Kanapathipillai, "July 1983: The Survivor's Experience". Other essays and texts include Uma Chakravarti and Nandita Haksar,

The Delhi Riots: Three Days in the Life of a Nation (Delhi: Lancer International, 1987); Mushirul Hasan (ed.) *India Partitioned: The Other Face of Freedom,* op. cit.; Gyanendra Pandey, "In Defence of the Fragment: Writing About Hindu-Muslim Riots in India Today", in *Economic and Political Weekly,* Annual Number, March 1991, pp. 559–72; E. Valentine Daniel, "Mood, Moment and Mind: Writing Violence", paper presented at the conference "Violence Against Women: Ideologies and Victimization", Sri Lanka, 1996; Pradeep Jeganathan, "All the Lord's Men? Perpetrator Constructions of Collective Violence in an Urban Sri Lankan Community", unpublished paper, n.d.

[17] Gyan Pandey, "In Defence of the Fragment," op. cit. p. 560.

[18] Recent attempts at rewriting Partition history from a subaltern and gender perspective include essays by Urvashi Butalia, "Community, State and Gender: On Women's Agency During Partition", *Economic and Political Weekly,* Vol. XXVIII No. 17, April 24, 1993; and "Muslims and Hindus, Men and Women: Communal Stereotypes and the Partition of India" in Tanika Sarkar and Urvashi Butalia (eds.), *Women and the Hindu Right: A Collection of Essays* (Delhi: Kali for Women, 1995); Dipesh Chakrabarty, "East Bengal and the Sense of Place in Bhadralok Memory", unpublished paper, 1995; Veena Das, "National Honour and Practical Kinship: Of Unwanted Women and Children" in Veena Das, *Critical Events: An Anthropological Perspective on Contemporary India* (Delhi: Oxford University Press, 1995); Karuna Chanana, "Partition and Family Strategies: Gender-Education and Linkages among Punjabi Women in Delhi" in *Economic and Political Weekly,* Vol. XXVIII No.17, April 24, 1993; Ritu Menon, "Reproducing the Legitimate Community: Secularity, Sexuality and the State in Post-Partition India" in Amrita Basu and Patricia Jeffery (eds)., *Appropriating Gender: Women's Activism and Politicized Religion* (New York: Routledge, 1997); Ritu Menon and Kamla Bhasin, "Recovery, Rupture, Resistance: Indian State and the Abduction of Women During Partition", *Economic and Political Weekly* Vol. XXVIII No.17, April 24, 1993; Gyanendra Pandey, "Partition and Independence: Delhi 1947–48" in *Economic and Political Weekly,* Vol. XXXII No. 36, September 1997.

[19] Examples of recuperating women in the history of the freedom movement and, thereafter, in social movements are Radha Kumar, *The History of Doing: An Illustrated Account of Movements for Women's Rights and Feminism in India 1800–1990* (Delhi: Kali

for Women, 1993); Bharati Ray, *From the Seams of History: Essays on Indian Women* (Delhi: Oxford University Press, 1995); Stree Shakti Sanghatana, *"We Were Making History. . ."*: *Lifestories of Women in the Telengana People's Struggle* (Delhi: Kali for Women, 1989); Geraldine Forbes, *Women in Modern India* (Cambridge University Press/Foundation Books, 1996).

[20] Joan Kelly, *Women, History and Theory* (Chicago: University of Chicago Press, 1984), p.1. Kelly's is still one of the most lucid texts on this subject.

[21] Joan Wallach Scott, "Women's History and the Rewriting of History" in Christie Farnham (ed.), *The Impact of Feminist Research in the Academy* (Bloomington: Indiana University Press, .1987), p. 36.

[22] Joan Kelly, *Women, History and Theory*, op. cit., p. 3.

[23] Ibid., p. 1.

[24] Ibid., p. 2.

[25] For deft summaries of how feminist historiography has progressed see Susan Geiger, "Women's Life Histories: Method and Content," in *Signs, Journal of Women in Culture and Society*, 11, no. 2, 1986, pp. 334–51; Sherna B. Gluck, "What's So Special About Women's Oral History?" in *Frontiers* A Journal of Women's Studies, Vol. II Number 2, 1977; Joanna Bornat, "Women's History and Oral History: An Outline Bibliography" reproduced in *Oral History in Women's Studies: Concept, Method and Use* (Bombay: SNDT, Research Centre for Women's Studies, 1990).

[26] See Joan Kelly, op.cit., Joan W. Scott, op. cit., and Gerda Lerner, *The Majority Finds Its Past: Placing Women in History* (New York: Oxford University Press, 1979), pp.145–80.

[27] Gerda Lerner, "The Feminists: A Second Look", *Columbia Forum* 13 (Fall 1970), pp. 24–30.

[28] Joan Kelly, op. cit., p. 6.

[29] Gerda Lerner elaborates these as being: sexuality; reproduction; the link between child-bearing and child-rearing; role indoctrination; sexual values and myths; female consciousness. Socialist feminists like Sheila Rowbotham have added class; black feminists rightly insist on race; and in South Asia the importance of caste, religion and ethnicity cannot be over-emphasized.

[30] Joan W. Scott, op.cit., p. 41.

[31] To paraphrase Virginia Woolf, it is the small *details* of a woman's life—did she marry? how many children did she have?

did she do the cooking? did she work outside the home?—that make up her personal history *and* a social history, and it is from this mass of information that we will be able to add what she called then, "a supplement to history. Calling it of course by some inconspicuous name so that women might figure there without impropriety." Quoted in Joan W. Scott, op. cit., p. 34.

[32] Women writers like Ismat Chughtai, Qurratulain Hyder, Amrita Pritam, Jeelani Bano, Krishna Sobti, Ajeet Cour and Jyotirmoyee Devi in India have written with great power on Partition. A careful analysis of their writing (not attempted here) will compare with men's fiction in interesting and unexpected ways, not least in their tangential comments on nation, country and religion.

[33] The original scope of this study was Punjab (East and West, i.e. W. Pakistan) and Bengal (West and East, i.e. E. Pakistan); after initial interviewing in West Bengal, however, and extended discussions with collaborators in Bangladesh we recognized that the Bengal experience was so different that it merited a separate study. The migrations here took place over eight to ten years, were not accompanied by the kind of violence that Punjab experienced, and consequently, the rehabilitation and re-settlement of refugees were qualitatively different. The Pakistan part of the study, however, is being carried out by Nighat Said Khan and Anis Haroon in W. Punjab and Sind. See an initial essay by Khan, "Identity, Violence and Women: a Reflection on the Partition of India 1947" in Khan et al (eds.), *Locating the Self*, op. cit., pp. 157–71.

[34] The literature on the use of oral history for feminist research is fairly extensive and varied. We do not propose to review it here, merely to direct the reader to the following which we have found most useful. Sherna B. Gluck and Daphne Patai (eds.), *Women's Words: The Feminist Practice of Oral History* (New York and London: Routledge, 1991); Ruth Linden, *Making Stories, Making Selves: Feminist Reflections on the Holocaust* (Columbus: Ohio State University Press, 1993); Michelle Perrot (ed.), *Writing Women's History*, trs. Felicia Pheasant (Oxford: Blackwell, 1992); Personal Narrative Group, *Interpreting Women's Lives: Feminist Theory and Personal Narratives* (Bloomington: Indiana University Press, 1989).

[35] Stree Shakti Sanghatana, op. cit., p. 26; SSS was one of the first feminist research groups in India to use oral history in order to establish and assess the contribution made by peasant women

to armed resistance in the Telengana district of Andhra Pradesh. See "*We Were Making History . . .*" for some of the most powerful testimonies on the place of women in history. Other women's groups that have used oral history are Stree Vani in Pune, interviews with Dalit women; Jagori, which has done several life histories of single women and Unmad, a group of health activists who have compiled stories of women with mental health problems.

[36] Gluck and Patai (eds.), *Women's Words*, op. cit., Introduction.

[37] Feminist historians and ethnographers have long been involved in a debate on the ethics of using personal narratives for research. Each exchange has led to refining our understanding of the implications of this methodology, but the debate itself has not been laid to rest. Judith Stacey in her essay, "Can There Be a Feminist Ethnography?" (Gluck and Patai, op. cit., pp. 111–20) details the complexity of the question, and the inherent "inequality and potential treacherousness" of the relationship between the researcher and the researched (p. 113). After a remarkably candid and soul-searching presentation of the issues, she concludes that "the relationship between feminism and ethnography is unavoidably ambivalent", perhaps even exploitative. Nevertheless, she does believe that "while there cannot be a fully feminist ethnography there can be ethnographies that are partially feminist", and research that is "vigorously self-aware and humble" (p. 117). Lila Abu-Lughod, on the other hand, in *her* essay titled "Can There Be Feminist Ethnography?" concludes that there can, and "that its time has come". (Lecture presented to the New York Academy of Sciences, February 1988. p. 28.) She argues that this is so because feminist ethnographers take the commonalities and differences between researchers and subjects into account, and contribute to the cause of feminism in special ways. A third view is put forward by Daphne Patai who says ". . . too much ignorance exists in the world to allow us to await perfect research methods before proceeding". ("Is Ethical Research Possible?" in Gluck and Patai, op. cit., p. 150.) However, she makes the important point that "ethical dilemmas subtly transform into political dilemmas" and need to be addressed as such. ("Ethical Problems of Personal Narratives" in *International Journal of Oral History*, Vol. 8 No. 1 February 1987, p. 24). For further discussion on the politics of representation see also, Personal Narratives Group, "Whose Voice?" in *Interpreting Women's Lives*, op. cit.; Anne Hardgrove, "South

Asian Women's Communal Identities" in *Economic and Political Weekly*, September 30, 1995, pp. 2427–30; Gillian Elinor, "On the Use of the Stolen and Given: An Essay in Oral History" in *Issues in Architecture, Art and Design*, Vol. 1 No. 2 Winter 1990–91, pp. 73–80.

[38] This last has come up especially with regard to Holocaust, incest and rape testimonies, and particularly with reference to Claud Lanzmann's video recording of Holocaust survivors, *Shoah*. See Judith Stacey, op. cit., and James F. Young, *Writing & Rewriting the Holocaust: Narrative and the Consequences of Interpretation* (Bloomington: Indiana University Press, 1988), pp. 157–71.

[39] Daphne Patai, "Is Ethical Research Possible?", op. cit., p. 147.

[40] James F. Young, *Writing & Rewriting the Holocaust*, op. cit., p. 165.

[41] For a most illuminating discussion of this, see Daniel Bertaux and Martin Kohli, "The Life Story Approach: A Continental View", *Annual Review of Sociology*, 1984, No. 10, pp. 215–37.

[42] James F. Young, op. cit., p. 161. The "reliability" of personal narratives as a historical document has been questioned by those who worry about its ephemeral nature, its distance from facts, its flexible and volatile character and its propensity to misrepresentation—by interviewer and interviewee, alike. See Ron Grele, *Envelopes of Sound: The Art of Oral History* (New York: Praeger, 1991); William Moss, "Oral History: An Appreciation", *American Archivist*, Vol. 40, October 1977, pp. 429–39; Samuel Schrager, "What is Social in Oral History?" *International Journal of Oral History*, Vol. 4, No.2, June 1983, pp. 76–98; Eva M. McMahan, *Elite Oral History Discourse* (Tuscaloosa: The University of Alabama Press, 1989.) Others see little validity in individual stories representing either group or collective interest and experience. The evidentiary value of oral history has been challenged most consistently by those who look at it as raw, unprocessed data, highly selective and untested. William Moss cautions that "recollection itself is a complex piece of evidence", involving three factors: the initial event or reality; the memory of it which is at least one step removed from reality; and the testimony which is yet another interpretive act. A fourth level of selection is that of the interviewer asking specific questions which elicit a specific response, and then reinterpreting them in his or her representation. Memory itself, he says, is

"tricky" with respect to reality. The historian or interviewer has no way of knowing from the testimony whether it is "distorted or accurate, deliberately falsified or spontaneously candid". Yet, he notes, "even as we move further from reality, recollections provide. . . a corresponding abstractive value of fascinating richness. . . Even when erroneous or misguided, recollections may, in their very errors provoke understanding and insight. Furthermore, the aggregate recollections of many people can provide a rough means for approximating historical truth where no transitional or selective records exist." (Moss, op. cit., p. 91.)

James Young, whose work on Holocaust testimonies discusses these issues at length, counters by saying, "The aim of testimony can never be to document experiences or to present facts as such. Rather, it is to document both the witness as he makes testimony and the understanding and meaning of events generated in the activity of testimony itself." Oral history, he believes, "is a matter of memory, reconstruction and imagination. Unlike written history that tends to hide its lines of construction, oral testimonies retain the process of construction, the activity of witness". He further notes the "constructed nature of all evidence" including that which is rhetorically objective like photographs, train schedules or eyewitness accounts from the era. Historical theorists now acknowledge that "the legitimacy of historical sources cannot rest solely on their factual element, in which case readers would be endlessly troubled by conflicting versions". Critical readers, thus, instead of "disqualifying" competing accounts learn to read "difference" and to incorporate that dimension in their analysis. James F. Young, *Writing and Rewriting the Holocaust*, op. cit., pp. 157–71.

Honourably Dead

Permissible Violence Against Women

In the villages of Head Junu, Hindus threw their young daughters into wells, dug trenches and buried them alive. Some were burnt to death, some were made to touch electric wires to prevent the Muslims from touching them. We heard of such happenings all the time after August 16. We heard all this.

The Muslims used to announce that they would take away our daughters. They would force their way into homes and pick up young girls and women. Ten or twenty of them would enter, tie up the menfolk and take the women. We saw many who had been raped and disfigured, their faces and breasts scarred, and then abandoned. They had tooth-marks all over them. Their families said, "How can we keep them now? Better that they are dead." Many of them were so young—18, 15, 14 years old—what remained of them now? Their "character" was now spoilt. One had been raped by ten or more men— her father burnt her, refused to take her back. There was one village, Makhtampura, where all night they plundered and raped, they dragged away all the young girls who were fleeing in kafilas. No one could do anything—if they did, they would be killed. Everyone was running for their lives. I saw it all—mothers telling their daughters they were ruined, bemoaning their fate, saying it would have been better if they hadn't been born. . . .

Durga Rani

. . . That day, my brother had his lunch and went out—it was namaaz time. He had taken two servants and a gun with him but some of the labourers saw him and shouted, "Catch him, get him!" My brother ran into the mosque. Maulvi Sahib was there. He said, not one hair on your head will be harmed as long as I am here. His wife said, "Beta, don't be afraid, they'll have to come for my son Noor Muhammad and Miyan before they hurt you. Don't worry." The attackers couldn't do a thing. They fought with the Maulvi but he said to them, "Come in, if you dare. You have eaten their salt and now you want to kill them!" They said, "Why did they harvest the rice?" He replied, "It was theirs, they harvested it. You will get your share."

*There were other attacks, but God was kind, he saved us each
time. There was a notorious gang in a neighbouring village who
went and looted people, attacked them. We were afraid they would
come for us. We put sandbags on the roof of our house, some people
put stones. We also had guns and sticks. . . . Our work was such
that our men had to go out at odd times, so they always had guns
with them. The leader of that gang tried to attack us three times but
something or the other stopped them. Once, the river swelled so they
couldn't cross over, another time he was on his way to our village
when he got the news that the roof of his house had collapsed. He had
to turn back. So we escaped, God was kind to us . . .*

Gyan Deyi

"August Anarchy"

The Hindustan–Pakistan Plan was an-
nounced on June 3, 1947 whereby a new entity called Pakistan was created, of which West Pakistan was to comprise
the Muslim-majority provinces of Sind, the North-West Frontier Province, and 16 districts of Punjab; the remaining 13
districts of undivided Punjab were to be part of India. Although the exact boundary line between the two countries
had still to be determined by the Boundary Commission,
the exchange of populations started taking place much before August 15.

Even earlier, however, in November 1946 in fact, Jinnah
had suggested such an exchange, referring to the exodus of
Hindus from Noakhali after the riots there in August. People were already on the move, he said, and it would be pru-
dent to devise some mechanism for their smooth and safe
transit.[1] In December 1946, Raja Ghazanfar Ali Khan referred
to increasing communal unrest and said the transfer of
populations was a necessary corollary to the establishment
of a Muslim state. Even Akali leaders changed their minds
afte: the Noakhali riots, and Sardar Swaran Singh, leader of
the Panthic Assembly Party, said in July 1947 that such an
exchange was the only solution to the problem of violence
against minority communities on either side of the redrawn

borders.[2] Only the Congress thought that the sporadic violence that had occurred was temporary; and Mahatma Gandhi unequivocally rejected the very idea:

> It is unthinkable and impracticable. Every province is of every Indian, be he Hindu, Muslim or of any other faith. It won't be otherwise, even if Pakistan came in full. For me any such thing will spell bankruptcy of Indian wisdom or statesmanship, or both. The logical consequence of any such step is too dreadful to contemplate. Is it not bad enough that India should be artificially divided into so many religious zones?[3]

To give Congress leaders their due, however, the unworkability of the idea was apparent: religious minorities were scattered all over the country, there were towns and villages even in Muslim majority provinces that had very large numbers of Hindus and Sikhs, those left behind would be more vulnerable than ever, and in any case, transfer of power was what had been agreed to, not transfer of populations. So, although people had begun moving out of villages as early as March 1947, much before the announcement of the Plan, the Partition Council nevertheless passed a resolution on August 2, 1947 to "arrest further exodus and encourage the return of people to their homes".[4]

The Boundary Commission announced its awards on August 16. Within a week, about one million Hindus and Sikhs had crossed over from West to East Punjab, and in the week following, another two and a half million had collected in refugee camps in West Punjab.[5] By November 6, 1947, nearly 29,000 refugees had been flown in both directions; about 673 refugee trains were run between August 27 and November 6, transporting more than two million refugees inside India and across the border. Of these 1,362,000 were non-Muslims and 939,000 were Muslims. Huge foot convoys, each 30–40,000 strong, were organized by the Military Evacuation Organization and the East Punjab Liaison Agency to move the bulk of the rural population, especially those who still had their cattle and bullock-carts with them. The estimate is that in 42 days (September 18 to October 29) 24 non-Muslim foot-columns, 849,000 strong, had crossed into

India.[6] Migrations varied in size and composition as well as in mode of transit. Some people moved in stages, first from small hamlets to larger communities, and thence to local transit camps; others travelled directly from the big cities by rail or air to the other side of the border. Families might leave together or in batches, depending on how permanent they thought the move was going to be. Many simply locked up their houses, entrusted their neighbours with the keys, and left with the assurance of returning. Others knew there would be no going back; and still others made the move, stayed for a while, and then returned.

As the violence increased, however, the migrations took on an urgent and treacherous character: convoys were ambushed, families separated, children orphaned, women kidnapped—and whole trainloads massacred. By the time the exodus was finally over, about eight to ten million people had crossed over from Punjab and Bengal—the largest peace-time mass migration in history—and about 500,000–1,000,000 had perished. The exchange, at least as far as Punjab was concerned, was as nearly equal as can be imagined: the total non-Muslim population of Punjab in 1941 was 4,357,477, the total Muslim population, 4,286,755.[7]

No one, they say, foresaw either the rivers of people that would flow from one part of Punjab to the other, or the blood that would be shed as they were killed in their tens of thousands. By the first week of March 1947 rioting, arson and looting had broken out in Punjab, beginning with the central districts of Lahore, Amritsar, Ferozepur, Ludhiana, Sheikhupura, Gurdaspur, Sialkot, Montgomery, Lyallpur, Gujranwala and the Jullundur Doab, and fanning out into the countryside. The violence was, by most reckonings, organized and systematic: Hindu and Sikh shops and businesses were singled out for burning and looting in West Punjab, Muslim property and homes in East Punjab. Allegations were made by both sides of the active involvement of political leaders, the Muslim League and the Jamaat, the National Guards, demobilised soldiers of the Indian National Army (INA), the Hindu Mahasabha and the Rashtriya

Swayam Sewak Sangh (RSS), with all claiming only to be acting in self-defence. Muslim leaders complained to Evan Jenkins, then Governor of Punjab, that Dr. Gopi Chand Bhargava and Lala Bhimsen Sachar were encouraging communal violence in Amritsar. They said the Muslim League had been non-violent for 34 days while the non-Muslims became violent on the first day of their agitation. Evan Jenkins replied that the Muslim League's agitation had been intensely provocative. "I did not know anything about Gopi Chand Bhargava," he continued, "but I did not believe that Lala Bhimsen Sachar was actively encouraging violence."[8]

The same day, March 4, non-Muslims in Lahore complained that a peaceful demonstration by non-Muslim students was fired at by the police at the behest of the Principal of Government College, Mr. Bukhari, and that another procession later that day was attacked by the Muslim National Guards.[9] In Rawalpindi and Lahore, Sikhs bore the brunt of the attacks, in Multan it was mainly Hindus, in Amritsar, Muslims. In a discussion between Governor Jenkins, Khan Ifthikar Khan of Mamdot, Malik Feroz Khan Noon and Mumtaz Mohammed Khan Daulatana on March 10, the Muslim leaders said they had heard that

> trouble was imminent in Ludhiana and Kartarpur. They also said there were large stockpiles of arms in the gurudwaras and that they would be quite prepared to agree to mosques being searched if we would search gurudwaras as well.[10]

Suspicion and mistrust ran deep, exacerbated by inflammatory pamphlets put out by both sides. One, with a picture of Jinnah, sword in hand, declared:

> Be ready and take your swords! Think you, Muslims, why we are under the Kafirs today. The result of loving the Kafirs is not good. O, Kafir ! Your doom is not far and the general massacre will come.[11]

Meanwhile, in a secret letter to Mountbatten dated April 9, 1947, Evan Jenkins warned of an organized attack by Sikhs against Muslims, and an appeal made by Giani Kartar Singh and Master Tara Singh for Rs. 50 lakhs towards a "War Fund". A pamphlet in Gurmukhi exhorted:

Oh, Sikhs! Read this and think yourself, what have you to
do under the circumstances? In your veins there is yet the
blood of your beloved Guru Gobind Singhji. Do your duty![12]

Calls to take up arms had their predictable consequences.
Between March 1947 and May 1947 the official figures for
deaths in disturbances in Punjab were 3,410–3,600, and the
loss of property, Rs.15 crores.[13]

Official versions of the violence in Punjab put out by India and Pakistan, post-Partition,[14] detail its occurrence district by district, village by village, mohalla by mohalla, and
trace its progress towards the "August Anarchy" which
marked the announcement of the Boundary Commission
awards. Swarna Aiyar[15] has given us an almost bogey by
bogey account of the great train massacres that were a feature of every train that carried fleeing refugees from one
side of Punjab to the other in the weeks between August 9
and September 30, until the Refugee Specials were arranged.
By August 13 it became impossible for passengers to reach
Lahore station because they were attacked en route; between
August 12–18, it became a veritable death-trap, and in the
rural areas, by August 15, nearly every east-bound train
passing through Montgomery and Lahore was stopped and
attacked. The North West Railway stopped running all trains
except mails, expresses and military mails. Train travel from
east to west was equally harrowing and hazardous, especially for those trains originating in or passing through
Patiala and Amritsar. Stoppages and derailment interrupted
each journey during which passengers were looted, slaughtered and unceremoniously pitched out. The dead and dying littered berths and platforms, and those who escaped
murder, died of thirst or starvation.[16] These "trains of death"
only repeated the savagery taking place all over the Punjab.
Foot convoys were ambushed, with escorts sometimes join-
ing the mobs and shooting indiscriminately; one such con-
voy, nearly six miles long, which left Lyallpur on September 11, 1947 was attacked several times during its journey,
and of the five thousand refugees, one thousand perished.[17]
Kidnappings and abductions were widespread; one account

has it that in Narnaul in Patiala State, 16,000 Muslims were killed and 1,500 women abducted.[18] Lorries and trucks were not spared either, and as late as July 1948, travelling by road in West Punjab was wholly unsafe. G.D. Khosla, who was in charge of the Government of India's Fact Finding Organization set up to enquire into the violence and the exodus, says:

> Day after day, week after week, non-Muslims from West Punjab continued to pour across the border in trains, lorries, aeroplanes, bullock-carts and on foot till, by the end of December 1947, four million of them had come into India. All of them had left behind their property and valuables, the majority of them had suffered bereavement; their bodies sick and wounded, their souls bruised with the shock of horror [sic], they came to a new home.[19]

The scale and intensity of the violence in Punjab continue to horrify us even today, virtually paralysing any effort to fully comprehend its meaning. The extreme difficulty experienced by all those who have attempted to "write" Partition violence finds its mirror-image in the difficulty which most commentators have in offering an adequate explanation for it. Nor is there any agreement on its primary causes. Early writing generally accepts that much of it was organized and orchestrated by law enforcement agencies and their functionaries, by willing henchmen of various quasi-political organizations, and a communalised bureaucracy. There was not so much a breakdown of law and order, as a suspension of it: brutality was allowed.[20] Had this not been the case, few would have been motivated enough to leave their homes and lands and livelihoods, and resettle in a new country. Time and again, in the course of our interviews we were told, "governments change, even rulers may change, but people are never exchanged". They were forced out of villages and towns by the ferocity of attacks on them, creating enough terror to banish any doubt or possibility of reconciliation. Why else would thousands from Patiala have resettled in faraway Sind? From faraway Peshawar in Dehradun?

The economic factor has also been considered a powerful motivator; so, agricultural labour was amenable to violently dealing with land-owners, debtors with moneylenders and traders, and assorted adventurers and opportunists who quickly saw a short-cut to betterment. Forty years later in Karnal Gyan Deyi said, "It was our own labour, people who worked on our land, they attacked us. Our own people did this." Economic considerations persuaded many who were propertied to accept conversion to one or other religion in order to retain their assets. Yet, according to other analyses, organized violence and economic factors, though important, cannot sufficiently account for the brutality; for them a good part of the explanation lies in cultural and psychological factors, and in the abiding nature of prejudice and deep-seated antagonism.[21] Latent in "normal" times, it erupts with extreme virulence during communal conflict and remains lodged in collective memory, to surface with renewed intensity in the next round. "Cultural memory," says Sudhir Kakar, "is a group's history freed from rootedness in time— it is as much imagination as the actual events that go into its construction." In his view, the retelling of Partition violence is the primary channel through which historical enmity is transmitted; the "truth" of these accounts lies not in their veracity but in the "archetypal material they contain".[22] The particular forms this violence takes—disfigurement, mutilation, disembowelment, castration, branding—are part of its pathology and must be recognized for their symbolic meaning. The brutal logic of reprisal thus realizes its full potential, with all parties to it fully cognizant of their role. In its own way this theory seeks to restore volition and "agency" to the actors and resists the passivity that more instrumentalist explanations assign to them, although, as Veena Das has noted, "there is no contradiction between the fact that, on the one hand, mob violence may be highly organized and crowds provided with such instruments as voters' lists or combustible powders, and on the other, that crowds draw upon repositories of unconscious images" to spur them on.[23] The exchange of violence that reprisal entails is justified by what some social scientists have called the language of feud. In this consideration, feud may be defined as "a pact of violence" between social groups in such a way that the "definition of the self and the other emerges through an exchange of violence". In this exchange, victims of feud are simply "bearers of the status of their group, the means through which the pact of violence continues to be executed".[24]

In our own time, analyses of ethnic violence in Bosnia, especially, but also in Sri Lanka, Sudan, Chechnya and Rwanda, see a strong link between ethnicity or religion-based territorial vivisection and ethnic "cleansing". Nationalist fratricide is part of the partition of countries when that partition is caused by the collision of two fundamentally opposed nationalist imaginations. Partitions in South Asia—India–Pakistan, Pakistan–Bangladesh, Tamil Eelam, among them—are the archetype of nationalist fratricide, the "conflict of people of a common cultural heritage in competition as 'nations' for control over land and government".[25]

Marking the Body

Women occupy a special place—and space—in such enactments of violence. Our own interviews with several women, survivors of the violence and the displacement, as well as with those who worked on their recovery and rehabilitation over an extended period of time corroborate, but also expand and elaborate upon what is found in written accounts.[26] In the next section, we discuss in detail the violence of abduction and forcible recovery of women; our attempt here is to look at the violence that women were subjected, to both, at the hands of men of the other community and within their own families, and to demonstrate how these diverse, yet linked, kinds of violence formed part of a continuum of violence that began pre-Partition and continued into the early Fifties. A careful consideration of such violence, specific though it may be to a particular historical moment and to communal conflict, may enable us to gain some insight into the more mundane violence and abuse that form part of the everyday experience of many women. It is also our hypothesis that the dramatic episodes of violence against women during communal riots bring to the surface, savagely and explicitly, familiar forms of sexual violence—now charged with a symbolic meaning that serves as an indicator of the place that women's sexuality occupies in an all-male, patriarchal arrangement of gender relations, between and within religious or ethnic communities.

The most predictable form of violence experienced by women, as women, is when the women of one community are sexually assaulted by the men of the other, in an overt assertion of their identity and a simultaneous humiliation of the Other by "dishonouring" their women. In this respect, the rape and molestation of Hindu, Sikh and Muslim women before and after Partition probably followed the familiar pattern of sexual violence, and of attack, retaliation and reprisal. What may be remarkable is the exultation that accompanied it. Stories of women been stripped "just as bananas are peeled",[27] and being made to parade naked in the market-place; or of being made to dance thus in gurudwaras; of being raped in the presence of their menfolk, recur both in written accounts and in our interviews. The Civil Surgeon of Sheikhupura, for example, testified to the Fact Finding Team mentioned earlier, on the violence in Guru Nanakpura on August 26, 1947 and said that, "women and young girls in all forms of nakedness" were brought to his hospital; "even the ladies of the most respectable families had the misfortune of having undergone this most terrible experience. The wife of an advocate had practically nothing on when she came to the hospital."[28] And the medical doctor at the refugee camp in Jhang testified as follows:

Apart from the injured from Jhang-Maghiana town (following the violence of August 26, 1947) over 500 seriously wounded persons were brought to the refugee camp from adjoining villages. One of the cases that I treated was of a woman from village Chund Bharwana who was the wife of a railway porter. One of her hands was chopped off above her wrist and then she was thrown into the fire, as a result of which her lower portion got burnt. But she escaped from there and was then thrown into a well with her two daughters and one son. She was taken out of the well later on and brought to the refugee camp.[29]

Among the chief types of injury inflicted on the wounded, the same doctor cites "amputation of breasts of women", and adds that "six such cases of chopped-off breasts were brought to the refugee camp and all of them proved fatal"

Very large numbers of women were forced into death to avoid sexual violence against them, to preserve chastity and protect individual, family and community "honour". The means used to accomplish this end varied; when women themselves took their lives, they would either jump into the nearest well or set themselves ablaze, singly, or in groups that could be made up either of all the women in the family; the younger women ; or women and children. The Fact Finding Team recorded that in Bewal village (Rawalpindi distt.) during the massacres of March 10, 1947, "many women and girls saved their honour by self-immolation. They collected their beddings and cots in a heap and when the heap caught fire they jumped on to it, raising cries of 'Sat Sri Akal'!"[30] A schoolteacher of government high school, Sheikhupura, who was in one of the three camps attacked on August 26, 1947, recounted the following:

> During the attack, my wife and daughter got separated. My wife took shelter in one house and my daughter in another. My daughter tried to put an end to her life by persuading a lawyer's son to strangle her. Three attempts were made but my daughter survived though she remained unconscious for some time. There were one or two girls in this house also, and they prepared a pyre with some quilts and charpayees.[31]

And the story of 90 women of Thoa Khalsa (Rawalpindi) who jumped into a well on March 15, 1947, is too well known to bear repeating.

Similar accounts abound but it is not our purpose here to repeat the litany of horror; it has been amply documented and can be easily located. Nevertheless, as we read and heard these reports, and as today we read and hear about similar violence in Meerut, Surat, Bhagalpur, Ahmedabad, we begin to discern some specific features of "communal" crimes against women: their brutality, their extreme sexual violence and their collective nature. The range of sexual violation explicit in the above accounts—stripping; parading naked; mutilating and disfiguring; tattooing or branding the breasts and genitalia with triumphal slogans; amputating breasts; knifing open the womb; raping, of course; killing foetuses—is shocking nc t only for its savagery, but for what it tells us about women as objects in male constructions of their own honour. Women's sexuality symbolises "manhood"; its desecration is a matter of such shame and dishonour that *it has to be avenged*. Yet, with the cruel logic of all such violence, it is women ultimately who are most violently dealt with as a consequence.

Each one of the violent acts mentioned above has specific symbolic meaning and physical consequences, and all of them treat women's bodies as territory to be conquered, claimed or marked by the assailant. Some acts are simultaneous or continuous (they may begin with stripping and culminate in raping, branding or tattooing); they may take place in public—market-places, temples or gurudwaras, the latter two signifying the simultaneous violation of women and sacred space—or privately, but with families as witness. Tattooing and branding the body with "Pakistan, Zindabad!" or "Hindustan, Zindabad!" not only mark the woman for life, they never allow her (or her family and community) the possibility of forgetting her humiliation. In the deep horror of its continuous and forever present recall of brutality, this particular violation has few parallels. In the context of Partition, it engraved the division of India into India and Pakistan on the women of both religious communities in a way that they *became* the respective countries, indelibly imprinted by the Other. Marking the breasts and genitalia with symbols like the crescent moon or trident makes permanent the sexual appropriation of the woman, and symbolically extends this violation to future generations who are thus metaphorically stigmatised. Amputating her breasts at once desexualises a woman and negates her as wife and mother; no longer a nurturer (if she survives, that is) she remains a permanently inauspicious figure, almost as undesirable as a barren woman. Sudhir Kakar, in his exploration of how communities fantasize violence, says that sexual mutilation figures prominently: the castration of males and the amputation of breasts "incorporate the (more or less conscious) wish to wipe the enemy off the face of the earth" by eliminating the means of reproduction and nurturing.[32]

Stasa Zajovic, analysing the mass rape of women in Bosnia-Herzegovina, says that as a result of rape "the female womb becomes occupied territory".[33] In Serbo-Croat, she continues, the term "cleansing" is popularly used for abortion, but abortion takes on a particular political significance in circumstances such as these. The idea of polluting and cleansing applies especially to women's bodies. In the process of rehabilitating women, post-Partition, many were regularly submitted to "medical check-ups" to eliminate the possibility of their bearing the enemy's children and "polluting the biological national source of family". Thus is a woman's reproductive power appropriated to prevent the undesirable proliferation of the enemy's progeny. Worse, the female body itself can be made to seem as if it has turned traitor.[34]

The violence against women during Partition cannot be separated from the violent hostility that erupted between Hindus and Muslims at that time. The repertoire of violence on all sides included profaning everything that was held to be of sacred and symbolic value to the Other—from pigs and cows slain in front of mosques and temples, to the circumcision of non-Muslim men, and the forced consumption of beef by Hindus—and this extended to sexually violating their women. The preoccupation with women's sexuality formed part of the contract of war between the three communities, and in our view, was of an even greater order of magnitude than circumcision or forcible conversion and marriage. So powerful and general was the belief that safeguarding a woman's honour is *essential* to upholding male and community honour that a whole new order of violence came into play, by men against their own kinswomen;[35] and by women against their daughters or sisters and their own selves. Three such accounts were given to us by the families of the women concerned, and one by a woman who barely escaped such a death herself.

Split Memory

*"Puttar, aurat da ki ai, au tan varti jaandi ai hamesha, bhanve apne hon, bhanve paraye."**

It has been almost impossible to write the accounts that follow with equanimity. Although we had read several reports and documents that describe the violence experienced by women in chilling detail, we were unprepared for what we heard from the women themselves about how many of them had been forced to die—at the hands of men in their own families, or by their own hands. Poisoned, strangled or burnt to death, put to the sword, drowned. It was made abundantly clear to them that death was preferable to "dishonour", that in the absence of their men the only choice available to them was to take their own lives. So many women told us how so many others had killed themselves, and so many men recounted with pride how their women "preferred to commit suicide" (*khudkashi*).

We could not, as some have done, accept these forced deaths as "suicides" with women "voluntarily" endorsing an honour code that requires their dying; just as we cannot consider the deliberate and premeditated immolation of widows on their husbands' funeral pyres, as sati. The circumstances in which many women took their own lives can hardly be said to have offered them much choice in the matter. When vials of poison or kirpans are handed to you; or quilts piled up, doused with kerosene and ignited so that you can jump into the fire; or wells and rivers pointed out

---

* "My child, what of a woman? It's her lot to be used, either by her own men or by others."

so that you can drown in them, can there be anything "voluntary" about such a death? With fathers, brothers, husbands, sons, mothers and aunts urging you to end your life swiftly and "courageously", such "suicides" in normal times would be called by another name. As we discuss later, these deaths were an instance of when, to acquiesce is not to consent, and to submit is not necessarily to agree. Notions of shame and honour are so ingrained and have been internalised so successfully by men and women, both, that a death which has been forced onto a woman may quite easily be considered a "willing sacrifice" even by women themselves.

Many women lived with the fear that each day may be their last and carried their poison packets around their necks. As they recounted their stories, simply but terribly, we realized that no description by us could adequately communicate the full import of what the imminence of death meant to them. The only way to do so is in their own words, with each narration describing another way of dying. And so, our first story is a first hand account by one who almost died. We sat in Taran's house in Kanpur in a middle-class neighbour-hood, listening to her as she reminisced; her memory moved back and forth between 1947 and 1984 when, as a Sikh, she was the target of another violent communal attack. In between, because we were with her for a few days, we laughed and joked, she read us her stories and poems, sang for and with us in a beautiful, mellifluous voice, cooked, even played cards. Around us swirled the city of Kanpur and the dailiness of her life flowed in and out of our conversation. She spoke of her children, her writing, her joys and despair, her dreams. And she spoke about 1947.

One night, suddenly we heard drums and our house was encircled. A mob gathered outside. I was 16, brimming with vitality. My two sisters were 17 and 14, and my mother was sick with worry. She trembled with fear. She took out all her gold, tied it up in handkerchiefs and distributed it among different family members for safekeeping. She made us wear several sets of clothes each, one on top of the other, shoes, socks, everything, and she asked us to hide the gold. We did not know where each of us would end up—this gold was our security. She kept crying and kept giving us instructions. The Muslims had brought *mashals* with them and were shouting slogans. The thanedar there was a Sayyid. He held the Qoran Sharif in one hand and warned the crowd not to touch the Hindus. They shouted back in anger and said they would not spare the kafirs. He said, " I am a Sayyid and you will have to walk over my dead body before you reach the Hindus and Sikhs." The mob left that night, but such incidents were repeated. They could attack at any time.

So we formed committees which met and discussed what to do. One day they were talking about what to do with all the young girls in the community. We would listen stealthily and overheard them saying that all of us should be locked up in a room and burnt alive. Our own families were saying this—they had seen what some Muslims had done to the women, raped and killed them. The ones who escaped and came back were in such bad shape—disfigured, mistreated. They felt it was better to kill their women than have them go through this.

Should I tell you what I felt when I heard this? I loved life, was in love with it. And I saw death staring me in the face. Just a few days earlier there had been a wedding in the family and we all had new clothes made. I started wearing a new suit every day, along with all the jewellery. I would dress up and call my friends over. I was going to die anyway, what difference did it make? My grandmother would get furious and say, "What do you think you are you up to? Why are you doing all this?" I said to her, "Beji, since we're going to die, why shouldn't I wear all my nice clothes now? Why should someone else wear them when I'm dead?

Taran survived Partition, as did her sisters, and then lived to experience the terrible violence against Sikhs in Kanpur after Indira Gandhi's assassination in 1984. But that's another story. Or is it?

Charanjit Singh Bhatia is a genial Sikh patriarch, head of a large family that came over to Rajasthan from Quetta in the NWFP, in 1947. We met him in Kota in his large, well-appointed house, evidence of his family's having made good in the intervening years. He listened politely as we explained our "research" to him, interrupting every now and again to add some bit of information or variation on an event that we recounted. Almost as if he was giving us just another detail, he told us about his uncle:

> He had six daughters, all of them very good-looking. He was well-to-do and also had very good relations with his Muslim neighbours. They told him to give his daughters in marriage to their sons—that way, they would all then be related and his family's safety assured. They could continue to live in the village without fear. He kept listening to them and nodding, seeming to agree. That evening, he got all his family members together and decapitated each one of them with his talwar, killing 13 people in all. He then lit their chita (pyre), climbed on to the roof of his house and cried out: *"Baratan lai ao! Hun lai ao baratan apniyan! Merian theeyan lai jao, taiyaar ne vyah vaste!"* (Bring on the marriage parties! You can bring your grooms now. Take my daughters away, they are ready for their marriages!) and so saying, he killed himself too.

Charanjit stopped. Then, shaking his head sadly he said, "That was a terrible time, people were made to do terrible things."

Part of the tragedy of those terrible times was that protection, both for those who offered it and those who could not accept it, was contingent upon a transgression—that of conversion and marriage—that in itself was equivalent to dying. By calling to his sometime friends and neighbours to come now and claim his dead daughters, Charanjit's uncle was reversing a fate that would otherwise have befallen him had he accepted their offer. This response that chose real, but honourable, death over the symbolic death that marriage and conversion entailed seemed not just preferable, but almost prescribed for Hindus and Sikhs. Another branch of this particular family succumbed and left behind a young daughter in exchange for safe passage to India, while three others were abducted in the confusion of moving. All were subsequently recovered and claimed by the family, one after ten years in Pakistan.

The Sheikhupura Tragedy: The district of Sheikhupura in West Punjab was a Muslim majority area but the Sikhs formed a substantial minority, 19 per cent of the population. Mainly agriculturist, they hoped that the Boundary Commission would allot the district to India because of its cultural association with Nankana Sahib, the birthplace of Guru Nanak, and Sacha Sauda, an important shrine glorifying the piety of his childhood. For this reason no large-scale exodus from Sheikhupura took place before August 16, the day the Radcliffe Award was announced. The Sikhs were at a disadvantage, arrangements for evacuation could not be made, and for several days no escape was possible. Sheikhupura became a byword for murder, arson, loot and rape; between August 17 and August 31 it was estimated that close to ten thousand people had been killed. They took refuge wherever they could, in Chuharkana and Sacha Sauda refugee camps, at the Namdhari Dharamsala, the government high school, the gurudwaras. The Sacha Sauda camp alone had over a hundred thousand people, as refugees from Gujranwala and the surrounding rural areas converged on Sheikhupura.[36]

In Amritsar in 1991, we heard the story of Sheikhupura many times over from various people, one of whom was a woman who herself had been a Search Officer working with Mridula Sarabhai on recovering abducted women. She recounted to us the story of a friend of her's and her husband's in Amritsar, a medical doctor who had died only a couple of years earlier. His name was Dr. Virsa Singh, and he came from Sheikhupura.

> Virsa Singh claimed he had shot 50 women personally. First he shot his own wife because the Muslims came to get them. Once he had done this, all the women in the neighbourhood gathered around, saying *"Viran, pehle mannu maar, pehle mannu maar."* (Brother, kill me first.) Some would push their daughters forward, saying, "Shoot her, put a bullet through her now." He says he just kept shooting and shooting. "They kept bringing them forward I kept shooting. There was shooting all around. At least 50 or 60 women I shot—my wife, my mother, daughter. . ."

I used to talk to him about it, ask him how he had killed like this. He would say, "How could I see my wife, my daughters fall into the hands of the Muslims ? I recalled Sikh history, the bravery of our people—I wasn't a murderer, I was their saviour." I said to him , "This must be a terrible burden for you to bear." He said, "Not at all, no burden." He subsequently remarried, had children, and wrote a book about it, called *Bhuler da Saka.*

"I don't know," said Mrs. Narindar Singh to us, "we were friends, we talked about it sometimes, I don't know how he did it."

Our last example is of a family of Khatris from Azad Kashmir all of whose women, save three, died so that there were hardly any female elders left on the paternal side of the family.* We heard the story of how they died first from Iqbal, their nephew, who was a young teenager at the time. We were introduced to him by his niece, Reva, in whose house we met one evening in 1991. Both keva and his wife were present throughout. Iqbal is a refugee twice over—first in 1947 from Muzaffarabad to Kashmir, then in 1990 from Kashmir to Delhi. As with Taran earlier, his retelling of events in 1947 was laced with references to his recent experiences in Kashmir, and particularly to the vulnerability of Hindu women in the prevailing tension between Hindus and Muslims in the Valley.

On October 17, 1947 he told us, the fourth day after Muzaffarabad was raided, the town was under curfew. In Baramulla the *kabailis* (tribals) looted jewellery off the women and took two truckloads of them back into the surrounding mountains. The Hindus then decided to collect in clusters and stick together for safety. They informed a senior officer of the impending attack and asked for protection. According to Iqbal this information was somehow relayed to the raiders by an informer, and they advanced their attack by two days. Here is how he recalled the events that led to the women's suicides, and to his assisting in the death

---

* Names in this account have been changed to safeguard privacy.

of his young cousin, a beautiful 18 year old whose husband strangled her to death with her own dupatta.

> On October 19 we noticed a massing of tribals on the hills around our village. Mehta Dhuni Chand, the DC, was the first target—he was killed. Many Hindu families, including ours, gathered in a large haveli. Some had rifles and guns with which we kept the tribals at bay for a couple of days. After this, we were overpowered and had to surrender. All our money was taken and we were told to march across the bridge over the Krishanganga. My three sisters swallowed poison—the hospital compounder distributed poison to any-one who wanted it— my bua gave the signal to the other women to jump by jumping off the bridge first. Then other aunts, my bhabis, six in all, killed themselves. No one tried to stop them, not even my father. We tried to persuade Veeran, a young cousin, to take opium, but she refused.

Iqbal himself didn't acknowledge the role the men had played in the women's deaths, nor would he admit to hav-ing helped strangle his cousin (the women of the family told us that he and her husband held one end of the dupatta each, and pulled). He kept repeating that the decision was theirs alone— they saw that they couldn't be protected any more and took their lives. But he also kept adding, "Natu-rally, if we (that is, the men) were going to be killed who would protect them? They had no choice." (Even as Iqbal was recounting this his wife kept interjecting: "They must have encouraged them, after all, what could ladies do in this situation? They must have persuaded them, what could the women do?")

We knew that two or three of the older women had not taken their lives and wondered what their memory of that incident was. Perhaps they could fill in some details, tell us how it actually happened. In a cool and darkened room on a hot summer afternoon in Delhi in 1992, we heard Bimla Bua's story:

> Two days before the attack people were already distributing guns and preparing for battle. We were told to leave Muzaffarabad and make for Srinagar and safety. But before we knew it 'they' arrived. We were asleep when they at-

tacked. We were first running, then we gathered in a few houses and stayed there till they burned them down. We never separated from each other. Outside, there were bullets flying, everybody trying to put out the fires. . . slogans, Pakistan, Zindabad! . . . They took everybody's gold, herded us out. We got separated, hid in a sugarcane field, didn't know where the others were. . . Somehow we came to the jail, next to which flowed the Krishanganga, and as we approached we saw women throwing themselves off it, bullets flying. . . we couldn't believe our eyes. . . .

Then they caught hold of a beautiful 17 year old and her sister who wouldn't let go of her hand. They dragged them for a long distance and the girls kept calling out, 'Bachao, bachao. . .' The *kabailis* were collecting all the Hindus and Sikhs in a hideout, Bala Pir. The two girls were already there . . . Night fell, they kept raping the women, then dumped them. Divided up the gold. They wouldn't leave the 17 year old and she decided she would commit suicide. But how to kill herself? She asked for a rope— but where to get it from? Her brother and husband then got hold of a scarf and decided they would strangle her with it. They were unarmed and helpless. She survived, despite their efforts to strangle her all night. During this she fainted, and in the morning they decided to throw her in the river. We didn't try to stop her—we, too, thought we would do the same, but we had the children to think of.

The next day they took her to the river, accompanied by the *kabailis* who kept saying, 'Give her to us, we'll restore her to health.' When she stirred and opened her eyes they tried to catch hold of her. Her brothers and husband then picked her up and threw her into the river.

They fed us only *gur ke chane*, no water, no food. In the evening they said the men and women have to be separated. Then they killed all the Sikhs and for some reason, allowed us to go. We crossed the bridge, it was dark, somehow we reached the jail where there were about 4,000 people. . . .

Bimla Bua says she kept a diary

. . . because I could never forget what happened during Partition, and because I wanted to put down what I had seen. I called it *My Recollections*. I simply couldn't forget that expe-

rience, it came before my eyes every waking moment. Now
when I walk the streets of Green Park, I think only of Nadir
Shah because I'm steeped in history. Partition was something
I experienced— how could I forget it ?

We stayed in jail for eight days, in a large hall. On Id, the
things I saw, I couldn't believe. . . how many women died by
their own hands, first with opium which was very slow, then
the hakims gave a poison which you just placed in your
mouth and died. . .

The *kabailis* were not interested in our lives, they wanted
young girls, they would kill any Muslim who tried to protect a Hindu. . . I had a ring left—and a pen. I kept hoping
they wouldn't steal my pen. . .

Reva's story:

Krishna (the cousin who was killed) was very young, very
beautiful. We often spoke about her when we were young. . .
the children would gather round to hear Partition stories.
The suicides and deaths were remembered with some kind
of pride by my male relatives—and women also. For us, it
was like a story, a kind of drama. We had photographs of the
women who died, the family kept their photographs, and
we would look at them sometimes. . . now we don't talk about
it very much. But then, we were also told some funny stories. . . there were very few aunts left in our family. . .

In Jammu in 1992, we met another branch of the family
which had left Muzaffarabad in 1947, five months after the
raid, but were on the move for ten years before they finally
settled down in Jammu in 1958. Many from their *biradari*
(kin community) live here in a kind of Muzaffarabad recre-
ated, intermarry within the community, and keep close family ties. Munni, another of Iqbal's nieces and Reva's cousin,
added an almost macabre twist to the story we had already
heard from Iqbal and Reva, and as she told it her father kept
interjecting, correcting her or providing details as he thought
fit.

Her part of the family, Munni said, prepared to commit
suicide by piling wood in the kitchen and setting themselves
on fire. Her mother threw Munni, who was just 10 months
old, on a lighted pyre but she was saved by a *kabaili* who

pulled her out just as her hair caught fire. He fed her with sugarcane juice till she revived and then handed her over to her mother. They escaped and stayed in a cave for four days but were separated from her father. When her mother heard (wrongly, as it turned out) that her husband had been killed, she killed herself too, by swallowing poison. Munni was brought up by her grandmother with whom she lived till she was an adult. Her father, meanwhile, had remarried.

Munni says her (maternal) grandfather could never reconcile himself to the suicides of the women in the family. He believed they had been sent to their deaths by one man in the family: his own brother and Iqbal's father. When the women turned to the latter for direction as the *kabailis* advanced and asked, "*Bhravan, hun ki kariye?*" (Brother, what should we do now?) he is supposed to have pointed to the Krishanganga and said, "There flows the river."

Only three women stood firm and refused to kill themselves or their children, despite the fact that packets of poison were ready for them all. "No more," they said "we're not going to kill our children." One aunt (Veeran) refused to take poison or give it to her 13 year old daughter, in spite of the menfolk urging her to do so. Later she justified her refusal by saying that "someone had to stay back and cook for the men if they survived", but she was made to feel ashamed of her "cowardice", her lack of courage in embracing her death.

Violent Means, Violent Ends

As our interviews progressed and we spoke to a wider group of people—survivors, men who had killed, families whose women were forced to die—we began to recognize some features of what we call a gendered telling of violence. No one failed to recall the violence of Partition, in general, and a particular moment of violence for themselves, personally; nor did anyone, man or woman, gloss over how women are dealt with in communal conflict. Yet, in the recounting of violence within their own families we noted an element of detachment in the men. The story is told in the heroic mode—the singular and extraordinary instance of doing a kinswoman to death is elevated to supreme and glorious sacrifice. So, one man's—or one family's, or one village's, even one community's—tragedy is sublimated and unfolds against the backdrop of siege and resistance, valour and vanquishment, honour and shame. The unhappy conjunction of all these made it incumbent on men to *act*, and to act almost on behalf of the collectivity of men. Although none of the men we spoke to (except Munni's father) admitted to it, the same unhappy conjunction may well have impelled them to kill members of the other community, too—that would not only avenge, it might even confer, honour.

For both men and women the trauma of Partition violence was difficult to articulate and this often made for a hesitant, disjointed or sometimes even "wordless" telling. We cannot say that men and women, as men and women, always spoke in different voices. Yet, as their accounts themselves indicate, the gendered nature of the experience of violence engendered its telling in specific ways. At least some part of this difference must lie in the fact that women, as Veena Das and Ashis Nandy have pointed out, were not only objects of, but also witness to, violence. Because they "retained the memory of loot, rape and plunder" in their bodies they remember it differently.[37] With men, the representation of violence may take a more formal or organized narration, like Iqbal's; be declamatory, like Dr. Virsa Singh's, or sadly matter-of-fact, like Charanjit Bhatia's. Occasionally it is distressed but, whatever the mode or tone, there hovers over their telling what Val Daniel calls "the protective shadow of a coherent narrative"; and even though there may have been ambivalence in their own actions, they are constrained from acknowledging it. Their telling has been incorporated into, and is part of, the master narrative, that male consensus which incorporates many singular voices into a whole. Its conceit, says Daniel, "is in its claim that it represents the truth or reality. . . This indeed is the mode of the narrative of modern history."[38]

The women's telling, on the other hand, exhibits what Daniel calls the "recalcitrantly ambiguous character of lived experience", and thereby challenges the normalising discourse of the men. Women's are the dissonant voices which are ordinarily "deflected, ignored, subordinated, excluded or destroyed";[39] and so, Iqbal's wife's is a questioning voice, a critiquing voice which avoids statements of fact even as it challenges the "facts" her husband offers. It is a voice which seems to account for the dead women's silence itself, fully conscious of male power to "encourage" and "persuade". Meanwhile, her husband keeps repeating "the decision was theirs", thereby attempting to speak *for* the dead women, in complicity with their men.[40] So, too, Bimla Bua's ambiguity with regard to their own (imminent) and Krishna's (real) death—"we didn't try to stop her—we, too, thought we would do the same but we had the children to think about"— is embedded in the larger social and historical discordance of the time and the crises and confusion it generated. Her account reverberates with its tensions, her recall is forever haunted by what she can "never forget". Her telling exposes the cracks in the family narrative at the same time as it exposes the celebration of "suicide", and punctures the coherence of the master narrative in which the death/sacrifice of women was considered the "normal", even inevitable, response to the chaos of an abnormal moment. In this scheme of things, Taran's defiant assertion of life in the face of death could only shock her grandmother because it turned the "normal" inside-out and showed it up for what it was—an inhuman code of conduct required almost exclusively of women. So, although she may have had no choice in the matter, she nevertheless demonstrated her disagreement by flamboyantly drawing attention to the very body that was considered a liability.

Reva's unexpected reconstruction, in hindsight, of women's mass dying as simultaneously heroic and humorous, and her non-committal recounting of one aunt's refusal to comply, has something of the detachment of her uncle's account. But it is drawn into sudden intimacy with the mention of the women's photographs and quickly identifies her now, today, telling the story, with them; there is a direct correspondence between her own vulnerability and theirs, always the potential sacrifice. The poignant, almost unconscious aside—"We used to look at (the photographs) occasionally, but now don't talk about it very much"—tries to distance that tragic (but necessary) event from her own life and circumstances, and is in striking contrast to her aunt's inability to forget.

Taran told herself she was "dying for freedom", not to save her "honour"; Bimla Bua rationalised her non-compliance in terms of maternal responsibility, almost as powerful a charge as safeguarding honour, but could not put it behind her. Fifteen years later she wrote her recollections ("in simple English" she said) in order to reconcile her life and her memories, but it was clear from her telling that neither reconciliation nor serenity attended her writing. If not serenity, then an element of recollecting in tranquility marked the accounts of Iqbal and Charanjit Bhatia. Shorn of the intimate detail that are present in both Bimla Bua's and Taran's accounts, they are more obviously representational: the words they use describe the events alright, but the relationship between themselves and what they describe is obscure. Neither Iqbal nor Munni's father were able to reflect on their own implication in the women's deaths: "What else could they do?" they asked, or simply, "They wanted to die." The normalising imperative that condoned, almost enjoined, such a violent resolution.

Gradually we realized that this violent "resolution" was part of a *continuum of violence* that had death at the hands of one's own kinsmen at one end, and rape and brutalisation by men of the other community at the other. In between lay taking your own life, sublimating your vulnerability and making of it something heroic. Also in between, and governed by the same logic, was the covert violence of the state exercised through the implementation of its recovery programme, a programme which forcibly recovered women abducted by men of the "other" community. In an attempt to resettle and rehabilitate them, it displaced and dislocated them once again. What connects the brutal and deliberate communal sexual violence against women to the desperate, but no less deliberate, doing to death of them by their own kinsmen? What links these two, in turn, to the equally deliberate and no less violent actions of the state in its apparently benign programme of recovery? What connects them, in our view, is a powerful consensus around the subject of violence against women. Neither absolute nor monolithic (obviously, not all men agreed that killing kinswomen was acceptable) this consensus is, nevertheless, at once deep and wide-ranging and encompasses most forms of violence, including the specific forms we have spoken of in this discussion. It has two critical and distinguishing features: it sanctions the violent "resolution" (so to speak) of the troublesome question of women's sexuality and sexual status—chaste, polluted, impure—and *simultaneously insists on women's silence regarding it* through the attachment of shame and stigma to this very profound violation of self. Thus, the woman raped, the woman who may be raped, the raped child, the young widow whose sexuality can no longer be channelised, the wife raped by kinsmen or others, the women who must be killed so that their sexuality is not misappropriated, the wives, daughters and sisters who must be recovered so that sexual transgression is reversed—are all compelled into acquiescing.* *

Some kinds of consensus are familiar, such as the patriarchal notion of safeguarding honour (male as well as community honour) through a control over women's sexuality. Most men and women we spoke to were agreed that honour—for losing or preserving—is located in the body of the woman. (Many women told us of how mothers would try to disfigure their young daughters who were attractive by smearing ash or mud on their faces to prevent them from

---

* Much later, and post-Partition, many of these same husbands and fathers would force their women into prostitution to enable the family to survive; now, male "survival" was more urgent than male "honour".

being molested.) Even Durga Rani who said, "What fault was it of the poor girl's? She didn't leave on her own, she was picked up . . ." had to admit that once abused, her "character" was now "spoilt". The consensus during Partition around killing one's own women is less common, and has to be considered in the context of general communal violence and forced evacuation. (Falling into the hands of men belonging to one's own community did not give rise to the same sort of shame-fear-dishonour syndrome, what Gananath Obeysekere calls *lajja-bhaya* [shame-fear]: a perceived loss of status is shameful; *bhaya* is the fear of losing status and of humiliation.[41]) Such an extreme circumstance transforms the deliberate taking of life into an act of humanity, easily accommodated in an unfolding scenario of shame, honour and martyrdom (*shahidi*). The consensus here is that actual death is preferable to death-in-life or the symbolic death of rape/abduction/conversion; the consensus is that murder is permissible. But the nature of the agreement is different, as we have seen from the accounts presented earlier: women can be part of the consensus and sacrifice themselves to honour; or they may agree on the importance of upholding honour but refuse to die in order to save it. Munni's story illustrates the ways in which women offer resistance even when they are most critically in jeopardy. The resistance of the aunt who refused to consume poison, justifying her non-compliance through a non-threatening discourse of respect and service; the resistance of the women who said, "No more", and the powerful memory of that resistance in Munni's narration; Taran's defiance; even Bimla Bua's ambivalence demonstrate the women's unwillingness to either consent to or acquiesce with an inhuman demand. And even when they do, they may well do so after weighing the consequences of both resistance and assent. With women, then, the shame-fear-dishonour syndrome presents itself differently: fear at the prospect of being sexually used; the unspeakable shame of being raped; fear of death and afraid because without defenders; and the twin dishonour of violation and consequent rejection.

The consensus is most successful when women "voluntarily" participate in the violence that is done to them, and ensuring their silence is a necessary part of the consensus. How often were we told of the courage and strength of women who came forward to be killed, or who set an example of self-negation by taking their own lives; and again and again, we heard men say with pride, "They preferred to die." This not only released the men from any responsibility for their deaths it also put a closure both, on the women's lives and on their speech. In much the same way the strenuous efforts made by families to protect their women at the height of communal violence were wholly consistent with later attempts to erase their very presence from their lives if they had had the misfortune of falling into alien hands; so too, the equally diligent efforts made by the authorities to eliminate any evidence of their having been so misused through large-scale abortions. The subsequent taboo on recall drove many, many women into silence and a willed amnesia regarding their violation. The consensus around the overt and dramatic violence of "suicide" and honourable killing, or rape and abduction also operated in the recovery programme; the state's ready consent to engaging in a similar violence (which, like the others, masqueraded as deliverance) lends piquancy to such a notion of partriarchal consensus.

The circumstances and particular violence against women that we have discussed may have been peculiar to Partition. Yet, as Pradeep Jeganathan writing on ethnic violence in urban Sri Lanka says, the "form and content of the extraordinary is deeply embedded in the history of the everyday, but nevertheless also stands outside the everyday".[42] So, moments of rupture and extreme dislocation, extraordinary as they are, underscore the more daily doses of violence against women and enable us to see them as part of the continuum—and, despite the shudder of horror, part of the consensus.

Notes

1 Satya Rai, *Partition of the Punjab* (Bombay: Asia Publishing House, 1965), p.102.
2 Ibid., p. 102.
3 Ibid., p. 103.
4 Ibid., p. 103.
5 M.S. Randhawa, *Out of the Ashes: An Account of the Rehabilitation of Refugees from West Pakistan in Rural Areas of East Punjab* (Bombay: 1954), p. ix. A Boundary Commission was set up under Sir Cyril Radcliffe to partition India and redraw her boundaries within 36 days. He was assisted by eight judges, four Hindu and four Muslim, in the task of dividing Punjab and Bengal; the cities, towns and districts awarded to East and West Pakistan, and to East Punjab and West Bengal were announced on August 16, 1947.
6 Satya Rai, op. cit., pp. 109–10.
7 Census of India, 1941, taken from M.S. Randhawa, *Out of the Ashes*, op. cit., p. 8.
8 Confidential Papers and Reports of Evan Jenkins. Note dated March 4, 1947 on "Disturbances in the Punjab". (London: India Office Library, R/3/1/176).
9 G.D. Khosla, *Stern Reckoning: A Survey of the Events Leading Upto and Following the Partition of India* (Delhi: Oxford University Press, 1949), p. 101. A total of 2,094 villages were covered by the survey in Punjab; 316 in the NWFP; and 216 in Bahawalpur.
10 Note dated March 10, 1947 by Evan Jenkins to the Secretary of State for India. Confidential Papers and Reports, op. cit.
11 G.D. Khosla, *Stern Reckoning*, op. cit., pp. 52–53.
12 Evan Jenkins, Confidential Papers and Reports, op. cit. Jenkins quotes from an appeal which appeared in *Ajit*, a paper published from Lahore, on April 5, 1947.
13 Evan Jenkins, Confidential Papers, op. cit. Report dated April 25, 1947.
14 For India, the Report of the Fact Finding Organization headed by G.D. Khosla, published its findings as *Stern Reckoning*, op. cit. The Pakistan government issued its version of events in five pamphlets: *Note on the Sikh Plan: an account of the secret preparations of the Sikhs; The Sikhs in Action: showing the Sikh plan in actual operation; The Rashtriya Swayam Sevak Sangh or the activities of the secret terrorist Hindu organization in the Punjab; Tribal Repercussions or what led the tribal Pathans of the north-west fron-*

tier to come to the aid of the people of Kashmir; Kashmir Before Accession: showing why the people of Kashmir rebelled against the Maharaja's government, what he did to suppress them and why he acceded to India. An unofficial contemporary account may also be found in the report put out by the Shiromani Gurudwara Prabhandak Committee, *Muslim League Attack on Sikhs and Hindus in the Punjab* (Amritsar: Sikh Publishing House, 1950).

[15] Swarna Aiyar, "'August Anarchy': The Partition Massacres in Punjab, 1947" in *South Asia*: Journal of South Asian Studies, Special Issue on "North India: Partition and Independence", op. cit., pp. 13–36.

[16] G.D. Khosla, *Stern Reckoning*, op. cit., pp. 102–05.

[17] Ibid., p. 230.

[18] Anis Kidwai, *Azadi ki Chaon Mein* (Delhi: National Book Trust, 1990), p. 306.

[19] G.D. Khosla, op. cit., p. 234.

[20] See, for example, G.D. Khosla, op. cit.; Swarna Aiyer, "August Anarchy" op. cit., M.S. Randhawa, *Out of the Ashes*, op. cit.; Kirpal Singh, *Partition of Punjab* (Patiala: 1972); Ganda Singh, "A Diary of Partition Days" in Mushirul Hasan (ed.), *India Partitioned: The Other Face of Freedom*, op. cit., pp. 27–96; and the private papers of Evan Jenkins in the India Office Library, among others.

[21] See especially, Sudhir Kakar, *The Colours of Violence* (Delhi: Viking, 1995); Veena Das (ed.), *Mirrors of Violence : Communities, Riots and Survivors in South Asia* (Delhi: Oxford University Press, 1990); and Gyanendra Pandey, "In Defence of the Fragment: Writing About Hindu-Muslim Riots in India Today," op. cit.; and "Community and Violence: Recalling Partition," in *Economic and Political Weekly*, Vol. XXXII, No. 32, August 1997.

[22] Sudhir Kakar, *The Colours of Violence*, op. cit., p. 37.

[23] Veena Das (ed.), op. cit., p. 28.

[24] Veena Das and Ashis Nandy, "Violence, Victimhood and the Language of Silence", in *Contributions to Indian Sociology* (n.s.) Vol. 19, no.1, op. cit.

[25] Jason Francisco, "In the Heat of Fratricide: The Literature of India's Partition Burning Freshly" in *The Annual of Urdu Studies*, op. cit.

[26] We have found almost no analyses of the specific violence against women during the partition of India. Descriptions abound, especially in fiction, but an analysis from a gender

perspective is generally absent. The essay by Das and Nandy,
op. cit., is an exception, as are the following articles by Urvashi
Butalia, "Community, State and Gender: On Women's Agency
During Partition", op. cit. Nighat Said Khan, "Identity, Violence and Women: A Reflection on the Partition of India, 1947"
in Nighat Said Khan, et al. (eds.), op. cit., pp.
157–71; and Ritu
Menon and Kamla Bhasin, "Recovery, Rupture, Resistance: Indian State and Abduction of Women during Partition," op. cit.
[27] Shorish Kashmiri, "Humiliated and Harassed They Left", in
Mushirul Hasan (ed.), *India Partitioned*, op. cit., p. 156.
[28] G.D. Khosla, *Stern Reckoning*, op. cit., p. 133.
[29] Ibid., p. 181.
[30] Ibid., p. 109.
[31] Ibid., p. 130.
[32] Sudhir Kakar, *The Colours of Violence*, op. cit., p. 37.
[33] Stasa Zajovic, "Women and Ethnic Cleansing", in *Women
Against Fundamentalism*, No. 5, 1994, Vol. 1 (London) p. 36. Trs.
by Cynthia Cockburn.
[34] In the rape camps of Bosnia-Herzegovina, Kadira who was raped
again and again (she has forgotten how many times) reports: "They
just came in and raped us and later they told us, 'Come on now, if
you could have Ustasha babies, then you can have a Chetnik baby,
too'." She said that those women who got pregnant had to stay in
the camps for seven or eight months so they could give birth to a
Serbian child. "They had special privileges; they got meals, they
were better off, they were protected. Only when a woman's in her
seventh month. . . then she's released. Then they usually take
these women to Serbia." In Alexandra Stiglmayer (ed.), *Mass Rape:
The War Against Women in Bosnia-Herzegovina* (Lincoln: University of Nebraska Press, 1994), p. 118. Accounts of the violence
against women in Bosnia and Herzegovina are the closest parallel we have found to Partition violence. Though the differences
are obvious, the two events nevertheless alert us to the link between a religion-based vivisection of countries, the sexuality of
women, and their role as upholders of honour and reproducers
of the community.
[35] It is commonly held that Hindu and Sikh women suffered such
a fate, but we were often told in Pakistan that Muslim women,
too, died in similar circumstances. For more details on this, see
Nighat Said Khan, "Identity, Violence and Women", op. cit.
[36] See G.D. Khosla, *Stern Reckoning* and M.S. Randhawa, *Out of*

the Ashes, among others, for detailed accounts of the violence in Sheikhupura.

[37] Veena Das and ·Ashis Nandy, "Violence, Victimhood and the Language of Silence", op. cit.

[38] Val Daniel, "Mood, Moment·and Mind: Writing Violence", op. cit.

[39] Ibid.

[40] We are grateful to Paola Bacchetta for drawing our attention to this important difference.

[41] As discussed by Pradeep Jeganathan in his unpublished paper, "All the Lord's Men? Perpetrator Constructions of Collective Ethnic Violence in an Urban Sri Lankan Community", n.d.

[42] Ibid.

Borders and Bodies

Recovering Women in the Interest
of the Nation

There are many young, half-mad women who keep laughing—
perhaps at all of us, at the country,
at religion and the propagators of these religions,
at governments and their laws.
Maybe they laugh at freedom—
who knows what they are laughing at?
                                    — Anis Kidwai,
                                    Azadi ki Chaon Mein

. . . *In the week ending May 8, 129 non-Muslim abducted women and children were recovered, and 495 Muslims; 13,277 Muslims were brought over, mainly forcible converts. There is much agitation about the failure, particularly in the States, to recover abducted women, and perhaps in answer to the lady hunger-striker in Bahawalpur (in Pakistan), you may have seen that two Muslim women social workers went for a time on a "hunger strike unto death" in Patiala (in India) in protest against lack of help received from State authorities.*

The fact is that whatever the leaders may say the plight of these women does not seriously touch the public conscience or even the conscience of a minor official, enough at least to induce him to co-operate against his own community to secure the release of women of a community he hates . . . too drastic action would merely lead to large-scale murder.

— Extract from a report dated May 24, 1948, from H.S. Stephenson, Deputy High Commissioner of the UK in Lahore, to the High Commissioner in Karachi.[1]

Recovery

In the aftermath of Partition the governments of India and Pakistan were swamped with complaints by relatives of "missing" women seeking to recover them, either through government, military or voluntary effort. Recognizing the enormity of the problem the two governments entered into an Inter-Dominion Agreement in November 1947 to recover as many women, as speedily as possible, from each country and restore them to their families. This agreement was followed by the passing of ordinances in both countries to cover the years upto December 1949, and in December of that year, the Indian Parliament legislated an act to facilitate the recovery operation in India.

The material, symbolic and political significance of the abduction of women was not lost either on the women themselves and their families, on communities, or leaders and governments. Leaders expressed their concern and anger at the "moral depravity" that characterised this "shameful chapter" in the history of both countries; the fact that "our innocent sisters" had been dishonoured was an issue that could not be looked upon with equanimity. Said one MP in Parliament:

> If there is any sore point or distressful fact to which we cannot be reconciled under any circumstances, it is the question of abduction and non-restoration of Hindu women. We all know our history, of what happened in the time of Shri Ram when Sita was abducted. Here, where thousands of girls are concerned, we cannot forget this. We can forget all the properties, we can forget every other thing but this cannot be forgotten.

And again, "As descendants of Ram we have to bring back every Sita that is alive."[2]

In a letter dated April 4, 1947 to Evan Jenkins, Nehru said:

> There is one point, however, to which I should like to draw your attention, and this is the question of rescuing women who have been abducted or forcibly converted. You will realize that nothing adds to popular passions more than stories of abduction of women, and so long as these . . . women are not rescued, trouble will simmer and might blaze out.[3]

Malik Feroz Khan Noon thought that the recovery of non-Muslim women abducted during the riots might be decelerated if amnesty were given; on a visit to Bihar, he made a public announcement that if women were returned within a week, it would be assumed that those returning them had been protecting them and had not committed any offence.[4]

At the level of policy, the first initiative was taken at the November 23–25, 1946 session of the Indian National Congress at Meerut, at which a resolution was moved by Dr. Rajendra Prasad, seconded by Maulana Abul Kalam Azad and adopted. It stated:

> The Congress views with pain, horror and anxiety the tragedies of Calcutta, East Bengal, Bihar and some parts of Meerut district. . . These new developments in communal strife are different from any previous disturbances and have

involved murders on a mass scale, as also mass conversions
... abduction and violation of women, and forcible marriage.
Women who have been abducted and forcibly married
must be restored to their houses; mass conversions have no
significance or validity and people must be given every opportunity to return to the life of their choice.[5]

Communal tension and the ensuing violence escalated at
such a rapid pace, however, especially after March 1947, that
on September 3, 1947 leaders and representatives of the governments of India and Pakistan met and resolved that steps
be taken to recover and restore abducted persons. Thus, on
November 17, 1947 the All India Congress Committee passed
a resolution which stated:

During these disorders, large numbers of women have been
abducted on either side and there have been forcible conversions on a large scale. No civilized people can recognize
such conversions and there is nothing more heinous than
the abduction of women. Every effort must be made to restore women to their original homes with the co-operation
of the governments concerned.[6]

On December 6, 1947 an Inter-Dominion Conference was
held at Lahore at which the two countries agreed upon steps
to be taken for the implementation of recovery and restoration, with the appointment of Mridula Sarabhai as Chief All
India Organizer. The recovery operation itself was in the
charge of the Women's Section, Ministry of Relief and Rehabilitation, with Rameshwari Nehru as Honorary Advisor.
The primary responsibility for recovery was with the local
police, assisted by a staff of one additional inspector general, two deputy superintendents of police, 15 inspectors,
10 sub-inspectors and 6 assistant sub-inspectors.[7] Between
December 1947 and July 1948 the number of women recovered in both countries was 9,362 in India and 5,510 in Pakistan. Recoveries dropped rather drastically after this date—
one reason put forward being the withdrawal of the Military Evacuation Organization from both territories—and it
was felt that a more binding arrangement was necessary for
satisfactory progress. Accordingly, an agreement was
reached between India and Pakistan on November 11, 1948

that set out the terms for recovery in each dominion. Ordinances were issued in both countries, in January 1949 for India, and May 1949 for Pakistan; in the case of India it was to remain in force till January 1950, in Pakistan, till it was abrogated.

The official estimate of the number of abducted women was placed at 50,000 Muslim women in India and 33,000 Hindu and Sikh women in Pakistan. Although Gopalaswami Ayyangar (Minister of Transport in charge of Recovery) called these figures "rather wild", Mridula Sarabhai believed that the number of abducted women in Pakistan was ten times the 1948 official figure of 12,500.[8] Till December 1949, the number of recoveries in both countries was 12,552 for India and 6,272 for Pakistan. The maximum number of recoveries were made from Punjab (East and West), followed by Jammu and Kashmir and Patiala. Within Pakistani Punjab, Gujrat district had the most recoveries; in Indian Punjab, Patiala, Ferozepur and Amritsar. The age-wise break-up of women recovered was as follows:[9]

	In Pakistan	In India
	(in percentages)	
> 12 yrs	45	35
12 > 35 yrs	44	59
35 > 50 yrs	6	4
50 and above	5	2

At the Constituent Assembly (Legislative) Session held in December 1949, considerable dissatisfaction was expressed at the low rate and slow pace of recovery in Pakistan, especially from Sind, Baluchistan, Azad Kashmir and the "closed" districts of Gujrat, Jhelum, Rawalpindi and Campbellpur. In addition, there was extreme disquiet at the mention of 2,000 non-Muslim women being held by government servants in Pakistan, and at a cease fire being agreed to in Kashmir without negotiating the return of Hindu women abducted there. Some members even went so far as to call for "open war to recover our sisters and daughters lying helpless in Pakistan", or at the very least, for retaliatory measures, suggesting that only an exchange of women be considered—what they give is what they will get.

To facilitate recovery and because the ordinance in India expired on December 31, 1949, Gopalaswami Ayyangar moved a Bill in Parliament on December 15 called The Abducted Persons (Recovery and Restoration) Bill, for the consideration of the House. It extended to the United Provinces of East Punjab and Delhi, the Patiala and East Punjab States Union (PEPSU) and the United State of Rajasthan, and consisted of 10 operative clauses which the Minister termed "short, simple, straightforward—and innocent"; relevant clauses are reproduced below. (See Appendix I for the full text.)

2. Interpretation

(1) In this Act, unless there is anything repugnant in the subject or context,

(a) "abducted person" means a male child under the age of sixteen years or a female of whatever age who is, or immediately before the 1st day of March 1947, was, a Muslim and who, on or after that day and before the 1st day of January 1949, had become separated from his or her family and is found to be living with or under the control of any other individual or family, and in the latter case includes a child born to any such female after the said date;

. . .

4. Powers of police officers to recover abducted persons

(1) If any police officer, not below the rank of an Assistant Sub-Inspector or any other police officer specially authorised by the Provincial Government in this behalf, has reason to believe that an abducted person resides or is to be found in any place, he may, after recording the reasons for his belief, without warrant, enter and search the place and take into custody any person found therein who, in his opinion, is an abducted person, and deliver or cause such person to be delivered to the custody of the officer in charge of the nearest camp with the least possible delay.

(2) In exercising any powers conferred by sub-section (1) any such police officer may take such steps and may require the assistance of such female persons as may, in his opinion, be necessary for the effective exercise of such power.

. . .

5. (2) In making any regulations under this section, the Provincial Government may provide that a breach thereof shall be tried and punished by the officer in charge of the camp in such manner as may be prescribed in the regulations: Provided that no abducted person shall be liable to be tried in a criminal Court in respect of any offence made punishable by any regulations made under this section.

6. Determination of question whether any person detained is an abducted person

(1) If any question arises whether a person detained in a camp is or is not an abducted person or whether such person should be restored to his or her relatives or handed over to any other person or conveyed out of India or allowed to leave the camp, it shall be referred to, and decided by, a tribunal constituted for the purpose by the Central Government.

(2) The decision of the tribunal constituted under sub-section (1) shall be final: Provided that the Central Government may, either of its own motion or on the application of any party interested in the matter, review or revise any such decision.

7. Handing over of abducted persons to persons authorised

(1) Any officer in charge of a camp may deliver any abducted person detained in the camp to the custody of such officer or authority as the Provincial Government may, by general or special order, specify in this behalf.

(2) Any officer or authority to whom the custody of any abducted person has been delivered under the provisions of sub-section (1) shall be entitled to receive and hold the person in custody and either restore such person to his or her relatives or convey such person out of India.

8. Detention in camp not to be questioned by Court

Notwithstanding anything contained in any other law for the time being in force, the detention of any abducted person in a camp in accordance with the provisions of this Act shall be lawful and shall not be called in question in any Court.

9. Protection of action taken under Act

No suit, prosecution or other legal proceeding whatsoever

shall lie against the Central Government, the Provincial Government or any officer or authority for, or in respect of, any act which is in good faith done or intended to be done in pursuance of this Act.

As is evident the Bill, although it may indeed have been short, was not as simple, straightforward or innocent as the Minister would have the House believe. More than 70 amendments were moved by 20 members in an extended debate on the Bill, that took a full three days to pass. Every clause, sub-clause and section was discussed threadbare, and serious objections were raised on everything from the preamble to the operative clauses. The main objections related to the definition of abductors and the time-frame that the Bill referred to (March 1, 1947 and January 1, 1949); the virtually unlimited powers given to the police with complete immunity from inquiry or action and no accountability at all; the denial of any rights or legal recourse to the recovered women; the question of children; the constitution of the tribunal; camp conditions and confinement; forcible return of unwilling women; unlimited duration for the Bill to remain in force; and the unequal and disadvantageous terms of the agreement for India vis-à-vis Pakistan.

The amendments moved by members sought to mitigate many of the gross irregularities they pointed out, and to qualify or modify certain other procedural aspects that were set out. But despite their strenuous efforts the Honourable Minister declined to incorporate a single amendment or modification proposed (bar one, limiting the duration of the Bill to December 1951); it was passed, unchanged, on December 19 and notified in the Official Gazette on December 28, 1949.

But more on this later; let us turn now to Kamlaben Patel, a social worker who was stationed in Lahore between 1947–52 and actively involved in the recovery operation. Kammoben said:

How I got involved in recovery work was by accident. I was supposed to go and work with Bapu at Sabarmati Ashram but

I didn't really want to go there. Mridulaben came to my rescue. She told Bapu, there are other things she can do, her health is fragile. I will find something else for her. So she asked me to work with her. I said, but what can I do? She said, "You be my personal secretary." But I can't type, I said, I don't speak English, how can I be your secretary? She said, "Look, all those skills can be bought, I don't need them from you—I'll give you a typist, a clerk, you don't worry about all that. What I want from you is that you should be able to take decisions on important matters if I'm not around, so that I know, Kamla is there, I don't need to worry."

I thought about it for a while and then said I would go on six months' probation. I first went to Pakistan in November 1947. Mridulaben sent me a telegram asking me to come to Delhi. When I reached there, she wasn't around but I was handed a ticket to go to Lahore. I didn't know why I was being sent there—I was just told, you have to reach there immediately.

Shri Prakashji, our first High Commissioner, was already there. He was quite adamant that proper arrangements should be in place before we went—he thought Mridulaben was crazy not to have insisted on it. However, we went. We had to establish a camp in Lahore, meet with government officials and start a dialogue. We had not attended any meeting regarding this work and so we were quite at sea at times about it, and yet we went ahead. Gradually, we learnt how to handle the work and situations as they arose. We made mistakes, small as well as big ones.

There were approximately 2,000 women who were in my charge. Those thousands of women who came from various districts of Pakistan, and so many others who came from several places in India, all had to be rescued. Now, when I look back at all that I was able to accomplish, I myself marvel at my own courage and the circumstances that pushed me into this work.

There was an ICS* officer, K.L. Punjabi, who felt that we had not recovered enough women in proportion to the money spent on this work. But I said to him, that's the nature of the

---

* Indian Civil Service.

work: when you see a family reunited, you see a father meet his daughter and the joy on their faces, you don't remember the lakhs that have been spent. When you see their happiness, you realize it is worth it. . . .

Let me tell you about Sialkot. . .

I went to Sialkot which was a closed district. I had no intention of going there because of the whole Azad Kashmir business. It was an anxious time because there was no agreement on Kashmir. I was instructed to go with the SP (superintendent of police) wearing a salwar kameez. No sari, under any circumstances. This SP was a complete rogue. He used to worm out all the information from us by being on his best behaviour. Often I told Mridulaben that I was afraid of dealing directly with him and because he was waiting to catch me out, I would make a mistake. And my mistake would be India's mistake. She said, "Don't worry, only you can do this work and I'm as capable of making a mistake as you."

You can imagine how I felt, an Indian woman entering a closed district at that time—we were fighting about Kashmir—but they were so excited that an Indian woman is coming! People came to see me, cried while asking about their relatives on this side. They asked about the situation obtaining on the other side. In their anxiety they asked questions which seemed foolish, like "My mother's relative went that side, would you know where he went? Did you ever meet him?" They were very hospitable towards me—a woman had come from Hindustan to see them—in spite of the fact that we were within five miles of the fighting. Suppose a crowd had gathered to throw stones, attack? But the opposite happened. On the way there nothing happened because the SP was in his uniform, but I was afraid that he himself might start something.

You see, Hindus never did accept the Muslims; if they had, these things could have been avoided. If they had looked upon them as one does on a younger or older brother in their homes, then they would not have developed this complex. Even the common people treated them like untouchables, never let them get close to themselves. Look, I am a Gujarati. Among us, there was not much warmth for them. In our place, Gujarat, there were no Muslim zamindars or highly educated people, only farmers or artisans. They could not equal either the money or education of the Muslims of Punjab or U.P. At the time of Partition when I went to Punjab for the first time, I realized that there was a lot of socialising and warmth between the two communities. They used to embrace each other and when they were forced to separate, they longed to see each other again. If they were alone together they would embrace, but in public they would shout slogans against each other. When the recovery work started progressing this antagonism became much sharper. Of course, it was an issue between two countries, then.

. . .Who leaves his home and goes away? But I think there were economic reasons (for Partition), too. The number of Hindus in Punjab was greater than the number of Muslims. Another reason could be that wherever the Hindus went, they exploited the Muslims. There were quite a few bania money-lenders who lent money at such exorbitant rates of interest that they were like blood-suckers. When an opportunity offered itself, they took their revenge. There were so many factors involved, it was not only one factor that brought about Partition. One cannot only blame the Muslims for subjecting Hindu women to violence, the Hindus also did it. In the Golden Temple 200 women were made to dance naked for the whole night in 1947. Not in the Darbar Sahib, but in its compound. And so many people were enjoying this unholy show. If I tell this to anyone they don't like it, but these are facts. I will talk on behalf of women and will not deviate from this fact. I am not a politician. If I had been one, I would have said that the Muslims did everything, we never did anything. But we were no less—how many we kept back, how many women we sold in the same way that baskets of oranges or grapes are sold or gifted—in the same way women were distributed. You asked me earlier why we uprooted these women again, but in my view they were never ever secure, had never put down roots.

Mostly the ones we recovered in India were sent back; theirs were approximately 12,000 women and ours were about 9,000 or a little less. We recovered them from Punjab, mostly from villages as well as towns, but more from the villages. That is because economic factors played a great part. Those nine to ten thousand women who were brought back from Pakistan were accepted by the Hindus. Why? Because of the economic factor. For the people had come from there as refugees and so they did not have any money. They did not have a woman to do the housework—a housewife. But here, there was a woman available. So forget everything, let's take her. They accepted them out of helplessness, not out of broadmindedness. It was not so important for the Muslims because they did not think of the woman as impure, but the Hindus did. With Muslims there was no problem about women's impurity and they hesitated much less when taking them back.

This was my experience. A Hindu woman felt that she had been made impure, had become sullied, was no longer *pativrata*. A Muslim woman did not feel like this. It was not in her blood, it is in our blood. We feel we have been polluted, we are no longer worthy of showing our faces in public. How can we face our families now when we go back? We would reassure the woman saying, "See how many times your father has come to fetch you." Even then they would feel ashamed of themselves because this tradition is so deeply ingrained in us. And Muslim women were not stigmatized by society. While our people would say that since they (the women) have lived for so long with a Muslim. . .Their parents would say that they had left their daughters with one or other of their aunts—they could not openly say that their daughters had been abducted.

This is our psychology. In the upper and middle classes this difficulty might have been there but not in the lower classes. A middle class woman might commit suicide—there were some cases like this, of course, but not too many. I have written about a case where the parents thought it was alright to sacrifice the life of a young girl in order to save a whole family. And when we were arguing about her recovery then the father said, this is our girl, and the girl denied it because she was terribly hurt by their behaviour. She said, " I don't want to go back. I have married of my own free will, I don't want anything from my parents." When she refused to return, it became very awkward. She was in the home of a police inspector. We felt that if we have found an abducted woman in the house of a police inspector, then how can we expect the police to do any recovering? That is why we had to bring her back. Our social worker went to Multan and met her. She said, "I will not go." Then we requested the Pakistani authorities to leave her in our camp in the Ganga Ram Hospital (Lahore) for a couple of days. Then if she says that she doesn't want to go back, it's fine, but she must come here and say that she doesn't want to. So she was brought by force. Her husband said, "I will take her back at night." I said, she will not return at night, she will stay the night with me. He said, "Why should my wife stay with you, what right have you to keep her?" Then I said, she is after all, our daughter, when a daughter comes to her mother's place she stays for a few days. She has no parents. That girl kept on saying that she didn't want to go to her parents, she wouldn't budge an inch. After two or three days she broke down, she told us that her parents had been told by the police inspector, "If you leave your daughter, gold and land with me, I will escort you all to the cantonment in India."

That man was already married, had children. He had told her father, you give me this girl in exchange for escorting you all to an Indian cantonment. Then her father gave him his daughter, 30 tolas of gold and his house. One night I called the girl to my bedside and said, if you want to go back (to the inspector) then I will send you. If you don't want to go back to your parents, don't go, but please tell me why. Then she became tearful and said, "Behenji, what can I tell you? I am not happy at this inspector's place. As long as he is in the house, I am alright, but as soon as he leaves on duty his wife harasses me, calls me the daughter of a kafir and so on. She makes me do all the work as if I were her maidservant. The man loves me, but he is under pressure from his family. But those parents who sacrificed me— I will never go back to them." I said, alright, don't go back to them, stay with us. We couldn't let her return to Pakistan, this was a prestige case. If we let it go, we would have to bite dust in front of Pakistan. We had to bring her before the Tribunal when it met. Just before that I thought that I would get her married off to a nice boy in India, specially because she was not happy with this man. If she had been happy I would not have thought like this, but she was unhappy and would have to spend the rest of her life in this fashion. There was one officer whose secretary was a very good man. I let the boy and the girl meet once, in secret, because it was against our policy. For this Mridulaben got very angry with me but I was quite obstinate. I insisted that we had no right to keep a woman in this manner. When everything was settled I decided that this young woman could now face the Tribunal without flinching. During the cross-examination, the Pakistan SP called for the inspector (her abductor) as a witness. Imagine that! But we were forced to agree because we were told that as a police inspector he could make trouble for us in our recovery work, later. So he came. Meera (the girl in question) was also called in and asked, "Where do you want to go?" She said that she wanted to go to India. The man glared at her and shouted, "So you want to go to India, eh?" She said, " Yes, I want to go to India." Then he yelled, "What do you think you are saying? I saved your parents, I have spent so much money on you. Even the bangles you are wearing are mine." I intervened and told them (the escorting police) that she should be taken in to change into her own clothes. Then I gave him back the clothes and gold and other things he had given her, saying she could do without.

She got married later, but not in Pakistan, obviously. We did it in Amritsar afterwards, with the proper arrangements. The boy got a posting to Simla* after a transfer from Pakistan. Her parents also came to the wedding. Five or six of us, friends, got together and arranged a tea party for her. Now this fact, after being exaggerated, got to Mridulaji's ears and, of course, she put me on the mat because these kinds of cases were outside our jurisdiction and we should not have been involved in them— they were really Mrs. Thapar's responsibility because they pertained to rehabilitation, not recovery. Mridulaben said, "You were my representative when you did this, you exceeded your brief." I said, well if you like, I will put in my resignation and go back to Bombay. I felt deep inside me that I had carried out my responsibility faithfully. If, because of me, their policy had been harmed then I would go back. At this she cooled down. Then, after a year when I was in Amritsar, this girl came to see me with her child. She came to see me specially, all the way from Simla. They were both very happy, she said. But I can't forget her anger at being sacrificed by her parents.

. . . One of the best things about our recovery work was the fact that all parties—Communist, Socialist, Congress, etc.— sank their differences and worked together. Our social work-

---

* Old and new spellings of place names—Shimla, Jalandhar—have both been retained.

ers used to accompany the police party—their women never did, they didn't have the motivation to go with the police. The police used to bring the women and leave them in the camp. We had several Congress, Socialist and even Communist members among our social workers. One day Begum Fatima of Lahore said to us, "I have heard that you have kept a Muslim girl as a prisoner and hidden her in the camp." What are you saying, Begum Fatima, I replied, we have hidden four crore people, if you wish you can take them all. And, in truth, I *had* hidden her! She was a disputed case. But one had to do these things because the circumstances demanded it. I said, for one thing, our girls have gone to sleep and for another, you are talking about one girl, but I have four crores here!

We were always being accused of keeping Muslim women. I was especially prone to this charge because I had to meet the Collector for sorting out problems relating to the camp—its site, rations and allotment of houses. Urdu newspapers published reports that India had sent very inexperienced young girls out to do the work of recovery!

. . . We recovered approximately 2,000 women from the Frontier. In my estimation, most of the recovered women were abducted, there was no abandoned person. But there were others who were kept in concentration camps or in somebody's house. Yes, concentration camps—because these ladies had been supplied to the military. This is not written in my book. You see, we used to send our military trucks to evacuate people who were left behind. For instance, one day, ten trucks would go to Lyallpur district (West Punjab) and the people who managed to climb onto those trucks were rescued, but there were others who could not make it. Suppose there was a large family and out of it only seven or eight persons managed to get out and the others got left behind—say, two girls were left behind. Now, they did not have the guts to go back for those two girls. When death stares you in the face then you worry about your own skin. And so, if your woman or child is left behind, either they will be abducted or they will be looked after by the local population. When they came with the Pakistani army, they were brought to the cantonment. Our own army was there and they established the camps where these women were kept when they were brought from the interior. Evacuations used to take place from there and their trucks would carry them to and fro. Those were known as camps and they used to call them "cantonments". If a woman found her way somehow to these camps then she would be sent to her own refugee camp, the one set up by her own country. But if she did not manage to reach this safe place and was picked up on the way, then either the man would keep her for himself or sell her off. No one could predict how long this sold-off woman would remain there. These poor women were housed by the government in the Kunja camp which was in Gujrat (West Punjab). Six hundred women had come to the Kunja camp as there was fighting going on in Kashmir. The army handed them over to us when they were useless. They were kept in the camp and when we celebrated Recovery Week and had used all our resources for this work, they brought these women into our midst. We felt so happy that 600 women had been sent by Pakistan.

All 600 had been used by the Pakistani army. Each one could not tell about herself but after talking with several of them one could make out that was the case. How did they become like this? When they were physically useless then they were brought to the camp and dumped there. There they could not get bathing water, food or salt. They also had some children with them who were very undernourished.

We got our independence in August 1947 and in November, there was the Inter-Dominion agreement. These 600 women were returned in February–March 1948. But this kind of situation existed in this area even earlier—it became worse during Partition. Rape and abduction of the other community's women—all this had started earlier. When they proposed to bring 600 women back to us we were very happy. We told everyone in the camp and asked them to prepare a fitting welcome for the Pakistanis who were returning such a large number of women. We were thankful to them. But when they came at 9 p.m. and I saw the state of the women, the ground almost slipped from under my feet. They looked like human skeletons—the women as well as children! They looked as if they belonged to another time. Those who were young had also become old by being used. I feel like crying whenever I remember that sight. They had been completely ruined. Now, when these women were brought to us in this state we were at a loss about how to handle this unprecedented situation. We had prepared a meal for healthy women. A savoury snack and rice and dal—in fact we had gone to a lot of trouble and had even got the utensils sent from Amritsar from the DAV camp. But now realization dawned that this food we had prepared was unfit for these ill and emaciated people. A few children died on the spot, one of them in my arms. The doctor also said that we could not give them the food we had made as they would get diarrhoea if they ate it. This put us in a fix—what were we to give them to eat? Where would we find milk and buttermilk for so many people at this late hour? We ourselves were strangers in this place, there was no way to order anything. And so we were constrained to give them that same dal and rice and mathri which we had brought.

In the morning, the doctor came and saw them and permitted us to give them simple food. We had our camp in the Ganga Ram Hospital where we had a very large community hall at our disposal. The next day Raja Ghazanfar Khan, the rehabilitation commissioner, and K.L. Punjabi came to see them. I could not stop the tears coming to my eyes while talking to them. Mr. Punjabi said, "Don't weep, Kamlaben, I already feel quite ashamed when I see these miserable creatures. I will just go and make arrangements for milk and food for them." He had to say this as food had to be sanctioned by the government, but he saw that these children had gone hungry for days. I told him, sanction or no sanction you must send enough food and oranges for them—even if I have to spend my own money. Each one was given one orange. The children ate the peels as well. You cannot even imagine all that I have seen. They would not sit in a row to be served food or, if our workers managed to make them do so, then they would sit and eat in one row and then go and sit in another to get another share. . .

Pakistan's attitude was that we should be thankful that it had managed to recover so many women. Naturally, they would not admit that they had any hand in the situation the women found themselves in. On the contrary, they claimed that they had been feeding these helpless women.

We asked them, what did you get to eat? Who was responsible for this miserable condition you find yourself in? How did you come to the camp? More than that they could not have answered as they were in a daze and so mentally disturbed. They had just been dumped. But this much they themselves told us, that they had been supplied to the army. Those who were older did not say anything but the young ones sometimes talked to us. I asked one of them whether they got food and she answered yes, we got very good food, but ever since we have come to this camp, our food has been stopped. I asked, what kind of delicious food were you given and she answered, "The meals of the men were very good." Then we understood what she meant. We had no definite proof, of course.

As far as I know, there weren't any women with infants of 4–6 months or babes-in-arms among these 600. But there were some who were pregnant. We used to make a list of all the pregnant women in Lahore and send it to Jullundar together with them. They used to keep these women for three months or so, give them a complete medical check-up (euphemism for an abortion) and only then would they try and find their relatives. Because if they came to know that the woman was pregnant they would say, let her stay in the camp and have her child.

It was my experience that women in the 35–45 age group felt very ashamed of having abortions. I felt that they had managed to acquire a certain status in their household and family. How could they show themselves to their husbands and children in this state? They wanted to burn themselves alive or die rather than face their people. They said they would rather go to hell. But they did not want an abortion, especially those who were in the third or fourth month of their pregnancy.

The government at this time passed an ordinance that those whose babies were born in Pakistan would have to leave them behind there and those children born in India would stay in India. I was in Lahore at that time. There was a conference held to discuss the implications and I was specially called. I said to Mridulaben that I will not attend this meeting because my opinions are the opposite of yours. I will say frankly what I feel about this matter at the meeting, otherwise I will not come. At that time there were a lot of very conservative people in rehabilitation work.

Mridulaben asked me, "Kamla, what do you want to tell me?" I said, a girl and a mother who has already been treated so cruelly should now be told that only she can go across and not her child—this is like stealing her child and this I will not do. Everyone has a right to her own opinions. Mridulaben was worried about the future of these girls, how to settle them. Who will marry them? Rameshwari Nehru was of the opinion that if they were Muslims themselves, then why should they leave their children in India? Our officers, Gundevia and others, also said, "What will happen to the children? Because if you are a Hindu then the children should also go." It was like a double-edged sword. There was one standard against which to measure on one side and another on the other. On the one hand the women were worried that they would lose their children, on the other there was this question, why should these children be brought back. I said, I will not do it. If any of you come there and do it I will help you, but I won't do it. I will not be a party to it.

At that moment, there was really no time to reflect on the future. Look after today and what tomorrow will bring, nobody could foretell. When you are faced with thousands of problems even when you are having your meals, there are fifty people crying in front of you, you don't see a single smiling face. . . All I knew was that one should not separate a mother from her child. Then finally these people agreed that these women would take their children with them to the Jullundar camp. After fifteen days we would ask them whether they wanted to take their children with them or not. If yes, they would take them, otherwise the children would be left in the Jullundar camp and suitable arrangements would be made for their care. I realized that women in the age group 30–32 were not keen to take their children with them for they had had other children earlier. But women who became mothers for the first time did not want to leave their first-born in Jullundar. When their relatives or parents came to see them they came to the Self Service Corporation, an all-India refugee organization, then these young mothers were very hesitant to see them. They felt ashamed of themselves and wept. They said that even if their parents took them back they would not accept their babies, their future prospects would be in jeopardy. And so they had to decide at that point whether they would go with their parents or continue living in the camp. But then they realized that they could not stay in the camp indefinitely, and finally they also agreed to leave their children behind. They wept and fell at our feet to beseech us but there was no other solution, and they had to leave their babies.

However, Mridulaben made some very good arrangements for these unfortunate children. She took over a whole wing in the Kamla Nehru Hospital in Allahabad. We sent her the children from the Jullundar camp. The procedure was such that you can't imagine it! There was an air service between Amritsar and Delhi. We wrote to the airline, which belonged to the Tatas, not the government, requesting them for a free passage for these babies. We would put each baby in a basket together with a bottle of milk and one bag of clothes and give the basket to the air hostess. Then our social worker would go to Delhi and collect the basket and deposit it in Lady Hardinge Hospital for the night. Then it (the baby in the basket) would be sent by the next flight to Allahabad to be collected once again by our social worker and taken to the Kamla Nehru Hospital. Each baby was sent with a sealed envelope in which was given the relevant information about the baby, such as its parentage, etc. Mostly we knew the name of the mother but not its father as the mothers would not disclose them. We must have sent between 200–250 babies.

If we had left them behind in Pakistan then it would have been like snatching, but now these women left them behind of their own accord. That makes a difference in a woman's life. The difference between doing something by force and doing it of your own choice. This can be compared to a two-edged sword where we don't know which edge will be sharper. I certainly wasn't able to tell.

A few of the fathers wanted to keep their children, but they were very few. But this was not for us to decide. When the party went with the police to recover the women, the fathers might have asked for the custody of the children and they might have agreed in some cases. But our job was to recover the women, no matter what, and if they came with their children we accepted them as they were. We did not refuse to take the children.

. . . Today we sit in a comfortable room and discuss and raise all these questions but at that time, neither did the condition of these unfortunate women permit nor did we have any time to spare, situated as we were in camps, to ask all these questions. One could not even think normally, the conditions were so extreme. Anyway, only special cases came to me. The normal cases were dealt with by the Pakistan police who were always sitting next door. All that had to be done in these cases was to give either the women's signature or thumb impression and say that we found such and such a woman and give their names and that was sufficient. They were treated like cattle. The next day we would send them on to Jullundar. Then it was the work of the Jullundar camp people to get information about them. In our Lahore camp, all this was not possible. Also, as I said earlier, I got only special cases—either those who said that they did not want to go or those women whose cases were disputed—where the men claimed that the women were not abducted but had been with them for a long time and therefore they would not give them up.

The Indian government agreement was quite dumb in this respect for it said that any person abducted after March 31st, either woman or child, must go to their respective country whether they desire it or not. One had to be careful about these disputed cases. There were lots of people who claimed that the women they were holding were with them for a long time, and they would bring a sealed certificate from the sarpanch to this effect. If this woman is not abducted, as you claim, then why should her parents have lodged a report, we would counter. Then the case became worse. There was a question in our Parliament that for this work of dealing with women, would it not be handled better by a woman rather than an SP? They agreed. Now the question arose that on the other side the work was being handled by Qurban Ali Khan. Then Mridulaben and I did this work for about five months with the Pakistanis. I said that I will speak for Pakistan. It's not a question of Hindus or Muslims; it's also not a question of politics. If it was, I would be able to follow my inclinations in India, which is quite big. I am a woman and, as such, if the matter involves any woman, I shall speak about it. Some people were nasty. They accepted me as an observer and not a Tribunal member, but whenever the Tribunal was convened, whether this side or that, I used to attend it. And it was also mentioned in the Indian Parliament that Kamla Patel was attached to the

Tribunal. Our SP felt very bad about it. When the Pakistanis
accepted me our SP got rather upset. He said I was doing too
much for these people. I said, I am a woman and I understand
women—I do not want to understand your politics. I have
written the story of a Muslim woman in my book. She belonged
to a rich family. To begin with, I should tell you that Alwar, a
place in our area has in some parts of the state, a totally Muslim population. This lady belonged to a family, some of whose
members had migrated to Pakistan so that her relatives lived
both in India and Pakistan. Now we had to decide who to hand
her over to since both Pakistan and India could call on her
relatives to come and take charge of her. Who would prove
more stubborn, Pakistanis or Indians, we did not know. But
the girl herself was quite abusive and demanded to know where
were the Muslims we would send her to.

At that time the situation in the Muslim camps had become
very bad because there were no proper social services for them.
The Pakistani SP requested me, rather requested Mridulaben,
to please send Kamlaben for ten days. He said, "Your camp is
running smoothly but ours is not." So I went for ten days to
Jullundar and would go to their camp for few hours. I found
that things were rather bad. Here in this Muslim camp there
was one woman whose father's brother was in Alwar and another uncle—aunt's husband—was in Pakistan. She was pregnant and after six months in the camp, she was about to deliver. I told the camp authorities that they must do something
about her. When I saw that they were quite nonchalant, I called
the girl myself and asked her where she would like to go for
her delivery, to which uncle's place. She answered innocently,
and as if she had no choice, "You tell me." I felt very bad for
her—neither the Pakistani uncle nor the Hindustani uncle was
willing to help her, evidently. The camp people were quite fed
up as well so I said, you give her to me. They agreed promptly.
They even handed her over to me formally; a resolution was
passed in the Tribunal that Masooma so-and-so has been
handed over to Kamla Patel. Having gone through with this I
wondered what I should do with her, for her delivery time
was very near. So, I took her to Amritsar and handed her over
to the camp superintendent, Ajit, who was very well known in
Punjab. I told his brother, Jagjit, to please look after her and

see to her delivery. Then I told Mridulaben what I had done. She said, "What will you do with her, having brought her, especially now that she has a baby?" Then she suggested that I go and see Apaji and tell her the whole story. (Apaji was Rafi Ahmed Kidwai's sister, Anis Kidwai.) So I went and told her the whole story. She said, "Why are you so worried about her, Kamla? Just send her to me without hesitation."

After some time I went to Delhi—while I was working for the Khadi Commission, in 1956 to be precise—and I met Apaji and asked her what had happened to that girl. "She is very well. Shall I call her for you?" she said. Then she asked how long I was going to stay. Apaji had married her to a farmer—according to Muslim religion there is no bar about marrying a woman who has children. Apaji told the groom, "I am giving this child (her baby) into your safekeeping; you will look after it." Then they had a second child and both husband and wife came to see me with both the children.

. . . These women—it was not a question of Hindu or Muslim, it was more a question of where they belonged. We had to return these girls to their people, whether they were Hindu or Muslim, they had to be given back to their parents, sons and other relations. Let me put it another way. Though the question of religion was dominant, yet it was also a question of citizenship. There was a certain insecurity involved in case they stayed back. A Hindu or a Muslim woman would feel insecure if she got left behind in a country where the other community was dominant and where none from her own family or community remained or her entire social structure had been destroyed. She did not come there of her own accord but was brought there forcibly. These women would have no future nor feel secure. It is quite different for you and me. But for these lakhs of village women security lies in the fact that they belong to a community, that they are with their husbands who have a social standing in the community and therefore the husbands are constrained. Husbands cannot throw them out. Except for this kind of security, the uneducated village women have no other. Suppose the man with whom the woman is living throws her out one day—how can one trust a man who abducts, will he look after her for a lifetime? But if she goes to the country which is stipulated for her, she will at least have the protection of her government. The women who came to our camp put us this question, "Where will we go if our relatives don't keep us?" And we used to reassure them. "You are India's daughter, Pandit Nehru's daughter, and as such the government is duty bound to look after you. We shall keep you in a camp." Here there was no need to worry about her future. That this promise proved correct, I can vouch for, from my work experience.

Of course, there were unfortunate cases, they had to sacrifice, but they only numbered five out of 1,000. What would have happened to the other 995 women? How could we make exceptions? As it is, for the exceptions that were made already, the dominant types, conformists, were carrying on a running fight with the Tribunal. So, among them only about four or five exceptions were made because that seemed to be the only practicable solution to their problems. And as for the 500 genuine cases, they might be valid today and invalid tomorrow. What would happen then? They will have no one, no parents, uncles, aunts or any other relatives. Though there were Nari Niketans in existence, they would not have looked after a woman professing another religious belief. All this is very specific to women because on the whole they are more vulnerable. This identification, however, was done according to the countries they belonged to, that this one is an Indian and that a Pakistani. Partition was internally connected with Islam and the demand for a separate country, for a separate community. And since this label was attached, how could women be free from it?

Rupture

Even were it desirable, it would be difficult to present an accurate profile of the abducted woman during that turbulent time. From the official figures quoted earlier, it is clear that of those recovered the majority were below the age of 35, and primarily from the rural areas. From what we have been able to gather through interviews, accounts by social workers and some documents, however, the circumstances of their "abduction" varied widely. Some were left behind as hostages for the safe passage of their

families; others were separated from their group or family
while escaping, or strayed and were picked up; still others
were initially given protection and then incorporated into
the host family; yet again as in the case of Bahawalpur State,
all the women of Chak 88 were kept back, and in Muzaffarabad
district of Azad Kashmir, it is said that not a single Sikh
male was left alive and most of their women and young girls
were taken away to the provinces. Some changed hands several times or were sold to the highest or lowest bidder, as
the case might be; some became second or third wives; and
very, very many were converted and married and lived with
considerable dignity and respect. Again, there were some
who, as Anis Kidwai says, belonged to poor families and
were now with such generous men who "gave them silk
salwars and embroidered dupattas, and introduced them
to the taste of ice-cream and hot coffee! Why would they
leave such nice men and return to a life of drudgery and
poverty?"

A Sikh schoolteacher we met had spent six months after
the October 1947 raid with a Muslim neighbour in
Muzaffarabad in Azad Kashmir, before she crossed over
safely to Srinagar; her younger sister who had been abducted
could never be located despite sustained efforts by the family and the International Red Cross. In the mid-Eighties she
returned to Muzaffarabad where she stayed for six months,
visiting every Hindu and Sikh woman who had remained
behind, talking to them of their lives and circumstances. Of
the 25–30 women she met she informed us that only one
could be said to be unhappy and in unfortunate circumstances. All the others, though nostalgic and distressed at
not being able to meet their natal families freely, seemed to
her to be settled and held in regard both by the community
and their new families. "After all," she remarked "where is
the guarantee of happiness in a woman's life anyway?" And
there were a few among them whose circumstances had in
fact improved.

It is by no means our intention to suggest that the predicament these women found themselves in was not trau-

matic or fraught with anxiety and uncertainty; merely that it would be false to presume that their lot was uniformly grim, their "abductors" without exception, "bestial" or unreliable and craven, and to assert as Mridula Sarabhai did, that recovery was "an effort to remove from the lives of thousands of innocent women the misery that is their lot today, and to restore them to their legitimate environment where they can spend the rest of their lives with *izzat*" (honour).[10] Nor is it our case that the recovery effort should never have been made; going by the few accounts that exist, and on the basis of the interviews we have conducted with women themselves and those whose care they were entrusted to, the majority of women recovered were rehabilitated in greater or smaller measure or restored to their families. Our purpose here is to look beyond these at the many discordant notes that were struck in the process of recovery; at the conflicting claims that were made and voices that were raised; at the silence that was almost unfailingly imposed on the women after the event, and at what these tell us about how, in times of communal violence, each one of women's identities—gender, community and nationality—is set up against the other and contested.

Two accounts, both by social workers who were at the Gandhi Vanita Ashram, Jalandhar, for several years and worked with recovered women, are illustrative. In personal interviews with us one of them spoke about the return of Muslim women to Pakistan; the other about the recovery of a Hindu woman eight years after Partition. Krishna Thapar said that:

> Some time in 1950 I was required to escort 21 Muslim women who had been recovered to Pakistan. They did not want to return, but the Tribunal had decided that they had to go. They were young, beautiful girls and had been taken by Sardars. They were determined to stay back because they were very happy. We had to use real force to compel them to go back. I was very unhappy with this duty—they had already suffered so much and now we were forcing them to return when they just didn't want to go. I was told, " *Ey tan aiveyeen raula pa raiyan ne, enada ta phaisla ho chuka hai, enanu ta bhejna hi hai.*"

(These girls are simply creating a commotion for nothing, their case has been decided and they have to be sent back.)

The girls were desperate. The news got around and I received two anonymous letters saying, "If you take our women away to Pakistan we will kidnap you too." Those women cursed me all the way to Amritsar, loudly and continuously. When we reached Wagah it was evening, and we found that there were about 15 other jeeps that had also accompanied us—all belonging to the men they were with! They were hoping that should any one of the girls manage to escape, they would pick her up and take her back. As far as I could see they were all Sikhs. I told the Pakistani SP who was with me that to transfer them at this point into Pakistani jeeps was a risky business—the girls will raise a real hue and cry and we won't be able to restrain them. We had no lady police—you see, in those days there were hardly any —and I won't allow the policemen to manhandle any woman, whether she's a Hindu or a Muslim. And if they resist, we will have no choice but to use force. Now our jeeps couldn't go across without permission. Eventually we managed to get cleared and as soon as we reached Pakistan, these same women who had made such a commotion, became absolutely quiet. This the Pakistani SP had already told me.

Naturally, as soon as we reached Pakistan the women realized their complete helplessness — what else can you call it? It was complete helplessness, they had been transferred from one set of butchers (*kasais*) to another . . . what could they do?

When the jeeps came to a halt the SP dismounted, went round to the back of the jeeps, opened the door and rained abuses on those poor women. He shouted at them and said, "Now tell me, which one of you wants to go back to India? Tell me and I'll let you off right now to find your way back. Let's see how far you get." They shouted back at me—after all, I was the one who had brought them—they kept saying, "Why are you destroying our lives?" Earlier, when I had brought them from Jullundur jail saying, this is a government agreement, our girls are also being returned, they had shouted at me : "Who are you to meddle in our lives? We don't know you, what business is it of yours?"

In Lahore, the camp for recovered Muslim women was in the Women's Penitentiary. When we reached there, the women got down and each one of them made a burqa of her chunni and emerged in parda. They knew that if they protested now, they would regret it.

Krishnaji told us many other stories like this, each equally poignant, but it was from her colleague, Dayawati Kalra, that we heard the most heart-wrenching one of them all.

B. was the eldest of seven sisters. Her family, brothers, wanted her to come and live with them but she refused because she knew she would not be fully accepted. . . I was very close to her. Her's is a difficult story. . . I don't feel like talking too much about her life. . . she was such a brave woman.

She went with me to Vaishno Devi. She happened to mention that she had some relatives in Jammu but she was not keen to meet them. My husband wrote to her relations and asked them to get in touch in Jammu. They came to meet her and all of them started crying. She was very, very upset. She said, "*Main kithe phas gayee. Mere kol kithe athroo paye ne ki main rovan.*" (Where have I got stuck! I don't even have tears to shed any more.) She came away. She sacrificed so much—she was such a generous woman. . . . She brought three children. She came after 8–10 years in Pakistan but she did not want to come. . . .

When she left in the caravan she was very young. Her father was worried about her and he told her, "B—*Tu choti hondi, yaa tu na hondi taan main saare dooje bacheyan noon bacha ke lai jaanda.*" (If only you were not so young, or didn't exist at all, I could have taken the rest of the family to safety.) She thought she could help her family by committing suicide. There was a three storey house next door—she jumped from it, broke her leg, but did not die. She was destined to go through all the hardships in life, so how could she die! The caravan left with all the members except B. and her father. The father admitted her in the camp. There was a Muslim tahsildar there who would take young Hindu men from the camp and kill them. Her father was taken and he told the tahsildar to look after B. and give her to his relations if he were to die. B. was about 16–17 years old. Her father was killed. The tahsildar took her home, got her treated. About two years passed. There was no hope of anyone coming to take B. The tahsildar's son was a thanedar. He got them both married. She was happy. But she said they wouldn't let her meet any Hindu girls who had been left behind and about whom she came to hear. She learnt Urdu. With her family she visited relations in different cities but they were afraid to let her meet other Hindu girls who had stayed on or who had been kept by Muslims. But she was happy.

Her brother kept going to Pakistan to look for her, and finally he found out that she had been taken by the tahsildar and that he may be able to provide some information. When her brother contacted the tahsildar he said he was not aware of her whereabouts. One day her husband asked her if she would agree to go to India if someone came to take her. She said there was no question of her going now that she had children and she was well adjusted, where was the question of going?

There was no pressure on her to convert—she was from a Brahmin family. She followed her own religion, prayed the way she wanted. Of course, she could not go to any temple. . .

The search for her continued. Her father-in-law and husband knew about it but she was not aware. Finally she was taken to the court to make her statement. The DC asked her to remove her *nakaab* (veil) to make her statement. The orderly in the court recognized her as soon as she lifted her veil. He had been with her father. That changed everything for her. She was forcibly taken to the camp. She kept saying she did not wish to go. What would she do there? Which of her relations would keep her? She said she wanted to stay on where she was. But there was a lot of official pressure from India. When she was being taken to the camp in Lahore she gave all the jewellery she was wearing to her husband and told him she would come back. There was no way they could take her away forcibly. In Lahore there was a lot of pressure on her. Her brother was given permission to take her. He gave her a knife and said, *"Tu beshaq naa chal par ai chhuri meri gardan te rakh de"* (If you don't wish to come you don't have to, but just kill me with this knife.) After such a statement and this kind of pressure she had to come. The husband did not know about her decision. He was certain she wouldn't go.

She came to the Ashram and refused to go to any relation. The brother tried his best but she said, *"Main aithe aa agyee aan, bas. Meri jo tabaahi honi si ho gayee hai."* (I have come here at your insistence, that is enough. I've lost everything

now. I have lost whatever I had to lose. I will not go anywhere.) She brought three children. The third child was born
in Lahore camp where she spent six months. This was in
1957–58.

... Her husband and his family must have been heartbroken—they lost her as well as their three children. . .Only I
know her story because we were very close. She did not talk
to anyone about it. That tahsildar kept her like a daughter
for over a year. Only when no one came for her did he suggest marriage to his son. No one else would have done so
much. He was honourable.

When we met her in 1991, B. was eloquent about her present
life, spoke with pride about having educated herself and
been able to stand on her own feet, and of being helped
greatly by the Ashram and the women there; but she absolutely refused to speak of her past. *"Dafa karo"*, she kept saying, *"hun ki yaad karna hai. Dafa karo. Main sab bhula ditta hai.
Hun main izzat nal rah rahin aan, main kyon puranian gallan
yaad karniyan ne. Mere baccheyan nu vi nahin pata. Hun sudhar
nahin ho sakda, kuj nahin ho sakda."* (Leave it. What use is it
recalling the past? Forget about it. I've banished it all from
my mind. I lead a respectable [honourable] life now, why
look back to the past—even my children don't know anything about it. Nothing can be done about it now. It can't be
resolved.) It is all over now, she seemed to be saying, her
past as well as her struggle to come to terms with her life.
For years she believed in no religion and no god, till very
recently, when she joined a Radha Soami sect.

In Jammu, in 1992, we met a man who told us about his
sister who had been abducted from their village in October
1947. He showed us letters from her, an embroidered Qoran
cover that she had made for him, and played a tape recorded
message from her, over and over again for us. Her story is
the mirror image of B.'s:

K. was 16, and had gone to visit her grandparents in village
Hattiyan Dupatta (Muzaffarabad distt. of Azad Kashmir)
when she was picked up by the tribals. She was passed from
one man to another, tried to commit suicide by throwing
herself off the roof of one captor's house, but was caught

and taken away by a zaildar. She was finally rescued by her parents' erstwhile neighbour, a patwari, who kept her in his house for some time before he persuaded her, for her own safety, to marry his son who was in fact younger than her. Her father went to Lahore and tried for three months to trace her through the Red Cross, but failed. When they finally managed to make contact with her, he went again to Pakistan and tried hard to persuade her to return. She did indeed journey to Lahore to meet him, but refused to return because she was carrying her husband's first child. Her father returned, heartbroken, and died shortly thereafter.

K. lived on in Pakistan, had two sons and four daughters and commanded great respect in her family and community. According to the accounts of those who visited her, she lived well and with great dignity. She had complete freedom, we were told, didn't believe in Islam, was not obliged to read the Qoran or say her namaaz. But her name was changed to Sarwar Jahan. The common description of her was that she was like a dervesh whose words had almost oracular importance. She never moved out without a pistol (is supposed to have shot dead three intruders who entered her house when she was alone), was quite militant—and wrote reams of mystic poetry.

K.'s brother said she was filled with longing for her family after she met her father, and wrote many letters that spoke heartrendingly of the wall of separation that had come between them, of the misfortune that divided them forever.

> Who has aimed these arrows of separation?
> Neither you, nor me.
> God has released these arrows of separation
> That forever divided you and me.

When once her brother wrote that for them she was forever lost, she responded with, "How can you talk of purity and honour? How can you denounce me for what was no fault of mine?" He recounted how, when he visited her 40 years later, she sat guard by his bedside all night, every night, for the two months that he stayed with her. But she did not visit her family in India even once, nor did she ever return to their ancestral village in Muzaffarabad.

These three narratives—as well as the disputed cases heard by the Tribunal, and the several stories we were told of women who had managed to escape from the transit camps on both sides—give us some clues regarding the circumstances of abducted women's lives. The individual adjustments they made did enable them to achieve a degree of equilibrium and take up the threads of living again. But many offered strong resistance and, often, refused to conform to the demands of either their own families or their governments and fall in line with their notions of what was legitimate and acceptable. Some who resisted resorted to hunger strikes, others refused to change out of the clothes they had been wearing, either when they were recovered or when they had been abducted. Their protest could be powerful and searing. One young recovered girl confronted Mridula Sarabhai thus:

> You say abduction is immoral and so you are trying to save us. Well, now it is too late. One marries only once—willingly or by force. We are now married—what are you going to do with us? Ask us to get married again? Is that not immoral? What happened to our relatives when we were abducted? Where were they? . . . You may do your worst if you insist, but remember, you can kill us, but we will not go.[12]

The challenge posed by those 21 Muslim women to the social worker—"Who are you to meddle in our lives?"—was a challenge directed at the state itself, a state that had already lost any claims it might have had to intervene in their lives by its complete failure to prevent the brutality and displacement that accompanied Partition. "There was so much distrust and loathing for us in their hearts," said Gulab Pandit, who was Rameshwari Nehru's right hand person for 18 years, "they would say—if you were unable to save us then, what right have you to compel us now?" To assurances that they were India's and Pandit Nehru's daughters and that the government was duty-bound to look after them, they retorted angrily, "Is this the freedom that Jawaharlal gained? Better that he had died as soon as he was born . . . our men have been killed, our homes destroyed."

For those who were recovered against their wishes—and there were many—the choice was not only painful but bitter. Abducted as Hindus, converted and married as Muslims, recovered as Hindus but required to relinquish their children because they were born of Muslim fathers, and disowned as "impure" and ineligible for membership within their erstwhile family and community, their identities were in a continual state of construction and reconstruction. How often were we told that women who had been abandoned by their families and subsequently recovered from Pakistan, simply refused to return to their homes, preferring the anonymity and relative autonomy of the ashram to a now alien family.

Resistance

In a letter dated March 3, 1948 to K.C. Neogy, Minister for Relief and Rehabilitation, Jawaharlal Nehru wrote:

> I have just had a telephone message from Sushila Nayyar from Patiala. She told me that a great majority of the (Muslim) women recovered refused to leave their new homes, and were so frightened of being taken away forcibly that they threatened to commit suicide. Indeed, last night 46 of them ran away from the camp through some back door. This is a difficult problem. I told Sushila that she can assure these women that no one is going to send them forcibly to Pakistan, but we thought it desirable for them to come to Delhi so that the Pakistan High Commission and others could then find out what their desires were. This would finally settle the question. In any event I assured her that we would not compel any girl to be sent to Pakistan against her wishes.[13]

The issue could not so easily be laid to rest, however, for it became a matter of prestige for both countries: how many Hindu and Muslim women were returned and in what condition, and how the authenticity of conflicting claims was to be established gradually took precedence over the humanitarian aspects of recovery. The focus of concern was primarily to identify the women as either Muslim or Hindu, but it also extended to them as citizens of their "respective countries", in need of being reclaimed. As Kamlaben Patel says in her interview, "the identification was done according to the countries they belonged to, this one is Indian, this one a Pakistani. And since this label was attached, how could the women be free from it?"

In all, approximately 30,000 Muslim, Hindu and Sikh women were recovered by both countries over an eight year period. The total number of Muslim women recovered was significantly higher—20,728 as against 9,032 Hindu and Sikh. Although most of the recoveries were carried out between 1947–50, women were being returned to the two countries as late as 1957, and the Act was renewed in India every year till 1956 when it was allowed to lapse.[14] Recoveries were more or less abandoned in the two or three years prior to this, largely because Mridula Sarabhai came in for some adverse criticism, and resigned. But the programme was beset with difficulties from the very beginning.

On January 16, 1948 Nehru made a public appeal through the newspapers in which he said:

> I am told that there is an unwillingness on the part of their relatives to accept those girls and women (who have been abducted) back in their homes. This is a most objectionable and wrong attitude to take and any social custom that supports this attitude must be condemned. These girls and women require our tender and loving care and their relatives should be proud to take them back and give them every help.[15]

Mahatma Gandhi who, after the Noakhali riots of October 1946, had resolved to go and "wipe away the tears of the outraged womanhood of Noakhali", expressed similar sentiments:

> I hear women have this objection that the Hindus are not willing to accept back the recovered women because they say that they have become impure. I feel that this is a matter of great shame. That woman is as pure as the girls who are sitting by my side. And if any one of those recovered women should come to me, then I will give them as much respect and honour as I accord to these young maidens.[16]

The appeals made by Gandhi and Nehru indicate that the number of families unwilling to accept women who had been "defiled" by the Muslims was by no means insignificant; according to Gulab Pandit the problem became so pressing that the Ministry of Relief and Rehabilitation was constrained to print and distribute a pamphlet that sought to educate the public on the subject: it said that just as a flowing stream purifies itself and is washed clean of all pollutants, so a menstruating woman is purified after her periods. Similarly, the All India Women's Conference Report of its 21st session in Gwalior mentions that the Delhi Branch organized public meetings in different localities during Recovery Week in February 1948. It says, "Some of the office bearers and a few members did propaganda work in connection with abducted women by going about in a van through the streets of New Delhi and speaking to the public on loudspeakers." No details of this propaganda are given but one can guess its contents without being too far off the mark.

The anticipation of just such a rejection by the very family and community that were to provide them support, was one reason why many women resisted being recovered. Pregnant women were obviously more vulnerable than others and, as Kamlaben said, the decision on whether to abort or carry their pregnancies to full term was an agonizing one for almost all women, especially young mothers. Those who were in an advanced state did not even have this choice: for them the question of whether or not to abandon their babies must have been even more painful.

Meanwhile the government passed an ordinance to say that those (Hindu) women whose babies were born in Pakistan after Partition would have to leave them behind, but those (Muslims) whose children were born in India, could keep them. According to Kamlaben:

> For the government this was a complex problem. In Indian society, a child born to a Hindu mother by a Muslim father was hardly acceptable, and if the relatives of the women did not accept such children, the problem of rehabilitation of a large number of women and children would arise.

A special conference was held in Lahore to discuss the implications of this; the opinion of a majority of the social workers was that it would be wise to leave all such children with their fathers instead of allowing their mothers to bring them over to India, where eventually, they were likely to end up in orphanages. A senior civil servant, joint secretary in the Ministry of Relief and Rehabilitation, said the only practical solution was to "treat such children as war babies" and not be guided by emotional considerations while arriving at a decision in this regard. At this point, Kammoben (Kamlaben Patel) told us:

> I said in the meeting: the soldiers responsible for their birth go back to their respective countries and the infants have to be brought up by their mothers. Nobody separates them from their mothers. The stalwarts and seasoned social workers like Rameshwari Nehru should therefore visit Lahore and impart necessary training for separating the child—on our part we had neither the strength nor the capability for that work. If all of you do not approve of my suggestion, I would like to dissociate myself from this work.

It was only a sharp difference of opinion between Rameshwari Nehru and Mridula Sarabhai on the issue, and the insistence of those social workers who opposed such a callous solution to the problem, that saved the day for the women. A compromise was arrived at whereby the women would take their children with them to Jalandhar and, after 15 days, decide whether they wanted to keep them or not.

The differences between Rameshwari Nehru (who opposed forcible recovery) and Mridula Sarabhai (who wished to press on) gradually came to a head; Mridula Sarabhai believed that no woman could be happy with her abductor, Rameshwari Nehru, not so. Within a year or so of recovery work having been undertaken systematically, she advised the government to stop it altogether because she was convinced that although "the figures of recovery have been encouraging, we have not achieved our purpose. . . Figures alone are not the only criterion against which such work should be judged." Viewed from the "human and the women's angle", as she proposed to do, removing them from the homes in which they were now settled would result in untold misery and suffering.

> . . . From what I have seen of the recently recovered women, the number of those who have adjusted themselves to their new lives, have married their abductors or rescuers and have happily settled down, is appreciably great. . . It is also well known that a very large proportion of the women recovered in India were unwilling to go to Pakistan. Many of them *even after months of detention in our transit homes* were steadfast in their determination to remain with their new relatives (emphasis added)
>
> . . . But I regret to say their protests, their hunger strikes, their pathetic and heart-rending cries of distress, widely witnessed by both workers and outsiders, were of no avail.[17]

Moreover, there was no follow-up system by which social workers could ascertain what happened to the women once they were returned. Often, the women's relatives could not be traced and they were married (again) to strangers or exploited commercially. Because social workers played no part in actually rehabilitating the women once in Pakistan, the work was left entirely in the hands of superintendents of police. "The defect arising out of such an arrangement," Rameshwari Nehru continued, "is only too obvious. By sending them away we have brought about grief and the dislocation of their accepted family life without in the least promoting human happiness." Finally, the woman's will was not taken into consideration at all; she was "once again, reduced to the goods and chattel status without having the right to decide her own future or mould her own life". Rameshwari Nehru's pleas found few supporters and little sympathy within officialdom, however, and in July 1949 she resigned as Honorary Advisor to the Ministry of Relief and Rehabilitation. Mridula Sarabhai was now in sole charge.

It would be incorrect to claim that the social workers did not also subscribe to prevailing notions of "difference" between Muslims and non-Muslims in the matter of "honour" and acceptability, and of social—and government—responsibility in the task of restoring these women to a life of "respectability" and "dignity". Indications are that they carried

out the search and "rescue" missions with some persever-
ance, especially in the first flush of recovery; in time, however, and with first-hand experience of the consequences of
their actions, they began to express their disagreement with
decisions that they believed worked against the women and
rendered their situation even more precarious. Indeed, when
it seemed to them that the women's plight was particularly
poignant, more than one social worker admitted to having
helped them "escape" the police and bureaucratic net. In
December 1949 Mridula Sarabhai was constrained to point
out that "the approach of the people *and even the social workers* is not correct (emphasis added). Public opinion must assert that the honour and dignity of women will be respected
and that in our country abduction will not be tolerated, as it
is in itself, immoral, apart from its being criminal. . ."[18]

These differences direct us to examine the role played by
social workers in the recovery operation, and the triangular
relationship that developed between the government, the
women to be recovered and their intermediaries. That this
relationship was ambivalent and became increasingly
troubled is, we would suggest, precisely because the
government's construction of the abducted woman's identity was being called into question. It was a construction
that identified her, first and foremost, as the member of a
religious community, and then invested her with the full
responsibility for upholding community honour; next it denied her any autonomy whatever by resolutely defining her
as the victim of an act of transgression which violated that
most critical site of patriarchal control—her sexuality. For
an elaboration of this however, we need to return to the Bill,
the circumstances under which it was formulated and the
debates around it.

A Nation and Its Women

"For me," said Mridula Sarabhai, "recovery
work is not only a humanitarian problem, it is a part of my
political ideology. The policy of abduction as a part of the

retaliatory programme has given a setback to the basic ideals of a secular state and Janata Raj."[19] Her statement is pertinent not only because it reflected, in general terms, government's—and the Indian state's—own image of itself, but because she was the moving spirit behind the 1949 Bill—just as earlier, the Inter-Dominion Agreement of November 1947 had been based largely on a 14 page document drawn up by her and handed over personally to Liaqat Ali Khan.

It was generally assumed that all abducted women were captive victims and wanted nothing more than to be restored to their original families as soon as possible. "Women or abducted persons are rescued from surroundings which, prima facie, do not give them the liberty to make a free choice as regards their own lives," said Gopalaswami Ayyangar in Parliament. "The object of this legislation is to put them in an environment which will make them feel free to make this choice."[20] Smt. Durgabai, supporting the move, went a little further:

Questions are asked: Since these women are married and settled here and have adjusted themselves to the new environment and their new relatives, is it desirable that we should free them to go back? May I ask, are they really happy? Is the reconciliation true? Can there be a permanent reconciliation? . . . Is it not out of helplessness, there being no alternative, that the woman *consents or is forced to enter into that sort of alliance with a person who is no more than the murderer of her very husband, her very father or her brother? Can she be happy with that man?* (emphasis added) . . . Is she not the victim of everyday quarrels in that house? The social workers can testify . . . that such a woman only welcomes an opportunity to get back to her own house . . . Sir, it may be that she has refused to go back. But on what grounds is this refusal based? . . . On a fear complex, on the fear of social customs and . . . that her relatives may not take her back.[21]

Other members disagreed and demurred at the arbitrary powers being given to the Tribunal to decide who was or was not abducted and should be sent back. Smt. Purnima Banerji cautioned the government against being over-zealous:

Time has passed, and in between (these girls) have lived in association with one another and have developed mutual

attachment as . . . couples. . . Such girls should not be made
to go back to countries to which they originally belonged
merely because they happen to be Muslims or Hindus, and
merely because the circumstances and conditions under
which they had been moved from their original homes could
be described as abduction.[22]

Shri Mahavir Tyagi, in fact, declared that such a recovery
was the real abduction, legally speaking ". . . My feeling is
that already violence has been committed on them once . . .
would it not be another act of violence if they are again uprooted and taken away to the proposed camps against their
wishes?" To this the Minister replied:

> . . . there has been hardly any case where, after these women
> were put in touch with their original fathers, mothers, broth-
> ers or husbands, any one of them has said she wanted to go
> back to her abductor—a very natural state of feeling in the
> mind of a person who was, by exercise of coercion, abducted
> in the first place and put into a wrong environment.

Despite the urging of some members that some mechanism
be devised to ensure that no unwilling woman was forced
to return to her country, the Minister declined to do so; simply gave a verbal assurance that no compulsion or coercion
would be used, and added, "I have not come across a single
case of an adult abducted woman who had been recovered
and who was pushed into Pakistan against her will."[23] The
clause in question was then put to the vote and passed by
the House. The recovered women themselves, although
promised a "free" environment and "liberty" were, by the
very terms of the Bill, divested of every single right to legal
recourse. The writ of habeas corpus was denied; their marriages were considered illegal and their children illegitimate;
they could be pulled out of their homes on the strength of a
policeman's opinion that they were abducted; they could
be transported out of the country without their consent;
confined in camps against their wishes; have virtually no
possibility of any kind of appeal (bar the compassion of the
social worker or the generally unsympathetic authority of
the Tribunal); and, as adult women and citizens, be once

again exchanged, this time between countries and by officials.

At least three members referred to the gravity of the measures proposed and pointed out that they violated the fundamental rights guaranteed by a Constitution that would come into effect the very next month (January 1950). They warned that the Supreme Court could not countenance the denial of the writ of habeas corpus, and that it was the right of every Indian citizen—which these women were—to choose to remain in India; by law and by right they could not be deported without their consent. Jaspat Roy Kapoor, objecting to the powers vested in the Tribunal said:

> What do we find in this Bill? We find that after release (these women) will have absolutely no say in the matter of the place where they are to live, in the matter of the companions with whom they are to live, and in the matter of the custody of their children . . . . I ask, in such cases, shall we be conferring liberty and freedom on her if we deny her these rights?[24]

As he was at pains to point out, unless children were included in the legislation there would be no chance of returning the women at all. And Mahavir Tyagi reminded the House that:

> These women are citizens of India . . . they were born in India itself . . . they have not yet gone to Pakistan . . . In taking them to Pakistan without their consent, even if the agency be the police or the sanction be the proposed Tribunal, shall we not contravene the fundamental rights sanctioned by the Constitution? . . . The fact that their husbands have gone to Pakistan does not deprive the adult wife of her rights of citizenship. They have their own choice to make.[25]

To this the Minister replied that he had himself proposed an amendment that would *extend* the powers of the Tribunal and allow it to determine not only whether the woman was abducted or not, but whether she be sent to Pakistan or allowed to stay back. On the issue of habeas corpus he said, "If the interpretations should be that what we have provided in this particular Bill is not quite in accordance with Article 21 or any other provision of the Constitution, then of course the remedy for a writ of habeas corpus will remain."[26] As mentioned earlier the Bill was passed, in toto, with no modification of its clauses. When the debate on it was over and some officials had adjourned to the Minister's room in Parliament House, an excited Mridula Sarabhai said to the Minister, "Thank God, Sir, it's all over and the women in both the countries are going to be grateful to you."[27]

Borders and Bodies

The Recovery Operation of the Government of India, albeit humanitarian and welfarist in its objectives, was nevertheless articulated and implemented within the parameters of two overriding factors; first, the relationship of the Indian state with Pakistan and second, its assumption of the role of *parens patriae* vis-à-vis the women who had been abducted. In the former, it was obliged as the "responsible and civilized" government of a "civilized" country to rightfully claim its subject-citizens; as the latter it was morally bound to relocate and restore these same subjects within their families, communities and countries. This dual role and responsibility simultaneously cast Pakistan itself as the abductor-country and India as the parent-protector, safeguarding not only her women but, by extension, the inviolate family, the sanctity of the community and, ultimately, the integrity of the whole nation. Additionally, and recurrently, the moral, political and ideological importance of India's secularism was held up as an ideal that had to be vigorously championed and defended for it was this, more than anything else, that enabled the Indian state to *define itself in opposition to the Pakistani one.*

The recovery programme, through its covert and overt rhetoric and operations, was as much an index of how India and Pakistan constituted themselves vis-à-vis each other as it was a contest of competing claims by Hindus, Muslims and Sikhs over each other's (and their "own") women and children. To this extent both countries were engaged in a redefinition of each other's (and their own) national "character", as demonstrated by a commitment to upholding honour and restoring moral order. The proper regulation of women's sexuality had to be restored, and the sexual chaos that mass abduction represented had to be reversed. Thus, the individual and collective sins of men who behaved without restraint or responsibility in a surge of communal "madness" had to be redeemed by nations who understood their duty in, once again, bringing about sexual discipline and, through it, the desired reinforcement of community and national identities.

Feminist and other scholars of nationalism in post-colonial societies have drawn attention to the place that the "woman question" occupies in transitions to modernity. In India, for instance, the preoccupation of the social reform movement with widow remarriage, sati or the age of consent was, in fact, a concern with women's sexuality. The movement's intention was to lift discussion of it out of the domain of the traditional, and insert it into the political and social agenda of modern nationhood; but as various analyses have shown,[28] the enterprise was confounded at the outset by the clear demarcation of public (represented as male and modern) from private (represented as female and traditional), and by the need to emphasize the purity and cultural superiority of Indian womanhood.

The rhetoric of modernity, however, could hardly be abandoned by a modernising state: it was constrained to undertake the kind of transformation that would enable it to weld a nation and build a citizenry that would recognize its fellow members as part of the same nation, sharing nationality. It would have to grant rights, assign responsibility and guarantee equality in an undifferentiated manner to all its citizens. Nonetheless, as Deniz Kandiyoti argues, definitions of "modern" take place in a political field where certain identities are privileged—even while equality is promised—and others subordinated. Whenever women serve as boundary markers between national, ethnic and religious collectivities, she says, "their emergence as full-fledged citizens" with concomitant rights "will be jeopardized".[29]

Other analysts have noted that women have been subsumed only symbolically into the national body politic, because no nationalism in the world has ever granted women
and men the same privileged access to the resources of the
nation-state. Moreover, as Mosse points out, "nationalism
had a special affinity for male society, and together with the
concept of respectability, legitimized the dominance of men
over women"[30] The passionate brotherhood of "deep comradeship" that Benedict Anderson talks about is an essen-
tially male fraternity in which women are enshrined as the
Mother, and the trope of nation-as-woman "further secures
male-male arrangements and an all male history".[31]

Floya Anthias and Nira Yuval-Davis have pointed out
how central dimensions of the roles of women are constituted around the relationships of collectivities to the state,
and that equally central dimensions of the relationships
between collectivities and the state are constituted around
the roles of women.[32] The reconfiguration of relationships
between communities, the state and women in the wake of
a bitter and violent conflict amongst Hindus, Muslims and
Sikhs and the division of India along communal lines, took
place in part around the body and being of the abducted
woman of all three communities. She also delineated the
relationship between India and Pakistan as they typified the
two principal "communities", Hindu and Muslim, eternally
and irrevocably locked in battle with one another. Each was
projected as an essentialized collectivity: Hindustan, land
of the Hindus, and Pakistan, Muslim homeland, closed to
non-Muslims, non-believers. In the classic transposition, the
woman's became the body of the motherland (Woman-as-
Nation) violated by the marauding foreigner.

The establishing of difference, or distinction, is a virtual
prerequisite for nationalism even though all definitions of it
remain elusive. What, asks Eva Sedgwick, distinguishes the
"nation-ness" of the United States from the "nation-ness" of
Canada or Mexico? From the Philippines? And from the many
nationalisms within itself? Recognizing the several differences she concludes that there is no "normal" way for the

nation to define itself:

> ... the 'other' of the nation in a given political or historical
> setting may be the pre-national monarchy, the local ethnicity,
> the ex-colony, the diaspora, the transnational corporate, ideo-
> logical, religious, or ethnic unit. . . the colony may become
> national vis-à-vis the homeland, or the homeland. . . become
> national vis-à-vis the nationalism of its colonies.[33]

Most theorists of nationalism have posited that nations are
haunted by their definitional others; implying "some element of alterity for its definition" a nation, according to
Perry Anderson, is ineluctably "shaped by what it op-
poses".[34] Benedict Anderson further suggests that nationalism should best be conceived "not as an ideology" but "as
if it belonged with kinship or religion rather than with lib-
eralism or fascism".[35]

In its own perception, three significant factors in the constitution of the Indian state set it apart from—and above—
Pakistan: it was *statedly* secular, democratic and socialist.
Pakistan was avowedly Islamic ("theocratic" to many), still
feudal, suspiciously "un-modern". This was at the level of
ideology. At the "imagined" level, however, other factors
informed the self-perception of the Indian state and its male
subjects, and both are important for an understanding of
the uncommon zeal with which the Indian government set
out to recover women. The idea of Pakistan as embodying/
representing the larger collectivity of Muslims, by definition inimical to Indian national interest; the sexuality of
women as transgressed by abduction and forcible conversion and cohabitation; and the question of the "legitimacy"
of children born of such "wrong" unions as future members of a community, are the three elements that we examine as forging the link between secularity, sexuality and the
state.

Again, the Debates provide the clues to all three. Chaudhury
Ranbir Singh, member from East Punjab said:

> Sir, our country is a secular State and it is in no way proper
> to compare an agreement arrived at in our country with that
> of the other. The other country is a theocratic State. We can

have doubts with regard to our sisters there but it is not justified for anyone to entertain the suspicion that fair treatment will not be meted out to women in this secular State.[36]

And, Sardar Bhupinder Singh:

> You are not prepared to go to war over this matter, I do not
> know why. If you are prepared to do so for a few inches of
> land in Kashmir, why not over the honour of our women? It
> is more important and is likely to affect our political pres-
> tige. . . Whenever outstanding disputes between this coun-
> try and Pakistan are enumerated they mention canal water,
> Kashmir and evacuee property—and such is the weakness
> of our government, they do not mention this question of re-
> covery of women.[37]

For the government, as for many leaders, Pakistan's intentions as far as the restoration of women was concerned never
quite squared with its performance. They disallowed the
MEO from conducting recoveries after July 1948; were tardy
in promulgating an ordinance based upon the November
1948 Agreement; appeared not to be co-operating on the
speedy recovery of those whose details had been furnished
by the Indian government; desisted from taking action
against those government servants who were supposed to
have possession of two thousand women; and failed to ensure that their police and social workers honoured the spirit
and letter of the Agreement. In December 1947, moreover,
Pakistan put forward the view that women ought not to be
"compulsorily" restored to their relatives because they were
"happy and content" in their new surroundings. In support
of this argument, it produced declarations to this effect made
by the women concerned, duly attested by magistrates.

Members of the house continually urged the Minister,
Gopalaswami Ayyangar, to impress upon the government
the need to put greater pressure on Pakistan for this purpose. Smt. Durgabai from Madras even went so far as to
say:

> Thanks to the leadership in our country, we have been able
> to get social workers who are not only public-spirited but
> non-communal in their outlook, and therefore, they are

inspired by the noble example set up by the Father of the Nation, Mahatma Gandhi, and also other leaders whose support and help are available in plenty for recovery activity. . .[38]

Another, Pandit Thakur Das Bhargava, declared ". . . so far as we are concerned, we know how to honour our moral obligations," implying that the Pakistanis did not.

As the discussions in Parliament continued it became clear that, in most members' view, Pakistan itself had become the abductor country mimicking, at a national level, the behaviour of its male subjects and guilty of the same moral turpitude. By contrast, India behaved like a responsible parent-protector, in turn reflecting what was the generally responsible behaviour of her people. There were aberrations, of course—"Some of our misguided brothers also share the responsibility to a certain extent"—but, in the words of one·member, "greater fault lies with the people and even with the government of Pakistan". In April 1948 the Lahore high court admitted a writ of habeas corpus requiring seven abducted women and children at the Sir Ganga Ram Hospital Camp to be produced before the court. When the women and children appeared the court ordered that they be released immediately because, in its view, the agreement between India and Pakistan regarding the recovery of women and children had no legal sanction unless it was made into a law through proper legislative procedure. Kamlaben Patel, who appeared with the seven recovered persons, recalls:

> No one was willing to accept our brief. At long last when a Christian advocate agreed to accept he was threatened with boycott. . . so he declined to appear. . . The matter fell on my shoulders and I had to step into the dock as the defendant. . . I was hooted down by the lawyers present in the court room . . . they shouted that they were not interested in my work and were not willing to repatriate recovered women and children. . . Their words upset me more than the order given by the court.[39]

As far as several members were concerned, Pakistan's duplicity regarding the return of women was consistent with its duplicity in all other matters under dispute—Kashmir, canal waters, and evacuee property—and provided proof enough (if proof were needed) of its indifference to honouring agreements in general. By proceeding as if Pakistan would indeed keep to its side of the bargain, India was guilty of weakness and irresolution. In the face of such provocation she had no choice but to depart from her moderate and "civilized" course and speak Pakistan's language. Pt. Thakur Das stated,

> The Pakistan government does not understand the language of morality, it only understands the language of force and retaliation. . . If this were a matter of mere international morality, I am at one with the Honourable Minister. But, all the same, when we have entered into a bilateral agreement—and with all solemnity they entered into the Agreement—let us see how it has been honoured in letter and in spirit by Pakistan.[40]

In at least two very significant instances Pakistan had betrayed its intentions:

> We knew on the 3rd of September 1947, an agreement was signed between the two governments and the ink was not dry when the Pakistan government, along with the Azad Kashmir government, raided parts of Kashmir and took away our women. . . For a government to be party to this loot, to this raid upon women and property and then to say that they were not. . . and ultimately to accept that they were. . . Nobody on earth can justify the Pakistan government.[41]

Nor could anybody countenance the fact that two thousand Hindu women were still in the custody of Pakistani government officials. That India should have signed a cease fire agreement before the captured women had been returned indicated that the government was neither "bold enough, good enough, sagacious enough, nor honest enough". Women had been spirited away to the closed districts of Jhelum, Gujrat, Campbellpur, the Frontier and Rawalpindi where no Indian recovery official was allowed to enter; they were stripped and paraded in Kabul; they were passed from hand to hand and sold in bazaars—still India stood silently by. If retaliation was the only language Pakistan could understand, then that was what India should speak, and speak it through those same sisters who "our country has a tradition of protecting". They would be the hostages. And if the state had cast itself in the role of Father to the women, then its male citizens would safeguard them like their brothers. "Sir," said Pt. Thakur Das Bhargava, "there is no reason why . . . a country is not justified in keeping these (Muslim) girls as hostages for some time. . . As a matter of policy, of strategy, it should have been done." If India could think of cutting off relations with Pakistan on economic matters, why could it not do so "to get our sisters back?"[42]

It could not, because then it would be no different from Pakistan. "Now I wish this to go on record," said Gopalaswami Ayyangar,

> that (making recoveries) is a thing which, as a civilized government, we ought to continue to do. Our own policy is that whatever may be done in the other Dominion, whether recoveries. . . are adequate or not, we owe a duty to a large number of Muslim women who are abducted within our territory.[43]

As powerful was the sentiment expressed by Shibban Lal Saksena:

> Sir, our country has a tradition. Even now the Ramayana and the Mahabharata are revered. For the sake of one woman who was taken away by Ravana the whole nation took up arms and went to war. And here there are thousands, and the way in which they have been treated was told by the Honourable Minister himself . . . what-not was done to them.[44]

Several other members concurred with this sentiment, reminding the House of its "moral duty" to behave honourably.

Two traditions are here being invoked: a tradition-in-the-making of responsible government, secular principles and democratic practice (anticipated even in these Debates in the discussion on the Constitution of India due to be introduced in Parliament in January 1950); and an ancient Hindu "tradition" of chivalry towards women and fierce protection of their honour. Such an invocation was consistent with what has been called the Janus-faced quality of nationalist discourse: as Kandiyoti points out, ". . . it presents itself both as a modern project that melts and transforms traditional attachments in favour of new identities, and as a reaffirmation of *authentic* cultural values culled from the depths of a presumed communal past" (emphasis added). In this case, it also necessitated the complete negation of any values of a shared Hindu-Muslim past (or present); indeed, one might even say that the attempt was to distance "civilized", "secular", Hindu India as far as possible from "irresponsible", "communal" Muslim Pakistan, and crystallize the difference in such a way that no other representation of either community or country could be accommodated.

Unlike community identities which most members assumed to be predetermined and unchanging, the identity of the Indian state was being newly forged. The Debates seesawed between those who were more concerned with establishing its secular credentials and adhering to democratic principles (among them members of the Communist Party of India and some Congress members, men and women), and those who were pressing for a more militant resolution as proof of the state's concern with its larger responsibility towards both its citizens and its *territorial integrity*. In the end, it was the latter who prevailed and the Bill was passed—but not without exposing some very fundamental flaws in its formulation, and unacceptable coercion in its implementation.

Boundaries and Being

It is important to note here that, from the very beginning, the concern with abducted women or persons went hand-in-hand with alarm at forcible conversions. This preoccupation continued throughout the Debates and, in fact, underlined another important factor in India's relationship with Pakistan: the loss of Hindus to Islam through such conversions, in addition to the loss of territory. Abduction and conversion were the double blow dealt to the Hindu "community" so that the recovery of "their" women, if not of land, became a powerful assertion of Hindu manhood at the same time as it demonstrated the moral high ground occupied by the Indian state. Nothing like this concern was evident with regard to the abduction of Hindu women by Hindu men, or Muslim women by Muslim men (by all accounts also very widespread), presumably because here no offence against community or religion had been committed, nor anyone's "honour" compromised.

Although there seemed to be a general consensus on both sides of the border that large numbers of women had indeed been abducted, a working definition of an abducted person was attempted by the Indian government only in 1949 in the Bill under discussion. Let us recapitulate this definition. It says:

> In this Act, unless there is anything repugnant in the subject or context, 'abducted person' *means a male child under the age of sixteen years or a female of whatever age* who is, or immediately before the 1st day of March, 1947 was, a Muslim and who, on or after that day and before the 1st day of January, 1949, had become separated from his or her family and is found to be living with or under the control of any other individual or family, and in the latter case *includes a child born to any such female after the said date* . . . (emphasis added)
>
> If any police officer, not below the rank of an Assistant Sub-Inspector or any other police officer specially authorised by the Provincial Government in this behalf, has reason to believe that an abducted person resides or is to be found in any place, he may, after recording the reasons for his belief, without warrant, enter and search the place and take into custody any person found therein who, in his opinion, is an abducted person, and deliver or cause such person to be delivered to the custody of the officer in charge of the nearest camp with the least possible delay.

The looseness (". . . had become separated from his or her family and is found to be living with or under the control of any other individual or family . . .") and arbitrariness ("If any police officer . . . has reason to believe that an abducted person resides or is to be found in any place . . .") of these definitions provoked intense debate in the Assembly. As mentioned earlier, many members were justifiably disturbed by its implications and by the extremely wide powers given to the police to determine exactly who would fall into this category; others drew attention to the significant departures made in this definition from the legal definition of "abduction" (to kidnap; to carry away illegally or by force or deception) and the consequent culpability of the government in a court of law.

Their misgivings were often fully borne out, not only by the actual process of recovery but also by the very impossibility of establishing, beyond reasonable doubt, that the person/woman "recovered" had in fact been "abducted" in the first place. Lists were compiled on the basis of claims filed by the relatives of missing women and sent to those in charge of the recovery operation in either country. These were then verified, if possible, and locating the women invariably required the help of local people. Needless to say, this was not always forthcoming. Kammoben told us that

. . . in Patiala, Nabha, Faridkot and other such states in East Punjab, and in Bahawalpur in Pakistan, there were innumerable difficulties in getting the approval and support of the local elders. . . and organising recovery in Jammu was like trying to chew iron.

Search officers and social workers told us that they used all kind of tactics to locate and "rescue" the women. "We had to go to far-off villages at all hours," said Kammoben, "sometimes walking for three or four kilometres. We didn't take a vehicle because the local people shouldn't get to know about the arrival of the police." The local police would often tip off families before the search party arrived so that they could remove the women from the premises. If this was not possible, they would be hidden in tandoors or where grain was stored till the police departed. They would then be spirited away to a safer spot. One liaison officer told us:

The operation was a raid in every sense of the word—we did many irregular things, like dipping a police officer under water and keeping him there till he told us where the

women were. . . sometimes I would slap the women and tell
them that I would shoot them if they didn't inform us.[46]

This was often necessary, he continued, because Pakistan
regularly put out "all kinds of false propaganda": the women
were told that many of their relatives had been killed and
the few who had survived were not likely to take them back.
They were also told that there was widespread starvation
in India and that a bucket of water was being sold for Rs. 5!
Or that they would be handed over to the armed forces for
their pleasure as soon as they got back. "It was but natural," Kamlaben said, "that the women were afraid to return
to India."

As we have seen, the circumstances of abduction varied
widely, and it was by no means possible to assume that any
and every woman located in a home or community was
eligible for recovery. Resistance to being thus recovered came
not only from their "abductors" but also from women themselves. A common plea was that their liaisons had been made
freely and under no compulsion; and indeed, many had
taken advantage of the social turmoil to marry men of their
choice from outside their community, something that would
almost certainly have been disallowed in more normal times.
The untidiness of the formulation in the Bill found its harrowing and messy consequences in implementation
throughout the eight years that the programme was in operation, but nowhere was this more disturbing than on the
issue of children. Just as leaders were beginning to take in
the enormity of the impact of delineating boundaries and
dividing people and territories, social workers, too, were
faced with the appalling consequences of dividing women
"like oranges and grapes" and deciding fortunes on the basis of who fell into which basket. And where did the children belong? With the oranges or grapes?

The two governments had agreed that neither forced conversions nor forced marriages would be recognized by either country. It followed then that children born of such
unions would be illegitimate, and for the purpose of the Bill
were defined as "abducted persons" if they happened to be

born within the time-frame set out in it. Now, those very members who had protested that no forcible recovery or return could be countenanced, and those who believed that every abductor had been guilty of a "shameful crime", was a murderer and could not be relied upon to provide either security or dignity to the woman he had forcibly converted and married, found that there were no grounds for their children to be treated as abducted persons. Why should they all be forced to go to Pakistan? they asked. "You must realise," declared Pandit Thakur Das Bhargava,

> that all those children born in India are the citizens of India. Supposing a Hindu man and a Muslim woman have married. Who should be the guardian of the offspring?. . . Now when a Muslim girl is restored, she will go to Pakistan; she may change the religion of that child. The child will be considered illegitimate and is liable to be maltreated and killed. Between father and mother, who is entitled to guardianship? . . . If the father insists that he will look to the interests of the child and will see it is properly brought up, I do not understand why, by executive action, that child should be given to Pakistan merely because we have written these words here in the ordinance.[47]

Other members differed. "Our society is different from Muslim society," said Brajeshwar Prasad from Bihar:

> My friends made the suggestion that the children of such abducted women should be allowed to go back to Pakistan. May I know whether these children are regarded as legitimate? They are illegitimate in the eyes of the law. . .our Hindu society has no place for illegitimate children. . . I do not know how a child born of a man and a woman can ever be illegitimate. . . but we have to take facts as they are. . . such children if they are to live in India will remain as dogs. . .[48]

Yet others cautioned that if the government did indeed regard such marriages as illegal and, consequently, the children as illegitimate, then according to the law only the mother could be the legal guardian. Those who professed to speak on behalf of the abducted women admitted that the abductor had been guilty of

> . . . highly reprehensible conduct; but let us look at the question from the point of view of the abducted woman. The children to her are a sign of her humiliation, are unwanted, and if she returns to Pakistan. . . I think we may feel almost certain that they will not be treated as members of their mother's family. . .Why should they not then be retained in this country where their father, *whatever his original conduct might have been* is prepared to claim them as his own? (emphasis added)[49]

Moreover, it was the opinion of yet others that if the Pakistan Ordinance had no provision for the return of children, why then should the Indian one? "It should be left to the discretion of the authorities to decide which children should be retained and which . . . sent away."

Once again the Honourable Minister assured the members that ". . . the mere inclusion of children in the definition of abducted persons does not mean that those children are necessarily sent away to the other dominion," for he too believed that ". . . children born after March 1, 1947 would not be welcome in the original homes of these abducted persons when they go back. . . in 90 cases out of 100". Indeed, government policy in its implementation actively discouraged women from taking their children with them, and pressurised those who were pregnant to have abortions before they returned to their families. Of the children born to mothers in Pakistan and recovered by India only 102 had come to India as on July 21, 1952. The total number of women recovered from there at this time was 8,206. The reason given by the Honourable Minister for including children in this Bill was that ". . . in the actual working of the law, our own officers felt that . . .their (the children's) presence was an impediment in the way of (the women) being taken out. . ." i.e., mothers would not leave without their children. He added:

> If the original (meaning, natal or marital) home is willing to take such children, they are sent to the other Dominion. If they . . . are not welcome there, other arrangements are made . . . I have already taken steps to persuade the Pakistan government to introduce similar words in the definition of an

abducted person in Pakistan, and I would ask that this very desirable improvement . . . should be allowed to remain.[50]

The contradictions between the earlier ordinance and the present Bill made for predictable confusion in understanding the scope of the legislation: Hindu fathers should be allowed to assert their right of guardianship, ("for no child born of a man and woman is illegitimate") but children born of Muslim fathers could not be accommodated in "our Hindu society". The definition of an "abducted person" included not only "any female" but also "any male child below sixteen. . . born before the 1st of March 1947" and "any children born after March 1947 and before 1 January 1949". Upon unravelling, however, the confusing nature of the Debates reveals a curious logic. For one, the concern with male children below the age of sixteen was clearly to do with forcible conversion, rather than sexual transgression. The first ordinance on children in 1948 (referred to by Kamlaben Patel in her interview) was an initial response to the experience of social workers and others, that Hindu families demurred from taking back daughters/wives/daughters-in-law if they had also had other children in the meantime. The ordinance laid down, and implicitly acknowledged, that *the child belonged with the father, Hindu or Muslim*, and should be left behind in either country. As recovery work progressed, it became clear that removing women without their children was proving intractable and in order to wrest both from their "captors", the children had to be legislated into the definition of "abducted persons" — primarily, we would suggest, to put pressure on the Pakistan government and on those men who were unwilling to let their children go.

The Debates reflect the intrinsic impossibility of legislating the boundaries of identity: were the children to be considered Hindu or Muslim? Illegitimate, because the conversions and marriages were invalid? Wards of their mothers or fathers? They also reveal the disjunction between the letter of the law and the spirit of the legislators. While the Bill called for the repatriation of all women and children who fitted the definition of abducted persons, the preoccu-

pation of several legislators was with maintaining community "purity" and difference, with blood and belonging.
More importantly, they underscore the deep ambivalence
of the Indian state striving to uphold its secular character
vis-à-vis Pakistan, but compelled to secure communitarian
interests at home in the aftermath of a division of the country on communal lines.

Secularity, Sexuality and the State

The single most important point about the
Abducted Persons (Recovery and Restoration) Bill was that
it needed to be legislated at all, since the maximum number
of recoveries had been made between 1947–49, before the
Bill was introduced in Parliament. Why then was the Indian government so anxious to reclaim women, sometimes
several years after their abduction? Why should the matter
of national *honour* have been so closely bound up with the
bodies of women, and with the children of "wrong unions"?
The experience of Pakistan suggests that recovery there was
neither so charged with significance nor as zealous in its
effort to restore moral order. Indeed, informal discussions
with those involved in this work there indicate that pressure from India, rather than their own social or political compulsions, was responsible for the majority of recoveries
made. There is also the possibility that in Pakistan the community stepped in and took over much of the daily work of
rehabilitation, evidenced by findings that the level of destitution of women in that country was appreciably lower. We
were told that both the Muslim League and the All Pakistan
Women's Association were active in arranging the marriages
of all unattached women so that "no woman left the camp
single". Preliminary interviews conducted there also hint
at relatively less preoccupation with the question of moral
sanction and "acceptability", although this must remain only
a speculation at this stage.[51]

Notwithstanding the above, some tentative hypotheses
may be put forward. For India, a country that was still reel-

ing from Partition and painfully reconciling itself to its altered status, reclaiming what was by right its "own" became imperative in order to establish itself as a responsible and civilized state, one that fulfilled its duties towards its citizens both in the matter of securing what was their due and in confirming itself as their protector. To some extent, this was mirrored in the refugees' own dependency in turning to the government as its *mai-baap* (provider) at this time of acute crisis. Organizations like the RSS and Akhil Bharatiya Hindu Mahasabha, for instance, were clamouring for the return of Hindu women and the Hindu Mahasabha even included the recovery of women in its election manifesto in 1951.

But the notion of "recovery" itself, as it came to be articulated, cannot really be seen as having sprung full-blown in the post-Partition period, a consequence of events that had taken place during and after the violence that accompanied the exchange of populations. If we pause to look at what had been happening in Punjab from the mid-nineteenth century onwards with the inception and consolidation of the Arya Samaj and the formation of a Punjabi Hindu consciousness, we might begin to discern some elements of its anxiety regarding Muslim and Christian inroads into Hinduness, and the erosion of Hindu dharma, values and lifestyle through steady conversion to those two faiths by Hindus.[52] With the creation of Pakistan this anxiety found a new focus, for not only had it been unable to stem conversions to Islam, it had also actually *lost one part of itself* to the creation of a Muslim homeland. Recovery then became a symbolically significant activity (its eerie resonance in the current frenzy to recover sacred Hindu sites from "usurping" Muslims is chilling), just as earlier the Shuddhi programme of the Arya Samaj, if it resulted in bringing only one convert back into the Hindu fold, served to remind the Hindu community that losing its members to Islam or Christianity was not irreversible. Recovering women who had been abducted and, moreover, forcibly converted, restoring them both to their own and the larger Hindu family, and ensuring that a generation of new-born Hindu children was not lost to Islam through their repatriation to Pakistan with their mothers, can be seen as part of this concern. Because, in fact, such recovery or return might not be voluntary, necessary legal measures had to be taken to accomplish the mission. In one sense, it would seem that the only answer to forcible conversion was—forcible recovery.

The key to understanding the unease surrounding the matter of the children of abducted women lies in the importance regarding the question of legitimate membership—of a family, a community and, ultimately, a nation.[53] The sanctity of all three lay in keeping the boundaries intact, in maintaining difference, and in refusing to allow sexuality to be contaminated by secularity. This is why the forced alliances resulting from abduction could neither be socially acknowledged nor legally sanctioned, and why the children born of them would forever be "illegitimate". This was also why the "faked" family had to be dismembered by physically removing the woman/wife/mother from its offending embrace and relocating her in the "real" one where her sexuality could be suitably supervised. (It is worth noting that though the legislation in India affected the recovery of Muslim women, the hidden referent was always Hindu women in Pakistan).

The unhappiness and, indeed, outrage at forcible conversion is palpable through all the debates on abducted women, and the extension of the definition of the term to *any male child below the age of 16* further indicates the depth of the disquiet. Although the state, especially one that called itself secular, could not be seen to be subscribing to this anxiety it could certainly act in the national interest, and in the interest of its citizens and their communities by upholding their honour—in this case, through restoring their "sisters" and its own subjects to where they belonged, with their respective Hindu or Muslim families and their own Hindu and Muslim countries. By becoming the father-patriarch the state found itself reinforcing official kinship relations by discrediting, and in fact declaring illegal, those practical arrangements that had in the meantime come into being, and were functional and accepted.[54] It was not only because abduction was a criminal offence that it had to be redressed—its offence was also that, through conversion and marriage, it transgressed the prescribed norm in every respect.

The Abducted Persons Act was remarkable for the impunity with which it violated every principle of citizenship, fundamental rights and access to justice, and for contravening all earlier legislation with regard to marriage, divorce, custody and guardianship and, eventually, inheritance, not so much to property but, more critically, to membership of a (religious) community. The freezing of boundaries, communal and national, calls for what Julia Kristeva terms "sexual, nationalist and religious protectionism", reducing men and women, but especially women, to "the identification needs of their originary groups", and imprisoning them in the "impregnable aloofness of a weird primal paradise: family, ethnicity, nation, race".[55] The state cannot absent itself while these negotiations are taking place; for, Kristeva continues,

> Beyond the origins that have assigned to us biological identity papers and a linguistic, religious, social, political, historical place, the freedom of contemporary individuals may be gauged by their ability to choose membership, while the democratic capability of a nation and a social group is revealed by the right it affords individuals to exercise that choice.[56]

Free choice, freely exercised, is what neither state nor community could allow abducted women in post-Partition India, so much so that it was legislated out. In its desire to restore normalcy and to assert itself as their protector, the Indian state itself became an abductor by forcibly removing adult women from their homes and transporting them out of their country. It became, in effect and in a supreme irony, its hated Other. In its articulation of gender identity and public policy, moreover, the state underlined the primacy of religious identity and, implicitly and explicitly, departed from its neutrality in assigning value to the "legitimate" family and community "honour". It did so through a regulation of women's sexuality; indeed, through legislation and executive and police action, it effectively reconstituted the multiple patriarchies at work in women's lives within the family and community, and as embedded in institutions and social mores.

Notes

[1] Reports from West Punjab, January–June 1948, India Office Library IOL/L P+J/5/332.

[2] Constituent Assembly of India (Legislative) Debates, December 15, 1949, p. 642.

[3] Evan Jenkins, Confidential Reports, April 1947. India Office Library R13/1/176. Weekly reports were submitted by the Governor to the Secretary of State for India.

[4] Ibid., March 1947.

[5] Constituent Assembly Debates, op. cit., p. 634.

[6] Ibid.

[7] Satya Rai, *Partition of the Punjab* (Bombay: Asia Publishing House, 1965), p. 113.

[8] Aparna Basu, *Mridula Sarabhai: Rebel with a Cause* (Delhi: Oxford University Press, 1996), p. 133.

[9] Constituent Assembly Debates, op. cit., p. 637.

[10] Aparna Basu, op. cit., p. 139. For details on Mridula Sarabhai's involvement in recovery work, see pp. 122–46.

[11] The Gandhi Vanita Ashram in Jalandhar was set up after Partition for the rehabilitation of destitute women. Subsequent to signing the Inter-Dominion Agreement on the recovery of abducted persons, it was designated the receiving institution for non-Muslim women recovered from Pakistan; its counterpart in Lahore was Sir Ganga Ram Hospital.

[12] Aparna Basu, op. cit., p. 131.

[13] *Selected Works of Jawaharlal Nehru*, Second Series, Vol. 5 (Delhi: Jawaharlal Nehru Fund, 1987), p. 114.

[14] Recoveries were temporarily suspended in September 1948 due to "propaganda" against social workers, in general, and Mridula Sarabhai in particular, and the Kingsway Camp in Delhi was closed down. Senior officials in the Indian government objected to Mridula's high-handedness and "non-official" functioning, and tried to bring the entire operation under their control. Recoveries resumed in December 1948. See Anis Kidwai, *Azadi ki Chaon Mein* (Delhi: National Book Trust, 1990), p. 306; and Aparna Basu, Second Series, Vol. 5 op. cit., p. 134.

[15] Appeal published in *The Hindustan Times*, January 17, 1948. *Selected Works of Jawaharlal Nehru*, op. cit., p. 113.

[16] Quoted in G.D. Khosla, *Stern Reckoning*, op. cit., p. 75.

[17] Memorandum on Recovery (Review of Position since October 1948) dt. June 20, 1949. Rameshwari Nehru Papers, Nehru Memorial Museum & Library, New Delhi.

[18] Report of the Relief and Rehabilitation Section presented at the Indian Conference of Social Work (Delhi Branch), December 1949.

[19] Aparna Basu, op. cit., p. 137.

[20-26] Constituent Assembly Debates, op. cit.

[27] Aparna Basu, op. cit., p. 139.

[28] See, among others, Partha Chatterjee, "The Nationalist Resolution of the Women's Question", in Kumkum Sangari & Sudesh Vaid (eds.), Recasting Women: Essays in Colonial History (Delhi: Kali for Women, 1989); Jasodhara Bagchi, "Ethnicity and Empowerment of Women: The Colonial Legacy", in Kumari Jayawardena & Malathi de Alwis (eds.), Embodied Violence: Communalising Women's Sexuality in South Asia (Delhi: Kali for Women, 1996); Lata Mani, "Contentious Traditions: The Debate on Sati in Colonial India", in Sangari & Vaid, op. cit.

[29] Deniz Kandiyoti, "Identity and Its Discontents: Women and the Nation", in Millennuim, Journal of International Studies, 1991, Vol. 20, No.3, p. 435.

[30] Andrew Parker, Mary Russo, et al (eds.), Nationalisms & Sexualities (New York & London: Routledge, 1992) p. 6.

[31] Benedict Anderson, Imagined Communities (London: Verso, 1992), Introduction.

[32] Floya Anthias & Nira Yuval-Davis, Woman-Nation-State (London: Macmillan, 1989), Introduction.

[33] Parker, et al, op. cit., p. 3.

[34] Quoted in Parker, et al, op. cit.

[35] Benedict Anderson, op. cit., p. 5.

[36] Constituent Assembly Debates, op. cit., p. 804.

[37] Ibid., p. 799.

[38] Ibid., p. 794.

[39] Kamla Patel, Mool Suta Ukhadela (Torn from the Roots, unpublished English translation), ms. p. 85.

[40-44] Constituent Assembly Debates, op. cit.; unless otherwise stated, all quotes in this section are taken from the Debates, pp. 640–44.

[45] Deniz Kandiyoti, op. cit., p. 431.

[46] Personal interview with K.L. Bindra, Liaison Officer, West Punjab, 1947–49.

47-50 Constituent Assembly Debates, op. cit.

51 We owe this information to Nighat Said Khan researching the Pakistan experience. See also Ayesha Jalal, "The Convenience of Subservience" in Deniz Kandiyoti (ed.), *Women, Islam and the State* (Philadelphia: Temple University Press, 1991), p. 88.

52 For a detailed account of this see Kenneth W. Jones, *Arya Dharm: Hindu Consciousness in 19th Century Punjab* (Delhi: Manohar, 1989).

53 Nira Yuval-Davis and Floya Anthias have put forward the viewpoint that there are five major ways in which women have tended to participate in ethnic and national processes and in relation to state practices. These are: a) as biological reproducers of members of ethnic collectivities; b) as reproducers of the boundaries of ethnic/national groups; c) as participating centrally in the ideological reproduction of the collectivity as transmitters of the culture; d) as signifiers of ethnic/national differences; e) as participants in national, economic, political and military struggles. Anthias & Yuval-Davis (eds.), *Woman–Nation–State*, op. cit.

54 We are grateful to Veena Das for having drawn our attention to this; for an elaboration, see "National Honour and Practical Kinship: Of Unwanted Women and Children" in Das, *Critical Events: An Anthropological Perspective on Contemporary India* (Delhi: Oxford University Press, 1995), pp. 55–84.

55 Julia Kristeva, *Nations without Nationalism*, trs. Leon S. Roudiez (New York: Columbia University Press, 1993), pp. 2–3.

56 Ibid., p. 16.

A Community of Widows

Missing Citizens

With tears in her eyes, a few days ago, a refugee woman went to see Pandit Nehru at his residence. Before India's partition, she belonged to a prosperous family in Pakistan but now she was homeless, with no money to buy food and no relations to comfort her in her distress: her only hope was her country's Prime Minister.

"I want a job," she pleaded with Panditji. The Prime Minister recommended to the Women's Section of the Ministry of Relief and Rehabilitation that she should be given a sewing machine. In addition, he paid her a sum of Rs 20.

The Women's Section has opened destitute homes and relief centres for such women, but then there are other problems worse than "unemployment". To find a solution for some of them would be a difficult task.

"What shall I do about utensils?" asked a destitute refugee woman who came to the Women's Section the other day. Her son had been shot, her husband murdered and daughter abducted. She did not know where to turn for support. The Officer-in-Charge of the Homes for Destitute Women and Children offered to help her.

"You will have a place to live where you will be provided with utensils and you can cook meals," said the officer.

"But how shall I cook my meals with these hands?" the woman replied, weeping, showing her right hand which had been chopped into half during the disturbances.

—Hitavada (a fortnightly publication), May 22, 1948

Homes for the Homeless

1947: Within the first few months of Parti-
tion about forty-five refugee camps had been set up in East
Punjab, varying in strength from 10,000–50,000 refugees. At
any one time there would have been at least 600,000–700,000
people in the camps. The largest one was at Kurukshetra, a
huge tented city, initially run by the army under the control
of the central government. In the course of time, and when
its population was down to about 300,000, it came under
the government of Punjab which carried out the dispersal
of refugees to other relief camps and thence to villages for
resettlement. Spread over an area of about nine square miles
it was divided into four townships, each with its own staff
of rationing officers, storekeepers, inspectors, assistants,
clerks, typists and record keepers. It had three full-fledged
hospitals and 14 dispensaries; a medical staff of over 1,000,
among them 80 doctors (17 of them women), 30 nurses and
midwives and 22 nursing orderlies. And by the end of December 1947, it had 17 schools in the camp area with more
than 5,500 students. Within three months the number of
schools had risen to 35 and the number of students to 18,200.[1]

Most of the refugees at the Kurukshetra camp were from
Sheikhupura, Multan and Muzaffargarh—shopkeepers,
traders, a few farming or land-holding families, predominantly lower middle class. Refugees were housed in clusters from the same village or district, two to three families
to a room, and in April 1950 the camp was finally closed
down.

The Karnal Mahila Ashram was set up in 1948 to look
after and rehabilitate "unattached" women and children. In
1950 there were about 3,500 women and children in the
Ashram, housed in barracks. They had come from the

Ramnagar and Kurukshetra general camps to the Karnal Widows' Home as it was then known, run by the government of Punjab till 1968 when it came under the government of Haryana. Each family cooked for itself, using the dry rations that were provided by the government. There was a school for women and children, tailoring and embroidery classes and production centres to provide employment to women, a dispensary, a temple and a gurudwara. Around 1955, as the women became self-sufficient, the government discontinued the supply of rations and gave them Rs. 12 per head if the family members exceeded two, or Rs. 32. As claims for compensation were settled and the women informed, the Ashram would give them one month's ration and discharge them.[2]

1997: Fifty years after Partition the Karnal Mahila Ashram is still there and so are seven widows from the Partition, who have survived. The Ashram is now also home to 40–50 Bengali widows and their families, brought here as refugees in 1971 after the creation of Bangladesh. The widows continue to live in tiny rooms, no more that 8' x 8', irrespective of the number of members in the family. The 1947 widows get Rs.150 per month from the government, an amount which they have been receiving for over thirty years. Now in their late sixties or early seventies, none of them is able any more to earn anything extra by sewing or doing embroidery.

The seven widows who still live in the Karnal Mahila Ashram are all mothers of daughters—only. Without husbands and sons, many thought of themselves as being doubly widowed. Rather than live their old age out with their daughters—despite the extreme and extraordinary course their lives had taken—and mindful, too, of the social conventions against prevailing upon the indulgence of sons-in-law, they chose (if one can call it that) to stay on in the Ashram. As more than one of them said to us: *"Putran waliyan dhar gaiyan, thiyan waliyan mar gaiyan."* (Those with sons have been able to settle themselves, those with daughters are as good as dead.) Although, in fact, these widows had brought up their daughters as if they were sons, educated them and sent them out to work, they couldn't actually expect to be looked after by them in the same way as if they had been sons. "*Bete vale ghar chaliyan gaiyan,*" they told us, "*beti waliyan ashram vich hi maran giyan.*" (The ones with sons, they've gone home, the ones with daughters will die in the Ashram.)

Widows with sons saw their plight as temporary. In time, the sons would start earning, get married, even get dowries, perhaps, and things would begin to look up—and they themselves would at last be able to feel "settled", physically, emotionally, psychologically and, hopefully, financially.

When we last saw Gyan Deyi in early 1997 (fifty years after she had been uprooted from her home in West Punjab), she was about 68 or 69, very fit for her age and for the kind of times she had lived through. Tall, erect, dressed as usual in her well- and self-tailored salwar-kameez, still looking strong, but her face was much more wrinkled than when we had seen her first, in 1989.

We visited her the next morning in the room which has been Gyan Deyi's home for almost 40 years now. She came here seven or eight years after Partition when she decided not to live with her brothers any more. She did not want to be a burden on others, she told us, especially as her brothers were so hard up themselves. The extreme tidiness and organization of her room are testimony to her strong will, her determination to create order in an otherwise quite shattered life. In the Ashram she learnt tailoring and embroidery and made a living from that till a few years ago, when the Production Centre became more or less non-functional. Her eyesight, too, was no longer good enough for this kind of work. She keeps in touch with her nieces and nephews, visits them occasionally, goes for weddings and deaths but has no desire to—or perhaps no possibility of—living with any one of them.

Half in earnest, half in jest, she said several times, "Most others from this Ashram have gone to *Rabb* (God), I am waiting for my invitation—any day now it may come."

Gyan Deyi: "You can't imagine how we lived. . ."

I've been in this Ashram for 32 years. In those days Miss Makhan Singh was here. I spent one year in the sewing section, I also learnt embroidery. I did that work for ten-twelve years. Then my eyes became weak so I had to stop. After that I started sewing—I had to do something, I couldn't survive without working. Pyjamas, frocks, petticoats, kurtas, suits. . .

After Partition for four-five years I lived with my brothers. When they moved I moved with them. Now I've been here 32 years. . . . I remember it's 32 years because that year my niece got married. I learnt sewing in Panipat for six months. I could have earned some money making clothes for others but my brothers didn't allow that. They said, it doesn't look nice your doing that. They were earning, I was living with them, for two years in Palanpur, one in Shahpur, that makes three, one year in Thirwa. . . in all four or five years. . .

. . . I remember from when I was ten or eleven. My father had wholesale shops, four shops where my bua's sons worked. They bought and sold gur and sugar. It was a big market. There were servants, munims. . . . We had 25 murabbas (units) of land. It was a lot of land. Muslim labour worked for us. We gave them ploughs and animals—there were no tractors then. Muslims did the work, my father supervised. Our lands were near the village of Gajranwali, tehsil Hafizabad, district Gujranwala. Nearby were Jalalpur Jattan da, Jalalpur Bhattian da, Kollon, Rampur. They were Muslim villages. There were Hindus there also, but mainly Muslims.

In our village how many were Hindus and how many Muslims, that I don't know, but there was no difference between Hindus and Muslims. We had very good relations. At marriages we exchanged gifts—if there was a marriage in our family we distributed sweets, half a seer for every member of the family. If there were ten members we sent five seers. Muslims got sweets made by Hindu cooks and sent them to Hindu homes. Only well-off families did this, not everyone. The Bhattis, Maulvis, Tarans—they had this exchange with us.

When we left the village the Bhattis really helped us. Bhattis and we were like one family—our houses were also nearby. We visited them, they visited us, on all happy and sad occasions we went to each other. We suffered only at the hands of the Malik Wassan (a local gang)—but actually they could never get to us. It was our own labour, people who worked on our land, they attacked us. Our own people did this. When the trouble started it was winter, the crop was ripe, ready to be harvested. We tried to cut it quietly at night. The house was full of paddy. They attacked my brother—I remember every-thing so clearly. I was sixteen or seventeen. When the trouble began my younger brother went to Amritsar to get trucks. Even the Bhattis advised us to make preparations to leave. They said, nothing can be guaranteed, we may not be able to help if the Malik Wassan come and attack.

All this started happening a month before we actually left. We escaped during that time. We had wanted ten trucks but only three came. How could we have brought all our things in three trucks? But almost the whole village, taking only very few belongings, left in three trucks.

I was living with my parents—I had come from Lyallpur to visit them. Those days girls would come for six months, eight months, to their parents. . . and I was still a child. I came here with my two brothers and their families. We took some jewellery, the rest we buried in our home thinking, not today, but tomorrow, in a few days we will definitely return. We never thought we would never go back. So we buried the gold under the grain. Twice my brother tried to return but he couldn't because our own labour had become our enemy. There were so many of them because we had so much land, not in our village, in four or five villages.

. . . We grew rice—we drew water from our wells for it with the animals, even camels. We had 15–20 buffaloes, so many buffaloes, so much milk—the nayans (women of the barber caste, Muslim) used to come to churn milk. Heaps of butter was made every morning—they took the buttermilk, gave us the ghee which they made from the butter. Most of our ser-vants were Muslims, they did the work. Churas (low castes) looked after the animals, nayans milked them, for the fields there were other labourers. Sharecroppers worked the land. For our own use, we churned the milk ourselves—my mother did that early in the morning.

We grew basmati—the basmati grown there was so fragrant you cook it here, you smell it out there. We had our own goats and sheep, they gave us so much wool, we produced our own blankets. We also grew our own cotton. Khes and bedspreads were woven in the village—we gave the weavers the thread, they gave us ready sheets . . . Just before we left we had 30–40 khes made. We had the yarn spun and carded—never did anything ourselves, the servants did everything. You can't imagine how we lived, rani, how we lorded it (*raj keetta*). . . . That's why we cry now. Even now I can see it all . . .

We escaped with such difficulty. What all we left behind— tins full of ghee, trunks full of blankets and quilts, so much. Our house in the village had four storeys. Many Hindu families had moved into our house for safety. We cooked for all of them. A mandir and gurudwara were set up in the house, paath went on all the time. There were very few temples in the villages, mostly gurudwaras. I took some rations, five or six plates, katoris, tumblers, some pots and pans. I locked the house myself and handed the keys to Maulvi Sahib. He brought us to the trucks, saw to our safety. He took the keys from me and said, "Beta, don't lose heart. Let the 15th (August) pass—we ourselves will come to fetch you and bring you back. Don't worry."

I was the last to leave, I was so scared. I locked the house from inside waiting for some of the men to come and take me. I put everything in order before leaving—I didn't want my brother and sister-in-law to say I didn't leave the house in order. I went to the roof of the house and looked out. I saw Gosainji passing and called out, "Brother, are you going to the trucks? Please send one of our men to fetch me."

I was so afraid the trucks would leave without me. People may not know I wasn't there—there was so much confusion, so many people. It was not a small village, more like a town, and there were so many people leaving. I was full of fear. After all I was still quite young and it was a frightening time even for older people.

We spent one night at Hafza, the second night in Tibbia College, Lahore, where there was a camp. . .

Our whole village moved together up to Amritsar. I had brought some cash with me, just a little, 1,000–1,200 rupees. My brother had come earlier, he had more. Whatever gold we were wearing was all we had brought. At Tibbia College there was a langar, people had contributed food. In Amritsar we lived for a month in tents provided by the government. Even after coming here we had hopes of returning. . . We were in touch with the Bhattis, we got letters from them. . .

Our younger brother located us through announcements. Much later, after three or four years, our village was allotted land near Karnal and Panipat. We got only a little land, not much. One of my brothers started farming again. My younger brother was educated, he had a B.A., so he got a job. I had always lived with my younger brother, so here also I stayed with him. They were all struggling so hard, they had to mai. ᵛ off several daughters, their income was not too much. They had just about enough, so I came away to the Ashram. We experienced real hardship—not enough to eat, not enough clothes to wear—but what is the point of talking about all that now? We saw such bad days in Panipat, in Garh Shankar. We had occupied a house left behind by a Muslim tehsildar. We farmed land that was not really allotted to us and later it was confiscated. I had two tolas of gold but I couldn't hoard it for myself when my brother's family was so hard up. If the children were crying for food, I couldn't sit tight on my gold. Slowly I sold everything. Three or four families got together to start a firewood business—it didn't work, they didn't know the tricks of the trade, they had never done it before. If someone asks me to start a shop, will I succeed? No, how can I? They had never farmed with their own hands, the servants had done it all. So they were quite lost. One of them started to trade in knives—got them made here and took them to Bombay to sell. It was difficult, difficult to live with sisters-in-law. . . .

We had no news about my husband, in-laws. After about five or six years like this, I heard my husband had died. Somebody told me. My in-laws didn't try to reach me. They were not poor people. They were quite well off, but they had small hearts. They had shops and orchards, houses. We didn't know them, my marriage was arranged by the village gosain (priest) who knew them.

My parents gave me 100 tolas of gold when I got married—11 tolas when I went to my in-laws for the first visit, 5 tolas when my nephew was born. One hundred and one suits, five buffaloes—actually three buffaloes and two cows—one mare, a camel which was used to draw water from the well. Eleven beddings, complete winter bedding—eleven quilts, eleven sheets, eleven pillows. Big beautiful beds with red payas (legs). There were no sofas in those days, no Godrej almirahs, no TVs, no radios. Things were given so we would remember them, things that would stay with us. Now they give useless things, nothing substantial, just a stupid show. The buffaloes given in my dowry were decorated with velvet cloth, the cloth for the forehead had silver bells which tinkled.

It was the talk of the town, my dowry. The wedding party stayed two nights—people couldn't believe it. But everything went to my in-laws. What else? The clothes given to me were full size—even those went to them. I was so young, how could I control anything? All my husband's relatives were given woolen clothes—his brothers, uncles, aunts, nieces, nephews, all of them. Kashmiri shawls were bought in Jammu and sent by one of our relatives. . . .

I was the last child of my parents. My father was quite old when I was born. He was crazy about me—he said, I have been giving so much for my nieces' weddings, when will a baraat ever come to my home ? When I was born he was in Hafizabad on some work. The nayan went to inform him about my birth and he bought a sackful of patasha, loaded it on a camel and distributed it all along the way home. I got married in January, he died in February, exactly a month later. For two months tailors sat at home making clothes for the wedding, and he had just finished off paying the tailors and the jewellers. Then he died.

. . . We all lived so peacefully, god knows how the differences (between Hindus and Muslims) came. Now look at the problems between Hindus and Sikhs —we all practised Sikhism although we were Hindu. It was all one. Now they are saying, these are Hindus, these are Sikhs. . . .

. . . I have just blurted out everything to you today, everything that was boiling inside has just come out. Well, we got what was in our kismat—what was taken away was not in our kismat. We must not have done good deeds in the past. But I thank god every day, I say, "Many, many thanks to you for giving me food to eat, clothes to wear." Most of my life is over, the remaining few days will also pass . . .

But sometimes when I'm sick or unwell, I miss children,

someone of my own. Of course I feel lonely. I feel it but who shall I say it to? Before whom should I cry? Will anyone solve my problem? No one can. I have to deal with it myself, I have to work on myself, on my mind and on my heart. Whatever I have to go through, I will. I have to.

As she pressed tea and biscuits on us, Gyan Deyi provided us with thumb-nail sketches of her companions in the Ashram, all of whom we had met in the course of our visits. Her special affection, however, was reserved for Durga Bhenji who had been the warden at KMA for many, many years, loved and missed by the widows who still live there.

Durga Rani retired as a senior officer in the social welfare department of Haryana, after serving for over forty years. At the time, and in the place she was born, no one could have predicted that she would spend most of her life as an active and dedicated social worker. A refugee and young widow herself, she spent all her adult life looking after other widows and their children. A life full of struggle, but also full of satisfaction derived from taking care of and supporting her in-laws, her own daughters, and a very large number of others. Now in her seventies, Durga Rani is still active and in good health. She lives in a comfortable house that she built for herself with her own money. Her two daughters, one a medical doctor, the other a housewife by choice, live with their own families but keep in close touch with their mother. Durga Bhenji showed us around the Ashram, introduced us to the widows still resident there, and spent many hours talking about her life and work.

Durga Rani: "I asked no one for charity."

. . . We left on August 22. The authorities decided that if the Hindus of Head Junu were killed, then those from all the other Head Project areas would take their revenge on Muslims. That's why we were saved. When my brother saw the corpses of Hindus at Maddon on August 15, he sent us a telegram to say he was reaching Sargodha and that we should get there by motor trolley. My father was superintendent there so he arranged for one.

Ours was one of the first trains out of Pakistan. As soon as we reached Jullundar, my father got a job in the social welfare department. I was living with him in Head Junu. My own house was in Multan, I mean my husband's house. I was not well so my father brought me to his house. After that the fighting started—I went to him in April, the troubles began in August. I had three little girls, I must have been 20 or 21 years old at the time.

All the trains were supposed to have an armed escort of Gurkhas, but often the Muslims would disguise themselves as Gurkhas. They would climb onto the trains and loot everyone. We had hidden some gold in my little daughter's underwear in a pocket—that was all that we could save, the rest was taken away, my mother's, my own. . .

When we reached Lahore, we were searched. Even Muslim women in disguise looted us, whenever they got a chance, they took it. Even though the first train was supposed to be the safest. We waited there for 45 minutes—other trains had also been stopped. Every time the train stopped, we were terrified. There was no police. It took us five or six days to reach Jullundar. On the way we could not even drink water. If we got out at the station we were afraid we might be killed. Sometimes we had roasted gram to eat, sometimes roti-dal. My in-laws went to Karnal, I remained with my parents. There were seven of us—my younger brother, parents, my three daughters and myself. My eldest daughter got cholera as soon as we reached—she was just four years old. We went straight to the camp. We had just one glass between us, but we got our rations at the camp. The camp was at the DAV college—they closed the college. Tents were put up, they made temporary arrangements for water, but there was a cholera epidemic very soon. My daughter died of it. After we cremated her, we found the younger one had it, too. But by then we heard of the Cholera Hospital in Jullundar and took her there—she was there for 25 days. My parents ate nothing—they said they would survive on cardamom water. I was with my younger daughter and an eight year old brother—if anything had happened to my parents, I wouldn't have known what to do.

My father made an announcement on the radio that those people who were still in Pakistan were surviving on neem and shisham leaves, and must be rescued. It was November when my husband finally came to India. He had contracted typhoid on the way. Till then he was in a Hindu camp in Multan, Khanewal. There was such a crowd there, he had to wait his turn.

We had a dry fruit shop in Multan, and about 50–60 acres of land in Bhulepur. My husband used to sit in the shop. He was 24 when he died. When fighting broke out in March (1947) we had to leave town—our Muslim neighbours threw burqas on us and escorted us back to our village on tongas. When rioting began in Lahore, Multan followed, and we were under curfew. We couldn't come out of our houses—that's when we escaped to the village, to Bhulepur, so that we could all be together. It was safe there. In Multan, Hindus were in a minority and in greater danger. By August, it too had erupted.

My husband went to the camp at Khanewal in September, stayed there for three months and came to Jullundar in November with his family. He knew we were there because my father had sent messages, announced it on stations—Amritsar, Atari—along the way. My husband was on the train to Karnal but he got off at Jullundar, his parents carried on to Karnal. My husband knew ten trains had reached Amritsar, ten had reached Jullundar and ten would go to Karnal. By then we had left the camp but someone informed my father that my husband was in Jullundar. We started looking for him and finally found him in a doctor's house. But he was already too ill. He had hidden in some sugarcane fields on the way. I didn't even get a chance to ask him how those three months had passed—he died as soon as he reached, on November 17. I couldn't even speak to him. He said to my father, "I took her from your house, now I am leaving her in your house." These were his last words.

By then, my father had been allotted a small house in Basti Godam—it had been abandoned by a Muslim family. After my husband died I realized that I had to stand on my own two feet now. I said to my father, I will have to be trained for some work. I will live with my in-laws because they have lost their only son, but first I must be educated. Then my father wrote to Rajkumari Amrit Kaur and to Rameshwari Nehru—he was also doing rehabilitation work—asking if they could help. They

said, send her to Delhi, and I left Jullundar on January 1, 1948.
I brought my youngest daughter with me and left the other
with my mother.

I had studied upto class V. If I hadn't been married at such
an early age—I was only 15—I would have wanted to study
further but my father-in-law never wanted me to work. At
Western Court I took a diploma in Hand and Machine Embroidery. Mrs. Sethi took my interview. Mrs. John Mathai was
also there. But Mahatma Gandhi was killed on the 30th so all
the offices were closed.

. . . I cried, of course, leaving my parents, but what else
could I have done? There were other widows at Western Court,
we often cried together. . . we would stay awake all night sharing our experiences, what had happened to us. There were
about 250 of us, refugees only, training at Western Court under Mrs. John Mathai and Mrs. Williams. We got a stipend of
Rs. 45 per month. We were two in a room. Slowly we became
friends, we would go out in the evenings, to India Gate, to the
Kasturba Ashram. . . But it was only after I started working
that I began to feel less sad. Before that I used to wonder how
I would cope, whether I could manage, how I would ever forget. . .

After completing my training I was given a cheque for Rs.
10,000 to start a tailoring shop in Lajpat Nagar (the normal
capital grant was Rs. 3,000 and a sewing machine). I don't know
how, but my room-mate, Satwant Kaur, took that cheque—I
had asked her to post it to my father. We never found that
cheque, so I took up a job in Meerut. But I didn't like it there,
there were too many Muslims, I didn't want to stay. So my
father took me back to Jullundar and I got a job in the Women's
Section where Premvati Thapar was the Director. I was an embroidery worker, I used to teach the girls at the Ashram. Then
my father was transferred to Karnal and I came here. Now we
were all together again. Then I taught for a while at Maler Kotla.

In February 1950 I started working in the Karnal camp—it
was near the railway station—my in-laws and daughter were
still living there. They had one room, a small veranda outside.
There were six of them in one room, my two sisters-in-law
were also with them. After some time, our claims were also
settled—we got 50 acres in Hissar as compensation—my sis-

ters-in-law got 12.5 acres each and so did I. But we never earned much from the land. As soon as claims were settled, you were discharged from the camp.

. . . It was not easy, in the Ashram. The women were unhappy at being uprooted like this. In their own homes they were settled, here they were dependent on us for every morsel. Standing in lines in the morning for their rations, waiting for three hours, and they were often cheated—it was hard, but at least they got something to eat. Sometimes they would protest, take out a procession against the management for being careless or indifferent. If the superintendents didn't do their work, sat with friends, didn't give them their rations, they would shout at them. They used to say the in-charges have all the facilities and we don't get our rations on time. There was a lot of *hangama* (commotion). But the government made sure everything was available—free food, electricity, water, shelter, medicines, schools. If they worked, they were paid. If the government hadn't stepped in, many would have ended their lives. There were emotional traumas—people's hearts and minds were never at peace—at least they didn't end their lives.

If I hadn't started working in the Ashram I don't think I would have been able to stand on my own two feet. I had offers to work outside at a good salary, but I said I didn't want to work with men, I wanted to be with ladies. I was afraid I would be taken advantage of. . .

We were often taunted by people when we went to the bazaar: they would say, we'll be at barrack number 18 or 19 tonight. We had peep-holes on our doors and would open them only after we had identified the caller, and there were four or five chowkidars on the premises. But cases did happen. Sometimes the chowkidars would take them away. Then we would "dismiss" the women, allow them to go away. We would say that her family has taken her, she has been discharged. What else could we do ? Once, a woman was asleep outdoors and a man jumped over the wall and came and lay down beside her. She got up, her child also woke up, and the man ran away. But he came back a few days later and went to many barracks. This kind of "attack", of harassment, kept occurring and we had to deal with it—we even had to ask the CID for help. Obviously some staff members were also involved. In 1953–54 there were many such instances, and the women were very insecure. Some lost their nerve. And we had to have many abortions done.

Slowly, the women settled down but there are those who could never accept what happened, either financially or emotionally. Look at S.—she had four daughters and a son, her son died when he was very young—she had to bring up her girls, educate them, look after them on her small stipend. She's still in the Ashram, has never settled down. Even today, she gets Rs. 100 a month. Mothers of daughters never quite settled down. Shanti Devi didn't settle down. . .

We tried to look after them as well as we could. I was quite strict, I wouldn't let them go out alone. We used to say, go out in groups of seven or eight. We tried to keep them safe. When the Ashram started there were about 2,500–3,000 women in it. We had 22 acres of land, eight supervisors, one superintendent. We used to keep 60 families in one barrack—they would use their *khats* (beds) as dividers. We gave the women dry rations—it was impossible to cook for so many—dal, rice, atta, salt, ghee, soap, oil, etc., so they could cook whatever they liked. I used to teach there and lived on the premises. My working hours were from nine to five but the supervisor or superintendent often called me even after that to help out. Slowly, families would come to claim the women and they left the Ashram.

Our aim was to make the women as self-reliant as possible, to keep them from going astray. Many of them we got married. Those who were on the lookout for other men, we let them find their own partners. Many of these marriages turned out quite well. There was one Divan Chand Thekedar who married one of our women—she now has five sons!—and there were a few widowers who also wanted to remarry. Three of our own workers married local men, widowers.

Lower class women went out to work, they worked as domestic servants, but those from a well-off background didn't. They wouldn't leave the Ashram, they sewed or embroidered and stayed inside its four walls. Women from poor homes worked as farm labour, went to the wholesale market, picked potatoes, cleaned cotton. Some did nursing. There was a lot of demand for such women, people used to pressurize us for them. Some women were afraid to work in other people's homes, afraid of harassment. Others used to say, what can they do to us? We are not a sweetmeat which they can eat. They can't do anything if we don't want it. There were all kinds of women. . .

. . . Sometimes when the women got together to tell their stories, their crying and wailing were almost unbearable. They would wear red dupattas and sit down and wail in different voices . . . from Multan, from Muzaffarnagar, Dera Ismail Khan, the Frontier. They cried so bitterly we never knew whether we would be able to sleep in peace. Listening to them cry, I learnt to forget my own troubles. . .

I never thought of remarrying, the question didn't arise. My father did ask me once, but the thought of marrying again never entered my mind. I was looking after my children, my in-laws, I had a job, I had my books—that was enough. I didn't need another "companion". I had never really been into my first marriage either—I don't know, I've been like this from the beginning. Now it's forty years. . .

If Partition hadn't happened, if I hadn't lost my husband and daughter, learnt to stand on my own two feet—I think life would have been more difficult! (*Laughs*) Perhaps I would have developed these concerns in that life too, I don't know. It was a tragedy, of course—I was quite alone, afraid to go anywhere, insecure. Even my children were afraid. It was only in 1965, after my mother-in-law passed away that I felt less fearful. I turned to religion. I have my own house now, I sold my land and got some money, I'm retired—happiness lies in this, and in the fact that I asked no one for charity, not even my own father. And I never allowed my mother-in-law to cry, to feel her son's absence. She never cried in front of me. God has helped me a lot.

Of course, then, in that life, we lacked nothing. One worries if there are problems, hardship. Yes, there are desires also. . . but perhaps I would not have had these desires then.

. . . This was all fate. We had to come and drink the water of this area, this water could not have reached Multan. To leave one's own country is fate. Now this is our country, this has become my place. I am settled here, wherever I am I want to come back to Karnal. Now Punjab is finished, India is my country. That is why I say a country should not be divided. But if it is destined to be divided, it will be. Whatever is written will happen.

Have I ever wanted to go back to Pakistan? No, one needs great strength for that and I'm not strong enough. It's a dream I can't afford to have.

Coping

The fact that the Karnal Mahila Ashram still has widows from 1947, and that the silai (sewing) centres set up by the Women's Section in Delhi at the same time also have about 200–225 women workers from then, is noteworthy. While the government's pledge to assume lifelong responsibility for the widows of 1947 has been redeemed, at least in all the ashrams that we visited in Punjab and Haryana and in Kasturba Niketan in Delhi, the present administration in all three states has, by and large, failed to live up to its responsibility. Bureaucratic insensitivity is partly to blame. The widows told us of difficulties in getting medical attention, in retrieving their monthly allowance, in even having simple repairs done to their rooms. Many said that it was the mutual support they derived from each other that enabled them to live with some dignity and humanity in their declining years. In addition to the indifference of today's social workers, are poor utilisation of resources and a reluctance to bend or, indeed, to extend the system in any way in favour of the women.[3] And yet, several of the widows we spoke to in the Karnal Mahila Ashram had chosen to stay on despite the fact that they did have families they could turn to and despite, too, the pitiful amount they receive as their due today.

It is obvious that over the years the government has departed from its professed welfarism of the Fifties. The benign—*mai*—face of the state has receded and its authoritarian—*baap*—aspect has assumed primacy. This is manifest in the manner in which it has dealt with other "victims"— of drought, flood, cyclones, toxic waste and, indeed, of its own more recent resettlement schemes, notably of those displaced by the construction of big dams. As the relationship between the state and its subjects becomes more confiictual and rights are demanded as well as exercised—in other words when "victims" themselves begin to demand and protest[4]—we have seen the state renege again and again on its commitment to the disadvantaged. At the same time it has become more coercive in its contractual exchanges.

The state's coercive potential, even immediately post-Partition, was seen in the discussion on abducted women when it acted as their custodian and guardian; but, as we hope the following discussion on the state's responsibility for the widows of Partition will show, we cannot characterise the post-Partition state as always authoritarian or acting against women's interests. Then, as now, the state was neither monolithic nor unified in its responses and policies. This was evident in the debates on abducted women where the discussion on the role and responsibility of the state went back and forth, with no real agreement on how recovery was to be effected or on the limits to state authority. In the actual implementation we have seen that there was considerable hiatus between the executive and legislative arms, and the police and social workers who were in direct contact with the women. With widows on the other hand, the state, sometimes inadvertently, at others consciously, acted positively on their behalf; one might even say that for many such destituted women state institutions were probably more efficient and accommodating than a beleaguered family, at least for a while.

The scale and incidence of widowhood in 1947–48 was so immense—as was the related task of resettling refugees— that it resulted in the Indian government setting up what was to be its first major welfare activity as an independent state: the rehabilitation of what it called "unattached" women. Never before in the country's experience had a government, either feudal or colonial, been called upon to shoulder social and economic responsibility for a circumstance as problematic as widowhood: ritually inauspicious, socially stigmatised, traditionally shunned. It is true that the colonial state had been compelled by social reformers to address the issue of widow remarriage and child widows and so intervene in social and cultural practice; but that exercise was qualitatively different from what the Indian state was called upon to do in the aftermath of Partition.

When the first onrush of destitute women and children poured into the country from West Punjab there was no single agency that could cope with the urgency of the situation. Voluntary workers of all descriptions organized themselves to assist in any way possible, but most immediately with food, shelter, clothing and medical aid. The government itself encouraged such assistance, in particular from the All India Women's Conference, the YWCA, and the Gandhians.

Rehabilitation on such a massive scale was no easy job for any government. In the first few months after Partition the Indian government sought the help of several service organizations like the Kasturba National Memorial Trust, the All India Save the Children Committee, the Trust for Sindhi Women and Children, the Jainendra Gurukul, Arya Pradeshak Pratinidhi Sabha, Nari Seva Sangh and Akhil Bharat Nari Shiksha Parishad, among others. The All India Women's Conference at its Twentieth Session held in Madras in December 1947 adopted a resolution in which it declared that:

> apart from giving immediate relief in the form of shelter, food, clothing and medical care, it was the duty of every member to work for: (a) the mental reconditioning of refugee women to enable them to become useful members in the new society in which they found themselves; (b) the provision of employment in the shape of industrial co-operatives for destitute women; (c) the education of young children and to provide training for women in nursing, mid-wifery, teaching and other professions; (d) the prevention of any further destruction of life by safeguarding the lives of unborn children and young mothers and instituting homes for expectant women and unwanted children; and (e) the prevention through social contact and propaganda of the spirit of retaliation being fostered in the minds of the victims of communal hatred, particularly the young.[5]

As a first step towards dealing with the situation the Congress appointed a Central Relief Committee with Mrs. Sucheta Kripalani as secretary, and a United Council for Relief and Welfare with Lady Edwina Mountbatten as chairperson. These associations operated in various refugee camps and relief centres and co-operated with the government in setting up schools, hospitals and production and training centres. In September 1947 the government appointed a small advisory committee of women social workers attached to the Ministry of Rehabilitation to direct the programme—this was the Women's Section.[6] Rameshwari Nehru, who had been looking after the evacuation of women and children from West Punjab during the worst disturbances, took over as Honorary Director of the Women's Section in November 1947, responsible for the "care, maintenance and rehabilitation of uprooted women and children from Pakistan".

In the initial stages the purview of the Women's Section extended to the whole country, but it found its time and energies taken up primarily by displaced women in Delhi. Regional organizers were therefore appointed for Bombay, Ahmedabad, Saurashtra and Rajputana to take up work in those areas; this system proved to be ineffective, however, and it was then felt that work in the states should be handed over to state authorities. Accordingly, at a conference of provincial chief ministers held in Delhi in July 1948 it was decided that where the number of displaced or destitute women was sufficiently large, separate women's sections should be set up to deal specifically with their rehabilitation.

With this revised policy it became necessary to bifurcate the functions of the Delhi Women's Section, and in March 1949 the Women's Advisory Section became an integral part of the Ministry of Rehabilitation. It was under the guidance of this Section that the rehabilitation of widows and other displaced women took place. The general pattern was: establishment of homes and centres; programmes of education; giving orphan children into adoption; arranging the marriages of young women; and financial aid and employment. Although all work relating to rehabilitation was handed over to local authorities, the cost was borne by the central government, and the number of those receiving gratuitous relief in 1949 was 73,000.

The functions of the state women's sections were: to formulate schemes for the rehabilitation of women and children; establish homes for them; run production and training centres; organize the sale of articles produced in work centres; run schools; arrange for the adoption of orphaned children; give financial or other aid to women; assist in finding employment; and, finally, arrange marriages for them wherever possible. Conditions varied widely in different places, so the women's sections followed different patterns of organization. In Delhi, authority was vested in an honorary director who had wide executive powers and worked under the rehabilitation department of the state government. The same was true of U.P. and West Bengal; only in East Punjab was the director of the women's section a regular salaried official of the state government. At the centre Rameshwari Nehru, Begum Anis Kidwai, Mridula Sarabhai, Sucheta Kripalani, Mrs. John Mathai, Hannah Sen, Raksha Saran and many others all worked in an honorary capacity, with executive authority.

In a note dated December 1949 Rameshwari Nehru stated that the number of "unattached" women looked after by the government in October 1948 was 45,374.[7] Although not all of these women were widows, a very large percentage of them was; indeed, it was the very size of this category that persuaded the government to set up a special section within the Ministry of Rehabilitation to administer to their needs. In a sense, the Women's Section of 1947 can be seen as a forerunner of the many government agencies that now exist for the welfare of women and children, for the disabled, for disaster victims, and for the destitute. At that time, though, it had another important dimension as part of the government's programme of resettlement: the rehabilitation of widows, apart from being an immediate and urgent necessity in the wake of widespread violence and the loss of homes and livelihoods, was a crucial factor in the state's perception of itself as benign and paternalistic. Stephen Keller, who did extensive fieldwork among Punjab's refugees in the '70s has observed that:

> In Punjab and other areas of north India, government has always been characterised as *mai-baap*. As such, it is duty-bound to provide a rich, warm, nurturant relationship (the *mai* part) as well as paternal protection from the dangers of life (the *baap* part). In times of national disaster, particularly, the more maternal aspect is emphasized.[8]

National disaster. It was obviously such an event that galvanized the government into responding; but having said that, it is worth examining both the conceptual dimension of the project of rehabilitating widows and its implementation, to arrive at some understanding of how, through government intervention, the status of Partition widows underwent some change. The first significant difference was that the widows of 1947 became the responsibility of the state. In acknowledging this and stepping in to mediate—and indeed, direct—their reabsorption into the social and economic life of the country the state had simultaneously, to perform two functions: that of custodian and guardian in the absence of actual kinsmen, and of an apparently benign and neutral agency which could not be seen to subscribe to or reinforce traditional biases against widows. This is not to say that in the course of rehabilitation patriarchal attitudes were suddenly and miraculously found to be absent; nor that taboos regarding the sexuality of widows were not reinforced. But the disruption of Partition meant that, in the absence of family and social constraints, ritual and customary sanctions against widows were temporarily suspended; and even though the state stepped in as guardian and pater familias, so to speak, the nature and scale of rehabilitation compelled it to facilitate their reassimilation into the country's economic and social mainstream as expeditiously as possible.

Since the widows of 1947 were, ironically, widowed by history—or as the government put it, "victims of a struggle that might well be regarded as a war"—it was proposed that they be classified as war widows and treated as such. This particular definition of widows and of the circumstances of Partition, enabled the government to deal with the crisis as a national emergency and, more importantly, to look upon the widows not as individual women inviting social ostracism, but as a community of hapless survivors to be accorded the same status as other refugees. With some important distinctions, however. In addition to being classified as "war widows" they were further classified as (a) those whose husbands and sons and other breadwinners were killed during the riots; and (b) those who, though "unattached" had relatives alive who were unable to maintain them because they had lost their jobs and possessions. These two categories were to be treated differently: the responsibility for the first had to be shouldered by the government for the *rest of their lives*, while that for the second could extend either until the time they became self-supporting or till their relatives were able to maintain them. Further, those in the first category who were not willing to lead the regulated (read restricted) life of the homes should be given allowances sufficient to maintain themselves because, it was thought, there would be very few of them.[9] The chief difference between the rehabilitation of men and that of women was that the government undertook life responsibility for aged and infirm women, and for unattached women and children, till they were able to maintain themselves.

By far the largest number of unattached women and children from West Pakistan were to be found in Delhi, Punjab, Bombay and U.P. Figures for Delhi in 1949 were: 1,173 women and children in six homes; 8,034 in seven homes in Punjab; 4,500 in Bombay in the Nari Seva Sadan in Kurla and at other centres; 400 in two homes cum infirmaries at Meerut and Mathura in U.P. The total number of unattached women and children in other states was 1,000, with state governments setting up 16 homes for them in Ajmer, Bhopal, Madhya Bharat, Rajasthan and Saurashtra.[10]

The situation in West Bengal was somewhat different with migrations continuing well into the 1950s. In 1948 the state government set up three camps exclusively for women and children, but they were closed in 1949 and the occupants transferred to a new camp at Titagarh. In 1950 there was a heavy influx of refugees from East Pakistan, and by 1952 there were eight camps set up exclusively for women with a strength of 7,400. Other eastern states had 5,400 women and children and homes were set up for them in Assam, Bihar and Tripura. Residential homes in all states were intended only for those women who were destitute but there were thousands of others who were not unattached, for whom other arrangements had to be made.

Often, entire families were destituted and lived in camps or makeshift shelters, eking out a living. For women of these families, work centres were established in different cities and towns from where they could take work away. In Delhi alone, some thousands of women graduated from the work-cum-training centres, as indicated in the table below:[11]

Centre	No. of wage earners	No. of trainees
Karolbagh	500	254
Subzimandi	401	102
Paharganj	260	133
Lodi Road	180	84
8, Central Lane	195	84
Connaught Circus	78	222
Mehrauli	350	150
Humayun Tomb	250	140
Bela Road	300	106
	2,514	1,275

Yet other women needed financial assistance or employment of a more regular nature to enable them to earn a living. Women seeking relief were mostly from urban areas; those from agricultural and other working classes in the villages were not entirely destitute and settled with their menfolk whenever land was allotted to them as compensation. The rehabilitation of women from middle or lower middle class business or trader families required much greater planning because these women had done little work other than looking after their own families, and had only a smattering of skills in embroidery and tailoring. Moreover, they needed living accommodation as well as training and work facilities.

In a report on the work done by the Women's Section from 1947–49 Rameshwari Nehru noted that:

> At the very outset the Section realised that rehabilitation is an intricate process and can be achieved only if adequate attention is paid to the psychological, educational and emotional needs of the women. It is of utmost importance to make them self-reliant and self-supporting, and restore their sense of dignity and worth.

The way to do this, in its view, was to treat them a course of occupational therapy, to pay attention not only to their physical needs but to "their intellectual and vocational development".

Without wishing to belabour the point or to put too fine a construction on stated intent, we would like to suggest that it was just such an approach that, in fact, enabled a large number of widows to be drawn into some form of economically productive activity. Despite the many shortcomings in the actual workings of the rehabilitation programme, especially after the mid-1950s, the formal recognition of the fact "that the care and maintenance of destitute women is a task in social reconstruction" indicates a critical shift in conceptualisation—in marked contrast to prevailing practice today, for instance, when they are considered a "liability".

The first endeavour of the Women's Section was to free the widows from economic dependence. It was hoped that, in the long term, specially planned women's settlements would develop, embracing not only the refugees of Partition but other categories of destitute women as well. State and central governments were therefore requested to make available suitable land, open and extensive, near large cities for this "new experiment": it was a matter of some conviction that, with proper facilities, the women (note that the official documents do not refer to them as "widows" although the majority of "unattached" women were just that) could be prepared for dairy farming and agriculture and for those "advanced industries which require meticulous training and skill in execution". Underlying this conviction, or experiment, was the hope that they would be absorbed into the economic reconstruction of the country. Renuka Ray, member from West Bengal, made the point in the Legislative Assembly (March 1948), thus:

> I want to note some specific points with regard to the rehabilitation of women. I do not think that the establishment of homes where some little occupation is given, is enough. In this country there is a very great dearth of women who come forward to be trained in different fields of nation building. . . This great tragedy has left thousands of women homeless and alone. . .The opportunity should be taken to train them to become useful and purposeful citizens. Tinkering with the problem by doing a little here and there will not be sufficient. What is required is a properly planned scheme of vocational training on a long-term basis.[12]

Women with some educational qualifications were offered training in "useful professions" like nursing, midwifery, teaching, stenography, accounts and office management. Those with very little or no literacy could take up the usual embroidery, tailoring, minor handicrafts and so on, although it was well understood that the scope for economic independence through these was quite limited, for the market was already glutted with fancy leather work and luxury articles. The excess of produce opened the way to exploitation of women's labour and they were paid ridiculously low wages for their work. But the women's own inclination had also to be considered and, as the Report notes, "despite our best efforts, it was not possible to enlist women's interest in any other work".

Women who were able-bodied and willing to do some physical labour were to be settled in what were called "agro-industrial" settlements. It was proposed that the settlements be built up on a few acres of land outside towns and cities, and women be trained in vegetable and dairy farming, oil pressing, and so on. A beginning was made by giving 60 acres of land near Kilokheri, near Delhi, to the Kasturba Seva Mandir. In all the work of training and engaging women in vocational skills, the Women's Section worked with a range of training centres, academic institutions and voluntary and social work organizations including the Tata Institute of Social Sciences, the Vocational Centres of the Ministry of Labour in Bombay and Delhi, the Kasturba Gandhi Memorial Trust and Lady Hardinge Medical College in Delhi. An Employment Bureau was set up in co-ordination with the Employment Exchange of the Labour Ministry, for placing women once they were trained. In March 1949, the Report noted that 500 women had secured employment through the Employment Bureau.

Durga Rani's and Gyan Deyi's stories are an indication of how the government's policies and programmes concretely benefitted widows and either equipped them with the means to become economically self-reliant, or provided the supporting facilities to make them independent of families, should they so choose. In her conversations with us Durga Rani was emphatic about the positive contribution made by the training programmes in enabling her to stand on her own two feet. Though Gyan Deyi did not express herself in quite the same way and was clearly unable to reconcile her present reduced circumstances with what she had left behind in Pakistan, it was impossible not to be struck by her poise and self-confidence. For her, the Ashram offered a viable alternative to a dependent and possibly less dignified existence with her brothers and, in her own way, she took advantage of her relative independence to help other women less capable than herself.

Missing Citizens

Following the partition of the country, the Indian government directly assumed responsibility for two groups of women. The first were those who had somehow been separated from their families, picked up while fleeing to safety, taken hostage, or kidnapped: these women were called "abducted"; the second group comprised those who had been displaced, destituted, widowed: these women were collectively described as "unattached". Both groups were obvious subjects for government intervention, and beneficiaries of rehabilitation programmes but their significance transcends this simple humanitarian concern: in a crucial way their very condition—"abducted" or "unattached"—defined their identity and in turn became the touchstone by which the government formulated and implemented policies with regard to their "recovery" and "resettlement". For both groups the common factor now was the rupture of normal familial arrangements and the absence of male kin. As surrogate parent, one of the state's principal concerns was with the women's sexual status. This concern was quite *explicit* in the case of abducted women, whose sexuality was perceived as available for exploitation by any transgressor and so had to be zealously guarded; it was *implicit* in the case of widows who were now assumed to be sexually inactive, but in need of rehabilitation, social and economic, for they were now without families or menfolk who would vouch for them. As abducted women they were sexual property and, simultaneously, upholders of honour, symbols of sacred motherhood, definers of community and national identity. As widows, they had to be liberated from the traditional stigma of widowhood and its consequent social death, and be activated as economic beings, part of the mainstream of national life.

Through its policies and programmes for both categories of women the government not only undertook its first major welfare and legislative responsibility as an independent state, it revealed the complexity of its relationship to gender and community, and secularism and democracy. In the early Fifties when the Indian state was defining its own political character and priorities, drawing up an egalitarian Constitution and safeguarding pluralism through a modified secularism, the interaction of gender, community and state acquired particular importance for women. It underlined the critical role played by the state in mediating gender and community rights in moments of political crisis, at the same time as it highlighted the differential approximations to citizenship of its male and female members. It exposed the state's tremendous internal dissonances in terms of how women were categorised and dealt with. Finally, it demonstrated the state's ambivalence regarding its own identity as secular and democratic, and how very nearly impossible it was for it to be free of patriarchal, communal and cultural biases.

Unravelling the complexity of the question of citizenship Helga Maria Hernes says:

> (It) refers to the bonds between stable and individual citizens as well as the bonds among individual citizens. These bonds are circumscribed by law. . . by custom. . . and by the material resources available to individual citizens. . . . They are, in addition, circumscribed by the political situation prevailing at any point in time. All the dimensions are gendered in a variety of ways, and states differ along all three dimensions: the nature of legal, social and material bonds among citizens; the nature of the institutions which define and defend these bonds; and their capability of handling political crises.[13]

Our discussion so far has only tangentially touched upon the contrasting, but not necessarily opposite, experience of citizenship by widowed and abducted women in such a time of political crisis. In the earlier discussion we explored the relationship between gender, community and state in maintaining the purity of the "legitimate" family and religious community. Our concluding comments in this section indicate how problematic the very notion of citizenship was with regard to both categories of women, and how it was negotiated by them, by the state, and by those responsible for their rehabilitation or recovery.

As with sexuality, the discussions around citizenship, too, were explicit in the case of abducted women; implicit—or shall we say, assumed—in the case of widows. Both were citizens of a secular democracy, but the exercise of the rights of such citizenship was far less contested where widows were concerned. As protector and provider (*mai-baap*) the state acted on *behalf* of widows and abducted women, both, but with the latter its actions had a rather different outcome. The Abducted Persons Bill denied them the possibility of asserting their political and civil rights, even as the state's own redistributive agencies ensured the realization of their social rights. Because widows' political and civil rights were not in conflict with perceived community "rights" or claims, they were never put to the test in the same way as those of abducted women.

The extended debate on forcible recovery as violative of the constitutional and fundamental rights of abducted women, *as citizens*, is evidence of this conflict;[14] the resistance by abducted women themselves further demonstrates their attempts to realize citizenship by acting independently and autonomously—of community, state *and* family. This attempt was thwarted through a consensus reached by all three on the desirability and *necessity* of women preserving community and national honour by subordinating their rights, as individuals and citizens, to the identity of the community and the will of the state. With widows, on the contrary, the endeavour was to facilitate their entry into the social and economic mainstream of the country as productive members of the citizenry, contributing to what Renuka Ray called the process of "nation building". The oppressive bind of conventional widowhood was thus loosened sufficiently to enable women to emerge into, and assume, citizenship with all its rights and responsibilities. This category of citizenship simply collapsed in relation to the abducted woman, the woman-out-of-place. The process of recovery, of putting abducted women back into place, was not conceived by the state as a relationship to *women as missing citizens* of the new state (if so, it would have endowed them with civil rights);[15] rather, it chose to treat them as *missing members of religious and cultural communities* on whose behalf choices had to be made. Widows were redefined as victims of a national disaster requiring a direct form of inter-

vention which did not end simply by restoring them to the
communities they belonged to; the attempt was to make
them viable in their own community, economically independent and rehabilitated as citizens.

In both cases, the state was acting as custodian and guardian on behalf of missing or wronged men—in the case of
widows, the men were permanently absent or missing; with
abduction, it was the women who were "missing". Its intervention was radical in the first case because it was liberatory
and progressive in a decisive way. Offering vocational and
other training, arranging for employment, providing hous-
ing, food and education for widows and their children, and
assuring them safe refuge for the rest of their lives, if necessary, *without the stigma of widowhood* was a most significant
departure from the norm. Its intervention in the second instance, however, was conservative, because it acknowledged the primacy of family and community as the legitimate keepers of "abducted" women. Thus, its first obligation was to restore them to where they "rightfully belonged"
and only later, and perforce, to provide for them should they
remain "unclaimed".

The post-Partition conjuncture was one of unusual flux
and formative capacity and made for some unprecedented
relationships between women and the state; some of these
continue, others have been closed off. A comparison of the
state's relationship with widows and abducted women
sheds some light on the nature of this relationship and its
implications for women. To begin with, it illuminates the
workings of a state-in-transition as it negotiates both post-
colonial independence and Partition at the same time, and
tries to put in place a relatively progressive political and
social programme. What is clear from our analysis is that,
for women, the state functions in interaction with at least
two other major institutions—community and family—and
that together, they constitute the contesting arenas for gender issues. Then, we have seen that the relationship between
women and state may be co-operative or conflictual; generally speaking (and as borne out by the experience of wid-

ows and abducted women) there can be co-operation on issues of welfare, and conflict on issues of rights. Post-Independence the state itself was a complex confluence: defining itself as secular, democratic and socialist but operating
in a politically charged atmosphere, keeping communal considerations in balance; incorporating a benign paternalism
while simultaneously upholding patriarchal codes and practices; ensuring the realization of social rights but withholding civil and political rights, even while it deliberated on
fundamental rights and guarantees.

Notes

1. U. Bhaskar Rao, *The Story of Rehabilitation* (Delhi: Government of India, Publications Division, 1967), p. 45.
2. Personal interview with Durga Rani Katyal, warden of the Karnal Mahila Ashram for many years. It was almost impossible for us to obtain any official records of the early years of the KMA. Because of changes in state administration, records had been transferred from one city and capital to another—Jullundar, Ambala, Shimla, Chandigarh—and could not be traced. Durga Rani told us that she had kept many case files in her personal custody for a long time but had destroyed them in the early 1980s.
3. See also, *Sadda Hak, Ethey Rakh*: A Report on Refugee Women Workers of Delhi (Delhi: People's Union for Democratic Rights, April 1989); and Latha Anantaraman, *"In Dependence"*, *The India Magazine*, August–September 1996.
4. See Rajeshwari Sunder Rajan, "The Scandal of the State: Women and Institutional Protection in Contemporary India", op. cit., for a detailed examination of these issues.
5. Report of the All India Women's Conference, December 1947.
6. Reports of work done by the Women's Section, Ministry of Rehabilitation. Rameshwari Nehru Papers, Nehru Memorial Museum and Library, Delhi. All details in this section are from the RN Papers.
7. RN Papers, op. cit.
8. Stephen L. Keller, *Uprooting and Social Change* (Delhi: Manohar Book Service, 1975), p. 47.
9. RN Papers, op. cit.
10. Ibid.
11. Report of the Women's Section, Ministry of Rehabilitation, February 2, 1949–March 30, 1949.
12. Constituent Assembly (Legislative) Debates, March 1948, Vol. III, No.5.
13. Quoted in Marie Leech, "Women, the State and Citizenship," *Australian Feminist Studies*, No. 19, Autumn 1994 (Adelaide: University of Adelaide), p. 81.
14. Pandit Thakur Das Bhargava in the Legislative Assembly Debates said, "Sir . . . yesterday when we were discussing clause 8, viz., that detention should not be questioned in any court, I submitted that that provision is against the spirit of the Con-

stitution. . . . I do submit that there is no reason why these girls, who are citizens of India, if they want to live here should be forced to go away." He added, "I further submit that this (clause 8) is opposed to the fundamental rights guaranteed in the Constitution and is opposed to Section 491 of the Criminal Procedure Code. The writ of *habaes corpus* is always open." Constituent Assembly Debates, December 1949.

[15] We owe this formulation to Kalpana Ram.

stitution. . . . I do submit that there is no reason why these girls, who are citizens of India, if they want to live here should be forced to go away", He added, "I further submit that this (clause 8) is opposed to the fundamental rights guaranteed in the Constitution and is opposed to Section 491 of the Criminal Procedure Code. The writ of habeas corpus is always open." Constituent Assembly Debates, December 1949.

We owe this formulation to Kalpana Ram.

Picking up the Pieces

Women Rehabilitate Women

Partition changed the direction of my life . . . I felt now was the time to work for the country. I felt if people like us who are quite well off shirk such responsibility, then who will do it?

—Nirmal Anand

We never probed their pasts. Our idea was to let them forget, not to make them remember, how to reduce the impact of everything they had experienced, to lessen its effect on them. I took a personal interest in each woman and child, but I did not want to dwell on their tragedies too much.

—Krishna Thapar

"Women with Spirit"

Miss Makhan Singh, Bhag Mehta, Gulab Pandit, Damayanti Sahgal, Mrs K.N. Sawhney, Purnima Banerji, Dr Sushila Nayyar, Sucheta Kriplani, Bibi Amtus Salaam, Begum Anis Kidwai, Mrs Handoo, Mrs. Shoba Nehru, Vimla Dang . . .

The real work of rehabilitating women fell to women; not just those whose names can be found in government records and ministry reports; not the score or more with whom we spoke but countless others, volunteers who worked in camps, in homes, in seva sadans and women's service centres as doctors, teachers, trainers, wardens, camp commandants, counsellors and companions in the painful and protracted business of relocating and rebuilding. These were the women of the YWCA, the All India Women's Conference (AIWC), the Women's Indian Association, women who belonged to the Indian National Army, the Rashtriya Swayam Sewak Sangh, the CPI and other political parties, to any number of voluntary organizations; and individual women, many themselves widowed by Partition or unmarried as a consequence of it. None of them can be said to have been trained for the job yet most of them brought courage and dedication to it. Indeed the tragedy of Partition created a cadre of women workers many of whom subsequently became employees of the government and retired only after thirty or forty years of service. Women like Premvati Thapar who was in charge of the Gandhi Vanita Ashram in Jullandar where recovered women were brought, identified younger women with leadership potential and encouraged them to shoulder this responsibility. In time, the more resourceful among them acquired considerable organizational skill in running their establishments, while also coping with the trauma of dislocation and destitution on a daily basis. Often they found themselves on the wrong foot with a government that was hard-pressed itself and a bureaucracy that was either unwilling or unable to respond adequately. "*Rehabilitation mein sarkar ka ravaiyya bahut zyada nafis nahin tha*," Gulab Pandit told us. "*Bhashan dene mein nafis tha, lekin jab meeting-on mein stipend ko 8 anna se bhi badhane ki baat hoti thi, to unhe tangi mahsus hoti thi.*" (The government's attitude as far as rehabilitation was concerned was not very sincere. They were quick to give speeches but when it came to increasing the [women's] stipend even by eight annas they found it difficult.) Yet they persisted.

Krishna Thapar was one such woman. She worked with Premvati Thapar at the Gandhi Vanita Ashram for eighteen years, then joined the Punjab government where she spent the rest of her working life. The dedication, imagination and real concern with which she carried out her responsibility left a deep impression not just on us but on the many women she had helped over the years. Indeed, we first heard of her from a woman who had come to the Gandhi Vanita Ashram as a child. A refugee from Sialkot, she had been separated from her mother and brothers and sisters while fleeing, and never saw them again. A kind neighbour rescued her and after many halts at refugee camps along the way, deposited her at Jullundar. She stayed here for about eleven years, during the time that Krishna Thapar was "principal" of the Ashram. She did her matriculation, then qualified as a teacher and, at Krishna Thapar's and General Mohan Singh's (of the INA) suggestion, married the Nepali orderly of an ex-INA officer.

Having heard about Krishna Thapar in some detail from her, we set out to try and find "Miss Thapar"—but she was no longer in Jullundar. Still, she was almost a legend in the city and, eventually, after enquiring about her whereabouts from other social workers we located her in Delhi and Chandigarh. Since her retirement she has been living in Chandigarh with her adopted son—an orphan whom she helped to rehabilitate at the GVA. In a conversation that extended over many hours in both cities, she spoke of her years in rehabilitation in different districts of Punjab.

Krishna Thapar: "My work is here."

In 1947 we migrated from Lyallpur. I had completed my B.A. and was going to do my M.A. but couldn't, because the trouble had started. I studied in Hansraj Mahila College, Lahore and lived in the hostel for two years. I did my F.A. from Government College, Lyallpur. My father was in jail at that time so I could not be admitted into B.A.—one year was wasted. After he came out of jail he admitted me to Hansraj College. My father was full-time in politics. His name was Lala Chint Ram, he was a member of the All India Congress Committee—he was known as the Lion of Lyallpur! In all he must have spent about eleven years in jail, sometimes one year, sometimes two. We had a family business which was looked after by my older brother. Actually my grandfather had earned a lot but gradually my father spent it all. We lost our own house, moved into rented spaces. We were forced to do all this.

My grandfather was a middle-man, a wholesale dealer when Lyallpur was set up by the British. He left Ludhiana and went there—he dealt mainly in wheat. Ours was a joint family. My grandfather was the only one in our family who was educated. He looked after everyone. My brother was influenced by my father's political ideas, plus he was educated at National College. Among his friends were Bhagat Singh Bhraji, Sukhdev Bhraji*. . . .

You know, everyone has his or her own nature, the influence of politics was on the entire family but everyone did not respond in the same way. All of us sisters wore only khadi, absolutely pure khadi, we all had nationalist views. But then the others got married, some before Partition, some after.

In college also the spirit was the same. Ours was known for its nationalist views. People with nationalist views sent their daughters to this college. They didn't like to send them to Kinnaird or National College, they preferred this college. Miss Thapar was the Principal, a very dedicated woman. From the

---

* The well-known militant freedom fighters.

very beginning she was a nationalist. There was an orphanage in our college with 20–25 children living there all the time. We hostel girls looked after it, partly, and partly the working committee. Miss Thapar went to hospitals to look for children. Her life was truly dedicated. She would bring illegitimate children to the orphanage—while I was in the hostel she brought a month old child from Sir Ganga Ram Hospital and handed her to us hostellers. We looked after her. All of us brought things for her. We used to teach the children in the orphanage and each of us was given responsibility for two or three children. I mean to say, she did all these thing with spirit, not for show. Today so much of such work is for show.

Of course, they had to be a little careful about political activity—it was a question of girls. Families had entrusted the responsibility for their daughters to the college so they couldn't take risks. When I got admitted I had this thought in my mind, how does it matter whether I do a B.A. or not, why don't I go to Wardha to Mahatma Gandhi? Every time there was some political excitement, I said I want to go to Wardha. I wrote a letter to Mahatmaji saying I am studying here, but my heart is not at peace, I want to come to Wardha and work. I wrote a big, long letter and I told Mahatmaji, either you call me there to yourself or show me a path so that my mind is at rest. I was bent upon going to Wardha and doing practical work.

Mahatmaji sent such a beautiful reply to me, written in his own hand. It was a postcard. He wrote seven or eight lines, no more. He said, "I have received your letter. I am happy to see that you want to lead a life for your country. But I want that girls like you who are young, who are students, you can do more work there than in Wardha. You want to work with spirit, with my guidance, then I suggest that you complete your education." I read it many, many times and I felt what he said was correct. All the work for the country couldn't be done at one place, sitting in Wardha. It had to be done in every corner, in every village. He had written that this spirit had to be imbued in every individual, only then could this country become something, only then could it attain freedom. He said, you work there and if you are confused you write to me. But with that letter I was so inspired. Every time I read it I said to myself, your work is here. Actually you should leave the city and go to villages. Go and work with the children in the huts, infuse life in them. This is his message. We can't all run to Wardha. But then Partition took place, and everything changed. . .

We had summer vacations and I had gone to my Mamaji (maternal uncle) Charandas Puri, a leading lawyer who lived in Dharamshala. Normally during summer we went to the hills, to my mother's family. But that year Father did not want us to go. He said, you might have been going every year but if you go this year, people will say I have sent my own family away while I am telling everyone else to stay on, not to leave, nothing will happen. This fire will subside, countries are not divided like this. There will be killings but for how long. So he said, no I won't let you go. He kept saying, no. No one knew at that time that Partition would take place. People were leaving temporarily out of insecurity. The Congress policy was that people should stay where they were because nothing will happen. Even if the country is partitioned nothing would happen. Those who are living in Pakistan will continue to live there, those who are living in India will continue to live there. Hindus and Muslims will live on both sides, what is the problem. People are never uprooted. No one imagined this would happen. Not even the big leaders knew this, that is why they kept repeating, don't leave, don't leave.

My father left only on 28th September. Partition took place on 15th August but my father, mother, brother, no one left. Only me and my younger sister fought with our father and said, why don't you let us go? Every night there is rioting, we can't sleep. You pick up your stick and leave the house. Here Mataji, Taiji (aunt) keep worrying. We were a joint family, my father was the head of the family. His older brother and younger brother were both dead. We girls were brought up like boys, educated like them even before Partition. There were no restrictions on our movement. So both of us left for Dharamshala and were there when the country was partitioned. We knew nothing about our family, where it was. There was no news. Then one day, sitting there, we heard on the radio—in those days they used to announce on the radio—we heard that our two sisters-in-law and one or two other ladies from the family had reached Delhi by aeroplane. They announced that my father's son-in-law had gone to Agra. But we did not know where our father was, where Mataji and Taiji were. These women told our father, "We will not leave if you don't leave." We were unable to get any news.

Our father was certain that all the rioting, killings would stop and all of us would return. He kept living in his own house in Lyallpur. He didn't move to the camp which was started for the people leaving the villages. Many of our relations came to stay with him. In fact, he took control of houses in the village deserted by the Hindus and Sikhs, saying his relations and others coming to Lyallpur would stay there.

But then the Muslim Deputy Commissioner there requested my father to move. Many Muslims were more pained by Partition than us. There were all kinds of people, we can't say it affected only us Hindus and not the Muslims. There were such wonderful Muslims with great character. The DC said, "Thapar Sahib I will never excuse myself if any harm is done to you. So many Muslims have now come from India, Muslims who are bitter, who have lost everything, who have suffered at the hands of the Hindus, they may do you harm." You see, we didn't do less to the Muslims—we had also become such brutes. Everyone was trying to be more cruel to the other. Someone slapped first, someone else did it in response, but all of them slapped. There was no difference. We all lost our humanity. It was their policy then to take revenge. Those Muslims ousted from India didn't leave the Hindus alone. If they saw a Hindu woman they didn't spare her. This is what happened at Partition. Although nothing much had happened in Lyallpur, but that officer did not want to take any risk. He told my father to go to India, get help from there, send some army men from there to control things here. So on 28th September my father left. The DC provided his own conveyance. My father and all his relations were given seven to eight trucks. They first came to Lahore—DAV College Camp, then he came to Amritsar. After that there was no question of going back. Pitaji did not pick up even a needle from his home saying he would return within a fortnight. Those people who thought they wouldn't be able to return brought a few things along, but those who did not want to leave their homes, who believed they would return after peace was re-established, they brought nothing. Things took such an unexpected turn. . .

See, the thing is this—in my opinion a large percentage of Muslims did not want the Hindus to leave. I was quite young at that time but on the basis of our relations, our association with Muslims who were of course Congress-minded, I never felt they wanted us to leave. Muslims also sacrificed a lot for independence. Such Muslims thought like us. But those who were mischievous, the Muslim League types, we had no understanding of their mind My father told his relations to take whatever they wanted but he said he was not taking anything because he was definitely coming back. We don't even have family photographs. No photograph of Sukhdev Bhraji. All we could think of was returning, living in Lyallpur. After all Muslims, lots of them, did stay on in India, all of them didn't leave. But the Hindus had to leave in the face of all the problems. They left for security. Some people thought things might return to normal after five-six months. Muslim League was also quite strong. If we did not talk of democracy and if all the Muslims from India had gone to Pakistan, what problems would Pakistan have had? There are still as many Muslims here as in Pakistan. Those Muslims who have stayed on might want another Pakistan here—who knew what shape things would take.

. . . As far as women are concerned, our women suffered more. I feel a large number of our women never returned. Many died there. I have no statistics, I don't know exact numbers, but this is my feeling. We had no time for collecting statistics. We were busy looking after those who came. I was involved with recovery on this side. If I saw Muslim women crying I was as unhappy as when I saw a Hindu woman in trouble. We couldn't see their suffering because they were of woman caste (*aurat jaat*). It is women who suffered whether they were Hindus or Muslims. When I say Hindus I mean Hindu and Sikh both because we did not consider them as different. We considered them the same, and actually they were the same. It is only now that they have created a rift between Hindus and Sikhs.

How I got involved in this work is a long story. As I told you, I was in Dharamshala. Gandhi Vanita Ashram was a government institution right from the beginning. I was the first one to start it, I was the first employee. Miss Thapar was the

Director of the Women's Section. At that time no salaries and
grades were fixed. No one told us what our salary and grade
would be. Appointment letters were issued six or seven months
later. At that time they were busy collecting ladies who would
do this kind of work, and putting them into positions. We asked
nothing. How much will we be paid? Where will we eat? No.
We just said, the country needs our services. Just as you located me now, Miss Thapar traced me. We lived in Jullundar
Cantt. at that time, because my father came here. One of my
cousins who was also a worker, lived here. In October my
brother came to Dharamshala to inform us about their whereabouts. He had an unshaven face, dirty clothes. We didn't recognize him at first. He reached there with great difficulty. We
hugged him and cried bitterly. He told us everyone had come
safely. After 15-20 days, a month, the route to Jullundar cleared.
Even on this side things were in turmoil. Movement of people
was continuing, trains were flooded. Peace came much later.
Then we came to Jullundar Cantt. where my father was allotted a house. I joined service on 21st February 1948. She (Miss
Thapar) first found about about my father. I was her student,
she knew all her students who were active. I was the mess
president of my college. She knew I was a fighter. I always
fought for the rights of students. Even fought with her ! She
knew I was tough. But, it was not just me. There was one
Nirmala Hoon, don't know where she is now. She also knew
Kamla's family, her spirit (Kamla Mehra, another social
worker). There was Kaushalya Bagga who went into education. At the time of selection they saw whether women had the
spirit because only women with spirit could do this kind of
work. But gradually things changed.

I remember that day so clearly. It was raining. We heard a
car honking loudly. We wondered who had come. Miss Thapar
herself had come in that rain. She first came to Sadar Bazaar,
inquired about us. I was so surprised to see her. We used to
call her Biji. Although she was the Principal, all the girls called
her Biji. She asked me what I was doing. I said I had just barely
come. She asked me to see her the next morning. I was the first
one in my family to do a government job.

I used to think of completing my studies, but none of us
knew what would happen. I told her I would come the next

day. She just said that she had some work. I said, "I will do whatever I can, you just have to order." The next day I went there and she told me about the recovered girls who were coming back. She took me to a camp, showed me things and that was it. I started working then and there. I got dumped in Gandhi Vanita Ashram on 21st February, 1948 (*laughs loudly*). That building was under construction, it was to be a college. There were no doors. We put up *chics*. We put up tents. . . . The maximum strength at one time must have been 4,000 to 5,000 women, including children. This was in 1950–51. Women came with children. Some children came alone, children from train tragedies whose parents were killed or lost.

In these camps there were two kinds of women, those who were recovered and those who were alone, whose men had died. These women were alone with their children. They were brought from general camps for security reasons. For such unattached women camps were started in Rajpura, Rohtak. The recovered women stayed only in Gandhi Vanita Ashram. This was the base for recovered women. They were mostly young. Even the widows were young and most of those who were picked up were unmarried. Muslims who abducted them married them, others perhaps just kept them. We had to perform abortions on many of those who were brought to us—they were expecting. For that we had Dr. Kapur's hospital in Ludhiana.

Those who came back wanted abortions. These were fresh recoveries, meaning they had been there just for two months, three months, four months. Most of them were raped. Many of them said nikah had taken place. The government however made a policy that every Hindu woman living with a Muslim, whether with or without nikah, should be brought back. The government recovered some, other women tried to escape themselves. Some women from good families had gone into the hands of bad Muslims. This was also there.

Normally most abducted women were middle-class—only the rare one was from a high-class family. Most of them did not stay with us for long. Their relations had already given us forms to claim them. I don't know of any family which came to me and refused to accept their daughter. Of course we never told them about abortions. That was our rule. It is only now that I am telling you this, even many of my own staff did not know. The doctor was our own. Dr. Kapur was given the authority to perform abortions on young women coming from Pakistan. At that time abortion was illegal, so a special authority had to be given. I myself used to take them to the hospital and then go to bring them back. But if they were in a very advanced stage of pregnancy then no abortion was done. A few children were born but such cases were rare, because very few pregnancies were advanced. But Dr. Kapur had such a good hand that even five month old pregnancies were done well.

But we never probed their pasts. Our idea was to let them forget, not to make them remember. How to reduce the impact of everything they had experienced, to lessen its effect on them. I didn't like to ask too much and I discouraged others from finding out, too. I took a personal interest in each woman and child but I didn't want to dwell on their tragedies too much.

As I told you we had two kinds of women, those who were recovered and those who were destituted. Those who were destituted, whose husbands died, other men died, were first kept in the general camps. After some time the government decided to separate them and put them in the women's home. They wanted to settle the men, give them land, jobs, etc. So we collected all those women from Kurukshetra where there was a very big camp. Then we started camps for women in Hoshiarpur, in Karnal, Rohtak—young widows, some with children, some 25, 30, 35 years old. . . . Slowly, these women's camps became destitute homes because we had our own poor and destitute women. The camps became production centres, employment centres.

At the Ashram, we used to measure out the rations on a scale—we had to have some way of keeping track of amounts. It was a decent amount, not little, enough for a normal diet. But for someone who hasn't seen food for six months—many of these women had to be hospitalised when they came to us— they fell on the food like hungry beasts. They couldn't really eat all they got, but they were like starving creatures. Then they started stealing food—we would find chapatis under their pillows, under their quilts, their beds. . . . Some of them had become psychological cases. I found the supplies were getting less—they were being stolen! Not because they wanted to eat it all, but because they were hoarding it. I was very disturbed by this—I felt, these women have been through such trouble and here we are giving out handfuls of rations. If there is a child in our homes, do we ration food like this? Some eat two phulkas, some three, we don't count how many . . . .

One day there was a big fight over food in the kitchen and that day, I thought I would resign. I wasn't fit for this job. I can't work unless I have full control over the stores so that I can feed anyone who comes to their heart's content. No one should go away hungry. So I told the Deputy Secretary, Rehabilitation, H.D. Shourie, I made quite a fuss I remember, I came down the corridor and I had the store keys and the register in my hands. I threw the keys and the register at his feet and said, "Shourie Sahib, here are your keys and here's the register. I can't work in a place where I can't serve people with humanity, with proper dignity. I am not working here anymore." I kept on babbling whatever came to my lips, we kept on walking and he kept on listening, he said nothing, and I went on and on about the rations and government policy and whatnot, and finally I stopped. I was out of breath. When I stopped we had reached the steps, he patted me on the shoulder and said very gently, "Keep the keys and your register, and you do whatever you think is right. You have complete liberty. Tell me what you want." I said, "I am not going to measure out food on the scales for the women. If you think the government will suffer losses because of this, then I'll make up the loss myself. I'll go to the mandi and get sacks of atta from the wholesalers—but I won't count rotis any more." Right there, as a special case, he wrote out an order that for GVA, as much ration as Miss Thapar thinks necessary should be sanctioned. The only condition was that I should be present when the supplies were taken. That was okay. I krew that within six to eight months their hunger would be satisfied. Till then, I didn't mind if they hoarded, stole, I wasn't going to stop them. After all, what else did we have to give them? They had come to us having lost everything, torn from their roots, and we were counting out rotis? I couldn't do it.

We had a common kitchen at the time—when the Ashram was at full strength, even two or three kitchens. . . every day women were discharged as their families came to claim them. Slowly we wound up the additional kitchens. It was important to give them cooked food, especially in the beginning. They came to us so disturbed. . . it was important that the government was feeding them. Later we gave them dry rations and encouraged them to cook—and actually most women wanted to cook and feed their children themselves. We understood this. This was part of their return to normal living—cooking and eating on time.

And then we stopped giving them dry rations also, we gave them cash, so that they could buy whatever they wished. Plus they would be encouraged to supplement the stipend we gave and start living a normal life. So normal that often they would make friends with the policemen outside the Ashram and we wouldn't come to know! So much so that I finally said, we don't really need the police here, please remove them—keep them at a distance, not right in front of the gates. Whoever had to run away would run from the back, not the front of the Ashram! They didn't want to be restrained any more. But we were responsible for them, after all—tomorrow their families would come to claim them and they would be nowhere. Then we would be blamed for leading them astray, for taking money from suitors and marrying them off to the first man who came along. And there were undesirable elements around.

We received women from Punjab only at our Ashram. In my opinion the Punjabi women, no matter how badly off, they never asked for charity. And they made their own lives. We educated women who were mothers of four or more children from scratch, teaching them *aa, ee*. . . making them take the eighth class exam, the tenth class. . . it means something. Then we trained them in some sort of activity so they could earn their own living. And these recovered women came only to the government-run institutions—they didn't go to another voluntary service like the Arya Samaj or others. They went to Rohtak, to Hoshiarpur, to Karnal later, to the homes where there were as many as 600–1,000 families at any one time. But yes, organizations like the Arya Samaj came to our help for school admissions for our children, and they were very good with them.

The ones who stayed in the Ashram were those whose families could not be traced. These were the ones we educated, trained, got them married. You come to me to Chandigarh, I will introduce you to many of them. Our girls have gone to very good, respectable families. I sent some of our unattached girls even as far as Pilani to study, to Vanasthali. It was according to their abilities. We used every opportunity to get them the best education, for which the government paid. One of my girls is a doctor in Jullundar, she has a big clinic. Her name is Dulari. Her family was recovered. Her father was a doctor in the military, he was killed. When this woman came she had a son and a daughter. Her son was educated by us, we sent him to the army, got him married to one of our camp girls. He left the army after some years and now runs a very successful workshop. If we had not put our protective hand on the heads of such women, and if we had not provided motherly treatment, such things couldn't have happened.

Now this girl, Dulari, whom we educated to be a doctor couldn't have done it only on government funds because those were limited, but I had no dearth of money in Jullundar. My voice was like god's voice in the city. If I needed funds for any individual girl, I could tell any man and say, this is your responsibility and you have to do it. No one ever said no.

Then I performed all those marriages. No girl ever left without a proper dowry of Rs. 5,000-6,000 or more. Government does not provide dowry, does it?

How did I do all this? (*Laughs*) Everyone was known to me. The wholesale dealers in the mandi (wholesale market)—I just told one of them, you give me five suits, told someone else to give something else, just distributed responsibility. I had nothing myself, I was just the organizer. Even my own salary was spent on similar things because I had no fear of starvation and I knew I would get another salary at the end of the month. So there was no shortage of funds. I gave my girls clothes, furniture, even clothes for their in-laws—exactly the way things are done in normal weddings when girls are sent from home. All my department people used to say, "This woman has never got married herself—now she is fulfilling her desires by getting so many girls married. God knows from where she collects all these things." We performed the weddings in our camp. Proper baraats used to come. We did everything according to the religion of the girl. Girls who had come as 5-6 year olds remembered their names. From that we could guess whether she was a Hindu or a Sikh. But we didn't look for men from the same religion necessarily. We chose the best man available and used those rites which they desired. Personally I preferred Sikh rites because they are the simplest, around the Darbar Sahib. I could also understand what they were saying because I don't understand all these Sanskrit mantras.

At the time of the wedding I wanted to send the bride with such dignity that no one should be able to say that she had no family, or she did not bring gifts for her in-laws. If she had two sisters-in-law, we gave suits for both of them. If at the time of engagement some children came along, we gave five rupees each to them as well. Everything was proper. Proper *milni* took place. We have a huge album in the Ashram of all these weddings—actually I don't know whether they still have them because I left the Ashram in 1963.

We didn't do any joint marriages—we wanted proper marriages. There was a Marriage Board consisting of eminent local women and men, the superintendent and Miss Thapar. It was the Board which scrutinised the boys, their background, their jobs. There were two-three boys whose families said they did not want the wedding to take place in the camp. They were very good families. I said it does not matter, we will do these weddings outside. I asked my brother-in-law to arrange for two wedding ceremonies in Ludhiana. He, my brother-in-law, is a leading lawyer, a well-off man. If I told him you have to spend Rs. 5,000 there, he would do that. I made him give scholarships to many of our boys. Some were sent to Kurukshetra for studies. As I told you, I never faced financial problems. Children only needed to come to me—after that the problem could be solved.

The wedding of one of my girls was done in my house in Chandigarh. We found matches for many girls with boys from decent families. Every marriage was a big social event and everyone in the Ashram contributed by making something for the bride. Every family contributed one rupee out of the Rs.15 stipend they got. After all, it was a daughter of the Ashram who was getting married. We had made a welfare society in the Ashram to look after unattached girls. The staff members also contributed Rs.10–20. This is how we collected dowries for these girls who had no one but us.

There was a PWD officer whose mother had left some gold to be given in charity. I knew this officer's wife and I said to her, where will you find poorer and more deserving girls than the ones in our Ashram. I convinced her to give three sets to three girls when they got married. I arranged to give at least one set for every girl's marriage. I did not ask for charity, I told the people in town that they were not giving *daan*. These were their own daughters and they owed something to them. I did not want my girls to be treated as beggars. They used to tell me, "But you have so many daughters." I said, well I do and you have to help, and I will tell you what present you will give because I do not want any duplication. I asked for tea-sets, crockery. . .

I do not remember how many girls I arranged to get married. I know that hardly any one of marriageable age remained unmarried. Out of the unattached girls, there must have been 20-25 girls whose marriages I arranged. In the camp, mothers looked for boys themselves but they did get our approval. They held these marriages outside the Ashram also.

One of my girls went to Pilani to study. For her I had my eye on a boy called Kranti. I had been eyeing him for a long time. He was well qualified, a worker, Congress and Socialist worker. I told him, Kranti when you think of getting married do consult me. He said, "Bhenji, this I have already decided, but I will only get married when I am self-sufficient."

He decided to have a civil marriage. He did not want any dowry but we of course gave whatever we could. He had a reception for which he got cards printed with his and my name as hosts. In that reception all kinds of senior officers came because that was his circle. Officers came for all our marriages, but this was special. He now lives in Parwanoo, has his own factory.

This was the spirit.

As we travelled through Punjab and Haryana and talked to people in Delhi who had worked on rehabilitation, we realized just how many women had been instrumental in resettling other women. We spoke at some length to more than 20 who were still alive, and from each obtained one or other piece of information, or an anecdote or insight that helped us appreciate the scale and complexity of their job.

Unlike other aspects of rehabilitation such as the allotment of land, the physical relocation of refugees or the settling of compensation claims on which there is considerable documented material, most records pertaining to the homes and ashrams for unattached women have either been lost or destroyed. In their absence, the detailed information provided by social workers on the actual process of rehabilitation is invaluable; and it is in the counterpointing of factual data with first-hand knowledge and personal experience that we find the richest resource. Each of the women we spoke to illuminated some aspect of this process and enabled us to see social work as one way of achieving social progress.

Nirmal Anand, who lives in Madhuban in Karnal district of Haryana, helped start the first widows' home in Karnal in 1947. She came to India from Lahore where she was teaching at Kinnaird College for Women; after she came here, she says,

I could not think of teaching again, although teaching was my passion and I was working on a geography book before the trouble started. I said, I will never do geography again. I will do relief and welfare for people who have lost everything. I wanted to work in Delhi. My brother had arranged a teaching job in Delhi, but I declined that and went to Mridula Sarabhai. She was a bit tough with me because she felt a girl with my class background would not be able to do welfare work. She did not seem to trust me. But I had already started a social work centre in Karnal. Mridula Sarabhai asked me several times whether I was sure I did not want to do a university job. I said I was very sure, and I wanted her to guide me in my social work. She took me to Lady Mountbatten who gave me a truck and asked me to go to East Punjab to see where I wanted to work. This was in November 1947. Lots of refugees had already come. Camps had been set up also, at Kurukshetra. Lady Mountbatten wanted me to work at Kurukshetra because I was very young, about 22–23, and I had no other experience. I went all over, right from Delhi to Gurdaspur and beyond, and saw all the refugee centres. Then I went to Lady Mountbatten and informed her that I wanted to work in Karnal because in Karnal nothing was being done. There was tremendous need for work there. She asked me to give her a scheme, which I did. I asked for Rs. 25,000 and she sanctioned the full amount and made me chief organizer of relief and welfare. I had gone to Mridula Sarabhai to get advice and direction in the art of social welfare because I had no experience. She was quite impressed with me and that is why she took me to Lady Mountbatten.

Mridula Sarabhai criticised us left and right because she felt the Relief Committee was instrumental in destroying Muslim property. In the public meeting which was held to bring relief to the Muslims in Dalhousie, we were attacked by her. Mridula Sarabhai spoke for an hour and a half, and after that I asked permission to speak and spoke for three quarters of an hour, and told her about all the good work we had done. I also attacked her and said these Congress leaders come from Delhi and without finding out, criticise us, without realizing what they are saying.

Mridula Sarabhai was a great sport. She took my attack very well, and just before getting into her car she shook hands with me and said I should consider her a friend and go to her if ever I needed any help.

I did all this alone. My family was now in Dalhousie where we had property. My father did not want to leave Lahore, he wanted to continue teaching in Lahore even after Partition because he felt he could adjust among the Muslims. His name was C.L. Anand. Later on his law college shifted to Simla and he went to Simla with it, remained the Principal. He was very popular both with the students and the staff.

. . . My Principal, Miss McNair, was very fond of me and she was very keen that I stay on in Lahore even after Partition. I told her I had also become very bitter after listening to all the stories of torture and killing on both sides. I said I loved my students, but after hearing all that I would not be able to feel the same affection for them again, wouldn't be able to love them. . . About the Hindus I did not hear so many stories. So somehow I felt in the new atmosphere I might not be fair to my students. But then, here, when I saw my people also behaving this way, I gave up teaching altogether.

This is why I came to Karnal.

Lady Mountbatten was a great lady, a great social worker and she was involved in rehabilitation and relief. She was interested in finding good workers so she took me instantly.

... I was not interested in politics at all. I was very fond of my students and fond of teaching. I was teaching at Kinnaird, then at the Foreman Christian College and then at the University M.A. classes. There was unrest among the students which was based on false stories on both sides. The students would lock me in the classroom and say, "Now we want to talk to you." The Muslims would talk about their affairs and the Hindus about theirs. I would tell them, look here, I am not interested in all this. I don't know what is true and what not so please let me go. They still insisted and discussed the details of the killings, burnings. They had a lot of faith in me and felt I could guide them. But I was not able to help them because everything seemed to have been going wrong. Both Hindus and Muslims were doing all kinds of bad things. There in Dalhousie we had a lot of Muslim friends and I was very hurt when I saw my own students burning their houses. So I felt, if I can save even two houses I would rather do that than go in for teaching.

... Somehow Muslims had not been absorbed in the Hindu community. This was the main reason for the hostility. Hindus always felt superior as a culture or as a community. Beef-eating went a long way in dividing the community. Hindus had never accepted Muslims so once Partition came, they felt they could not trust the Hindus. Then the politicians came in and they felt unless there was enough violence the Hindus won't leave, for the Hindus had not decided to leave Pakistan. So it was all power-politics. The violence was engineered to compel them to leave. This was the main reason. Without the violence how would they get Hindu property and all the important jobs? The Hindus were in all the important jobs—that is why they started all the violence.

Eighty per cent of the motivation was political according to me, about 20 per cent was economic. To say it was due to religion is not correct, it is an uneducated way of thinking. We had very close Muslim friends. In Aligarh I was the president of the students' union although I was the only Hindu girl in the hostel. When I went there my Hindu family and Hindu friends reprimanded my parents for sending me there. When I reached there all the Muslim girls asked what were my conditions for living there. I said I would not like to eat beef, that is all. They said, "What! We will not have beef served even to Muslim students." They treated me very well. But there also I had trouble because I thought I would be murdered for political reasons. This was in about 1944. I started teaching very early because one of our teachers who had come from England died of brain haemorrhage. There were very few people who could have taken geography so I was accepted as a teacher.

I went to Aligarh on a scholarship. There was a Silver Jubilee Scholarship for going to England but because of trouble at that time, it was difficult to go. Then it was given for going to Aligarh, Rangoon and one other place. So I went to Aligarh. AMU was the only institution besides Rangoon teaching geography. Rangoon was further away so I went to AMU. I was the first Hindu girl to stay in the hostel. I did not want to stand for presidentship but they said, no, you come from a very brilliant institution and we would like to learn from you. The girl who stood against me apologised because she said she was being made to stand to make it an open competition. In fact she herself voted for me. I was elected unanimously.

I was a complete vegetarian, but there was no problem in the hostel. These prejudices were prevalent outside. In fact the Hindus in Aligarh told me I should wear a red bindi because I belonged to them—the Hindus. I said no. If this is a sign of being a Hindu I will never put it on. I wanted to mix with them, wanted to make them feel I was one of them.

I think the main thing was the food. The rift was primarily because of beef. If they had not been eating beef they would have been accepted more easily. On the one hand they were eating a lot of beef and on the other hand the cow was revered by the Hindus. Every Hindu book is full of praise for the cow. Other prejudices would all have been forgotten by the Hindus if the beef issue wasn't there. We had lots of Muslim friends, but I felt most of my relatives spurned the Muslims because of beef. You probe into this and you will come to the same conclusion. I don't think there is so much bitterness in Jammu & Kashmir because there they have very strict rules against killing the cow. Beef-eating is allowed but not cow slaughter.

. . . In the University we were just too academic and were concerned about our courses. We were not politically inclined. Our institutions were very, very academic. The students and the staff talked about the subjects and ignored politics. Perhaps because I was not interested in politics, no one talked to me about it. But when the massacres started then they all wanted to talk to me. I talked from the social angle and not from the political angle.

I lived on campus in Kinnaird College. It was a very beautiful campus and every staff member had two or three rooms. We had a joint mess, very good community life. There was only one Muslim and two or three Hindus on the staff, all the rest were Christians. Majority of the students were Hindu. There were very few Muslim girls but there was no discrimination—students were admitted on the basis of their marks, so in my time the great majority with high marks were Hindus so there were more Hindus than Christians or Muslims. Government College was equally good. So was DAV. Kinnaird was a missionary college.

. . .When I came to Karnal I was working directly under Lady Mountbatten. We had a school and a welfare set-up in the camp. We were conducting classes in embroidery, knitting. I had started a Widows' Home in Karnal city. I travelled all over and collected widow refugees. There were a very large number of them, some in the camps, others spread all over the city. They came from all over West Punjab. There was no town or village where there was no burning or looting. Trainloads of people were looted on both sides, terrible atrocities were committed. We could see all the fires and smoke in Lahore. The administration had lost all control.

We must have had about 50 women in our Home. Later on I handed the Home over to the government and it became the Mahila Ashram—I was an employee of the United Council of Relief and Rehabilitation under Lady Mountbatten, I had nothing to do with the government of Punjab. The great majority of women in our Home had no families, the menfolk were not there. They were from villages and towns. There were no women from the very well-off families—those from well-off families were absorbed by their relatives. People were very kind to each other. Those who were educated found it easy to adjust and rise up the ladder.

I used to have satsang (prayer meetings) with them—that was our mainstay. That was one reason why I could hold them together and hold them to my discipline. We organized readings from Ramayana, Gita, Japji, Sukhmani. They would love to gather together round me. That was very dear to them. They always talked about their problems, of course, but I would evade the subject because that would only lead to more bitterness. It was not very constructive.

I had lots of village centres for handicrafts, balwadis, crèches, etc., after I gave up working in the Ashram. I expanded my work. This work was also with refugees who had got settled on their own. They just went and started living in homes left by Muslims. We created work for their women, embroidery, etc. We used to do this also through the United Council. This work continued until Lady Mountbatten died. After her death I did not want to continue with the Relief Committee. I started my own institution, doing the same work. That work continues till today, even after 40 years.

I had no contact with the Ashram after I left. Miss Makhan Singh came to see us sometimes at formal functions. I only collected the widows, handed them over to the government and left to do my own work. I don't remember the details now.

I put in Rs. 5,000 of my own to start the work centre. Then the turnover started and after three years, after I was sure I would be able to manage things, I started raising donations. Today this institution is entirely looked after by the local people. We have more than 1,200 members who contribute regularly. There is a margin also on things we produce and sell. The money we earn and collect is used for our activities. Our members give between Rs. 2 to 200 every month. We do it this way because it is convenient for them. They give it willingly—*Haath jod kar dete hain.*

Forty years ago I decided I did not want to teach, I wanted to do social work. I am very glad that I took this decision. I am very happy with the people I am working with, and very happy with the people for whom I am working. I am very happy with the society, the local people, the way they have helped me, the way they have honoured me. Isn't it a great honour to have people who do whatever you ask them to do? Indirectly, so many people are helping me.

If Partition had not taken place I would have been a writer and a lecturer. I would have taken up a job in Dayal Singh College. So Partition changed the direction of my life. And if my students had not misbehaved in Dalhousie perhaps I would not have been here today. Since I saw them burning the houses I felt ashamed as their teacher. Now my students are doing much bigger things. I was not made that way. I could live simply. Work was my mission. The choice of this work was based on a line in Japji which says, *Seva karo hove nishmami uske hot prapt swami.*

The way the missionaries work also inspired me. I had a lot of contact with them also in Dalhousie where there was a Mission House. The ladies working there used to come to our house and relate what they were doing. All those things had an impact on my mind. I wanted to do that kind of work and I got this opportunity when Partition took place. I felt now was the time to work for the country. I felt if people like us who are quite well off shirk such responsibility, then who will do it?

The Social Workers: Betwixt and Between

There would not be many, we thought, like Nirmal Anand who looked upon Partition as providing a welcome opportunity to change the direction of their lives. It is true that she alone of all the social workers we spoke to expressed herself in this way; yet we could not but be struck by how each of them, from Kamlaben Patel and Mridula Sarabhai to Miss Makhan Singh and Durga Rani Katyal seized the moment and infused it with her particular sense of mission or purpose. Indeed, it was the "spirit" (to use Krishna Thapar's word) they displayed that somewhat changed the meaning of social work itself just as, in the Fifties, discussions on social welfare for women routinely included policy recommendations for political emancipation and economic betterment.

Those were extraordinary times, and theirs an extraordinary task, one without precedent. As "social workers" their role was that of intermediaries between government policy and its beneficiaries, the women they were responsible for.

Yet, they were not just workers responsible for the rehabilitation of women but individual women negotiating and
transacting between women and their families, society and
the government in a time of enormous flux and instability.
Who were they?

To start with, a large number of them had been involved
in one way or another in the Independence movement: some
were in active politics, others belonged to highly politicized
families; yet others were committed Gandhians. We met
some who had started out as destitute women but ended
up as camp commandants, wardens, superintendents or
supervisors with first-hand experience of what the process
of rehabilitation entailed. The women we spoke to personally, those whose written accounts we have read as well as
those whose names figure in government and organizational
records, came from predominantly urban, middle and upper middle class backgrounds; often professional, occasionally trader or landed. Almost all were formally educated, at
least matriculate; and had they not been catapulted into social service as a consequence of Partition they would probably have led the conventional lives of women of their social and economic class. They may have married; they may
never have been widowed in such circumstances. For some,
like Anis Kidwai whose husband, Shafi Ahmed Kidwai, was
slain in Mussoorie, working with women refugees was almost therapeutic; for others, like Mridula Sarabhai, social
work was the other face of politics. Many responded to
newspaper advertisements asking for volunteers, many others, themselves dislocated by Partition, needed to work.
None of the many women we met thought of their work as
just another job; nor can they really be seen as government
employees engaged in the bureaucratic exercise of handing
out dole.

At least, not post-Partition. In the decade following independence the work of resettlement was, in some way, linked
with national reconstruction. If Partition had sundered the
country, rendered people homeless and evacuated stability
then the task of restoration had to be imbued both with a

sense of compensating for the loss, as well as striking out, starting afresh. By no means are we suggesting that this by itself was sufficient or that it excused workers from responsibility for their actions; simply that it would be unfair to judge them only from the perspective of today, a perspective that might discount their very real attempts at anchoring the women in their charge in a community of, and for women, one that they hoped would ease their transition to well-being.

Nevertheless, they functioned very much within patriarchal structures, often displayed rather patriarchal attitudes and were influenced by urban middle-class conceptions of socially appropriate roles for women and men. How then do we understand their role? Did they work for women or—for patriarchy? One way of looking at it would be to see their intervention as a two-way process: of attempting to free women from their disability and destitution through economic sufficiency and imbuing them with a sense of worth, and restoring them to social "acceptability" through a repetition of restrictions on sexuality and mobility. Underlying Krishna Thapar's preoccupation with getting her "girls" married, for instance, was an understandable concern that they might be drawn into prostitution or be lured by men who thought of them as "available" for casual relationships. As she said, "There were undesirable elements around", and the social workers might easily have been accused of "leading the women astray". The marriages she arranged were primarily of young girls who had been orphaned, or of unattached women whose families had either been slain or were missing. Those who showed an aptitude for learning were fully trained and educated, even sent as far away as Pilani or Vanasthali (in Rajasthan) if necessary. She organized admissions in non-government institutions (like Arya Samaj-run schools) for them, arranged for funds or scholarships when required, and "used every opportunity to get them the best education" whether or not the government paid for it.

Marriage then, was only one aspect of her effort to rehabilitate women, never the only one. Very few widows were remarried, she said, and to the best of her knowledge none of the recovered women were married while in the Ashram. In their case the objective was to train them in some sort of activity so that they could earn their own living; if this entailed educating mothers of four or more children "from scratch", then that was what they did. Moreover, the support they offered the women was of different kinds, and extended to personally providing childcare while the women worked or were being trained (many women corroborated this and said they would never have been able to complete their training or study without it); or to specially nurturing those who were more traumatized than others by their experience. Both Krishna Thapar and Kamlaben Patel told us how, often, such women would simply move in with them till they felt able to cope on their own, and how their children looked upon them as surrogate mothers.

In the Recovery Operation Rameshwari Nehru and Mridula Sarabhai represented the two opposing poles on whether or not abducted women should be recovered against their wishes. One, Rameshwari Nehru's, was primarily a moral and ethical position; the other, Mridula Sarabhai's, a moral and political one. The strength of Mridula Sarabhai's conviction eventually overrode the courage of Rameshwari's, who resigned in protest. In the former's assessment, recovering abducted women was not only a moral duty, it was a social responsibility and a political compulsion; for her, there could be no separation of the human angle, the political angle and the women's angle, such as that proposed by Rameshwari Nehru. Nor, as we were told again and again by social workers and police officers, was she open to any reconsideration on this score.

By contrast, in Rameshwari's view the human and women's angles subordinated all others. While presenting a review of recovery work done between October 1948 and July 1949 she referred to the dissatisfaction among Hindus and Sikhs regarding the "disparity of figures of recovery in the two Dominions"—1,030 Muslim women and children from India, 158 Hindus and Sikhs from Pakistan. As she said, "I personally would not have taken any notice of the disparity. . . if I were confident that we were doing something that was right and just. But under the present circumstances, I feel we cannot have even that consolation."[1]

Although, initially, both Mridula Sarabhai and Rameshwari Nehru were responsible for recoveries—Mridula in Amritsar, with the Central Recovery Operation, Rameshwari in Delhi, in the Women's Section—by mid-1949 it was clear that the driving force, in every sense of the word, was Mridula. Tireless in her zeal and unflagging in her pursuit of "offenders" she alternately galvanized and bullied all concerned into attacking the problem with the same energy as hers. After Rameshwari Nehru resigned in June 1949 the implementation of the programme passed entirely into Mridula Sarabhai's hands; she was formally given complete control over it and its administration was transferred from the Ministry of Relief and Rehabilitation to the Ministry of External Affairs. It was only after this that the Recovery of Abducted Persons Bill was passed, largely due to Mridula's insistence that drastic regulation was necessary in order to effect the recoveries: because abduction was a criminal offence.

Henceforth, the Recovery Operation bore the stamp of Mridula's personality as well as evidence of her ability to ram through agreements and negotiations between India and Pakistan, and legislation in India because of her proximity to those in power—Nehru, Gandhi, Liaquat Ali Khan, Patel. As her biographer, Aparna Basu, puts it: "She was a mere social worker, but because of her political contacts and status she had access to ministers and senior officials whom she could bully and order around."[2] Despite contacts (because, in fact, Rameshwari Nehru also came from a powerful political family), it was Mridula's particular brand of fiery political activism in the early Fifties, her allegiance to Sheikh Abdullah in Kashmir and open differences with Nehru and others on Kashmir's status that led to her being forced to resign from all government-related agencies, and consigned to virtual political oblivion. Almost everyone we spoke to who had worked with Mridula on recoveries between 1947–53 expressed their differences with her on how the programme was being conducted. Difficulties on the ground and the experience of the Special Tribunal on disputed cases, as well as growing resistance by the women themselves should have been reason enough to reconsider the desirability—or even advisability—of continuing as before. But, as senior police officer, Ashwini Kumar, said, "Miss Sarabhai was like a woman possessed, wouldn't listen. She was a smouldering bomb, ready to explode. She saw the suffering of women—they were poor, helpless victims and she wanted to do something. Then, women's pleading did not matter."[3]

Unfortunately, only a handful of those engaged in recovery and rehabilitation have left accounts of their experience, and it is possible that a more in-depth analysis of their lives and work will make for greater understanding of their own attitudes and compulsions. In the absence of such material we have had to rely on our interviews and a few published sources for the discussion that follows.[4] Begum Anis Kidwai put together her diaries and notes on rehabilitation work in 1949, but they were published in book form only in 1974. In *Azadi ki Chaon Mein* (In the Shadow of Freedom) she says:

> Because I am a woman my pen finds it difficult to describe the kind of horrible sexual marauding of women in both parts of Punjab and in the Riyasats (Princely States). Moreover, what would one gain from such a description, other than loss of our own dignity and respect. Talk of this incident, there is shame, describe that, there is shame.[5].

Nevertheless, she (like Kamlaben Patel) makes a moralistic distinction between those women who were genuinely abducted and those "who were by nature inclined towards irresponsible fun. Once they got an opportunity they had no desire to return to a *life of decency and control.* (Emphasis added.) However filthy the atmosphere, it suited their inclination."[6] She admits that most social workers were unequal to the task of dealing with this far from simple work:

> I regret to say that we didn't prove worthy of this task. . . .
> None of us had the ability to understand the psychology of
> these women, nor did we try. The few sentences that are
> spouted at such occasions proved totally ineffective, and
> often we ended up saying very unpleasant things to them.[7]

Although we refer to all those whose writings we have
been able to access, we will use our extensive interviews
with Kamlaben Patel and her own book, *Mool Suta Ukhadela*
(Torn from the Roots) to elaborate what we think is indica-
tive of the general impression we gained from other social
workers we spoke to. In the Introduction to her book
Kamlaben says:

> On August 15, 1947 when India obtained independence and
> Pakistan came into being as a new nation, an upheaval fol-
> lowed which has no parallel in history. Genocide, arson, loot
> and abduction took place on such a large scale in East and
> West Punjab that it is impossible to write its history. I, for
> my part, have briefly narrated a few incidents which have
> made a deep impression on my mind and are still fresh in
> my memory. In fact, these are the narrations of my inner con-
> flicts which tormented me while engaged in the recovery of
> abducted women.
>
> When I arrived in Bombay from Delhi at the end of De-
> cember 1952, the common topic of discussion with friends
> and relatives was the recovery of abducted women and chil-
> dren and the experience which I had in Punjab. My friends
> and well-wishers often put pressure on me to write about
> those experiences but I could not muster up enough strength
> as I was overcome by emotion. Why should I write the tales
> of suffering of the women of Punjab who had been the prey
> of such brutality? The feeling of aversion for males had gone
> so deep that whenever I recollected the horror of those days,
> I got terribly upset and lost my sense of balance. Besides, I
> wondered within myself whether it would be any use writ-
> ing about the brutality I saw in Punjab in its most naked
> form. Will it be of any use if I expose the so-called bravery
> of the people of Punjab who, under the pretext of religion,
> butchered innocent, unarmed persons and forcibly snatched
> away the women of the minority community in their respec-
> tive regions ? All these thoughts clashed so violently in my

mind that I could not write anything at that time. More than thirty years have passed since then. With the passage of time the feeling of aversion has died down. Now, in the evening of my life, I have begun to view those problems in a dispassionate manner.[8]

When we met her in Bombay in 1989 a few years after she had written her book, she told us that she had not been able to digest normal food after her return from Punjab in 1952. But this is the same Kamla Patel who also wrote:

The pious work entrusted to me by God, of restoring thousands of abducted women to their own families, of rehabilitating them in a new life gave me the opportunity to understand human emotions and pain. I am grateful to God for giving me the power to work.[9]

Kammoben was a Gandhian for the better part of her life, having lived at Sabarmati Ashram for many years after she was widowed at a young age. Yet, so great was her revulsion against orthodox Hinduism and the traditionalism she found in Gandhian thought, that when she was asked to speak at a function commemorating Kasturba Gandhi in 1988, she refused. Her reason: Ba personified the subordinate status of Hindu women; she, Kamla Patel, could not endorse or celebrate that in any way. Yet she spent four long years in recovery work, believing genuinely that women who had been forcibly abducted should be returned to their "real place". In this she supported Mridula Sarabhai but, as is evident from her interview, made it clear that she would go thus far and no further.

Speaking of Lahore in 1948 she says, "Since there were no set precedents or beaten paths in this type of work" (or indeed in this kind of rehabilitation) "no comments or criticism came from any quarter. I myself had to assess and reassess my own decisions in order to make suitable modifications." To the general absence of precedent add the pressure of the times and the urgency of the situation and we have some idea of the circumstances under which the social workers discharged their responsibility. Yet it was important for them to establish a rapport with the women in their care, to hear their harrowing tales, be on their guard against threats of different kinds both from abductors and relatives, to say nothing of the women's own abusive hostility when recovered against their will. How then should one interpret Kammoben's remark, "The most important responsibility was to ensure that the recovered women who were rebellious did not vitiate the camp atmosphere by creating trouble."

What constituted "rebellion" and "creating trouble"? Could she have been referring to those women who tried to escape, refused to be "recovered", resisted returning to their "own" countries? Or did she mean those who might be "misled" by people in the camps or even outsiders who managed to sneak in? Certainly she considered the plight of abducted women to be akin to that of slaves, imprisoned and helpless. She was also initially in agreement with the official view that forced conversions and marriages were illegal and could not be sanctioned. But, then again, she was firm in putting the women's interests first, as stated in her interview and as she said to "Sudarshan" in her book:

> I would not like to separate a wife from her husband and I don't approve of the provisions of the Indo-Pak Agreement being misused in that way. You make up your mind and let me know what you want. I will allow you to escape from this camp if you so desire.[10]

As her work progressed and she heard the many disputed cases in the Tribunal her disquiet grew:

> I lost my appetite and sleep. My mind was in conflict—wondered why I should carry on this work any longer. I could not decide whether the real object of helping abducted women and children had been achieved. . . . I was inclined to feel more and more that we had not. . . . And we, the so-called social workers, were engaged in transferring them from one country to another under the false notion that we were doing some noble and humanitarian work. . . . Even after a lot of soul-searching I could not decide to what extent individual freedom be curbed in the larger interests of society.[11]

In her extended conversations with us she recounted the many times she had crossed swords with police officers in the Tribunal, with bureaucrats and even Mridula Sarabhai when it seemed to her that women were being victimized by political wrangling or subordinated to the "shackles of rules and regulations".

Kammoben's ambivalence, Krishna Thapar's zeal in getting her women married honourably and her equal distress at having to repatriate those who did not wish to go back, Mridula Sarabhai's insistence that a woman outside her own community was a woman dishonoured, and Rameshwari Nehru's refusal to continue to rob women of their choice and chance of happiness, all indicate how women's agency is situated in a contradictory way, as both complicit and transgressive, in patriarchal structures.[12] They may well subscribe to an overarching patriarchal ideology, but it was they, as women who were most familiar with the ground reality, who understood the suffering of other women in their care and were able to challenge this ideology when required. Kammoben's response to the official who objected to her unconventional decision on Meera is an instance of this: "I am a woman and I understand women—I do not want to understand your politics." As far as the social workers were concerned, the question can be asked as to when and on whose behalf their social agency was activated, for they could be charged with perpetuating power structures. But, as Kumkum Sangari has cautioned, unless the "co-ordinates of women's agency are established—the conditions of possibility, of proscription, of loopholes, of contradictions",[13] it is difficult to come to any conclusions about it. It is also to recognize that agency cannot be understood apart from the very particular contexts in which it occurs. The issue, in Joan Scott's words, "is less one of opposition between domination and resistance, control and agency, than it is a complex process that constructs possibilities for and puts limits on specific actions undertaken by individuals and groups".[14]

The social work relationship itself is an ambiguous one. In response to our question about her own feelings regarding the forcible return of women to Pakistan, Krishna Thapar said, "I felt such force should not be used on women. If they are happy here, well settled, then why should they be sent? I said, force should not be used—I did not say whether they should go or not go." A few months into their work hardly any of the social workers we met remained adamant in their views regarding recovery or rehabilitation. They changed their minds about the status of the women and how best to care for them, they redefined their own roles, and they redefined the problem. It is the contested definition and redefinition of problems that makes for social change, that can make "social work" the basis of political action; and so the fairest assessment, in our view, would be to see their role as sometimes complicit, other times transgressive, but never entirely passive. For, as Rajeshwari Sunder Rajan has pointed out, "social work activism has subversive and destabilising potential even when it functions within the broad parameters of patriarchial reformism".[15] The social workers' bargaining with patriarchy in the course of their work for, and with, women had an impact on their own lives and relationships too, and such an interaction can become the catalyst for withholding consent to the more coercive of patriarchal practices.

This is how one must read Rameshwari Nehru's passionate critique of the recovery programme as well as Kamlaben Patel's and Krishna Thapar's readiness to help women exercise their choice and defy the norm. So, too, must one consider the ways in which they acted for or on behalf of the women in their care. Could they, in good conscience, have been unmindful of the women's desire for "normalcy" or social acceptability, even though this raises many questions about reconstituting patriarchy? Feminists today have learnt to accommodate those women who suffer physical and mental abuse but are nevertheless unable to leave the violent marital home, even as they have continuously provided shelter to those who choose to leave. And they have tried to understand the choiceless-ness and vulnerability of those who see marriage to their rapists as the only way to salvage their "honour". Precisely because Partition was such a disruptive moment and a time of great social dislocation, the women social workers found it possible to slip through the cracks and exercise their agency on behalf of the women whenever they could. But it should not surprise us if they often ended up reinforcing patriarchal attitudes, for it is characteristic of patriarchies that they implicate women in a consensual relationship even as they create the necessity for their resistance.

Notes

1 Rameshwari Nehru, "Memorandum on Recovery of Women" (Review of Position since October 1948), dt. June 20, 1949. Rameshwari Nehru Papers, op. cit.
2 Aparna Basu, *Mridula Sarabhai: Rebel with a Cause*, op. cit., p. 108. Mridula Sarabhai's political biography is illustrative of her ardent and sustained involvement in the freedom struggle and women's emancipation from her early twenties. Born into a wealthy industrialist and politically prominent family of Ahmedabad (Gujarat), she was initiated into political activism through her father, Ambalal Sarabhai's proximity to Mahatma Gandhi. She was active in the Congress as a Seva Dal volunteer, participated in the Salt Satyagraha and was jailed several times between 1930–1944. For a detailed listing of her many political and social offices, see Basu, op.cit., pp. 238–48.
3 Ashwini Kumar in a personal interview, 1993.
4 Mridula Sarabhai's private papers are the property of the Sarabhai Foundation and not open to researchers or scholars. Even her biographer, Aparna Basu, had limited access to them. Kamlaben Patel's book, *Mool Suta Ukhadela*, Anis Kidwai's *Azadi ki Chaon Mein*, Rameshwari Nehru's private papers, and our detailed interviews with many social workers have comprised our main sources.
5 Anis Kidwai, *Azadi ki Chaon Mein* op. cit., p. 306. Trs. by Kamla Bhasin.
6 Ibid., pp. 143–44.
7 Ibid., p. 144.
8 Kamlaben Patel, *Mool Suta Ukhadela* (unpublished English translation), Introduction.
9–11 Ibid.
12 Kumkum Sangari, "Consent, Agency and Rhetorics of Incitement" in T.V. Satyamurthy (ed.), *Region, Religion, Caste, Gender and Culture in Contemporary India* (Delhi: Oxford University Press, 1996), p. 470.
13 Ibid., p. 474.
14 Joan Scott in a review article, *Signs*, Summer 1990, pp. 851–52.
15 Rajeshwari Sunder Rajan, "The Scandal of the State: Women and Institutional Protection in India", op.cit.

Learning to Survive

Two Lives, Two Destinies

Partition provided me with the opportunity to get out of the four walls of my house. I had the will power, the intelligence, Partition gave me the chance. In Karachi I would have remained a housewife.

—Bibi Inder Kaur

Even today there is no peace. No peace outside, no peace inside. There is no peace even today. I don't sleep, there is a feeling of being unsettled. My daughters are also not at peace. There is no well-being.

—Somavanti

A Future Claimed

Very large numbers of women who had never before stepped out of their homes joined the workforce after Partition. Force of circumstances, economic necessity and the urgency to rebuild homes and futures pushed many women of all classes into earning and supplementing family incomes. This also resulted in delayed, or no marriage at all for an appreciable number, although we have no statistics to prove this. Apart from the women who were trained and provided employment by the Women's Section there were thousands who rehabilitated themselves, so to speak, enabled to do so by the breakdown of traditional constraints on their mobility. They educated themselves, ventured out into offices, schools and colleges or hospitals—or stayed home, worked, and made a living.

The January 1949 issue of *Rehabilitation Review* records the fact that in Delhi 100 girls were enrolled in the Mehrauli Residential School for girls, and 225 in the Balniketan and Gram Sevika Shiksha Kendra; eight primary schools with a strength of 1,000 children—half of them girls—were started. The number of girls receiving training in nursing was 10, in basic education, 25 and in fruit and vegetable preservation under the Ministry of Agriculture, 40. In Hoshiarpur (Punjab), 230 boys and girls attended the district board school attached to the Camp; in Jalandhar, senior boys and girls in Seva Sadan attended the local public high school, and 40 ashram girls and 110 non-ashram girls attended an industrial training school set up by the government. At the Baldev Nagar Refugee Camp in Ambala, 400 girls were enrolled in the district board middle school attached to the camp, and about 200 attended the district board school at the Gandhi Nagar Camp. At the residential middle school for girls started by the Women's Section in Delhi, there were 60 boarders.[1]

The unexpected spurt in the education of girls immediately after Partition is reflected not only in the figures put out by the Women's Section for government initiated schemes, but by the records of voluntary organizations strung out across northern India, engaged in relief and rehabilitation. The Sharanarthi Sahayak Trust and the Mahila Udyog Mandir in Meerut helped women and girls gain admission into schools, and many individual women started *kanya patshalas* for young girls. The Arya Samaj which had had such an impact in Punjab, was very active in the field of women's education but, like all such organizations, has left few documents detailing their work in the education of women and girls after Partition. Karuna Chanana in her study on family survival strategies post-1947, notes how Partition narrowed the physical spaces available to women but enlarged their social space, thereby affecting not only traditional seclusion and marriage practices but also educational mobility and employment for girls and women.[2]

Indeed, even a casual glance at educational records for the years 1946–47 indicates a significant shift in the enrolment of girls in schools and colleges. Not all of this can be put down to Partition alone but the figures for Delhi, for example, settled largely by refugees, are notable. In the years 1946–47 the number of girls' colleges in Delhi was two, with an enrolment of 580. (By contrast, the numbers for Punjab were 18 and 2,418 respectively.) In 1949–50 the number of women enrolled in Delhi had increased to 1,927 and in Punjab, had dropped to 1,575.[3] Clearly, a large part of this difference is accounted for by refugees who now pursued their higher studies in Delhi rather than in Punjab. To this extent, Partition made for a *relocation* of female students rather than a dramatic new enrolment. Nevertheless, the fact remains that these figures only indicate formal enrolment and not the total number of women and girls educated and trained through diverse programmes, both government and private. It is these latter that account for new entrants, class-wise and occupation-wise, those who had earlier been both, uneducated and "unskilled" in the technical sense.

A similar trend was evident in West Bengal. Scores of women joined the labour force in the 1950s as teachers, office-workers, tutors, tailors and small shop managers. As Rachel Weber notes, "the working woman with broken sandals became a presence on the crowded streets of central Calcutta, and of various forms of public transportation."[4]

Unfortunately there are no figures available for those who did not avail of the many government schemes for women; an informal survey by us in Delhi among families who resettled in the city, and Karuna Chanana's study of three generations of women refugees indicate that the need for educating girls was articulated quite clearly by those mothers who felt their own vulnerability acutely. With the dispersal of families and the break-up of the joint family system, sisters and daughters could no longer expect to be looked after by their male kin. Therefore, it was expedient to equip them with the minimum skills to fend for themselves. In a study done in 1955 of attitudinal changes among refugees in Dehra Dun (U.P.), 56 per cent agreed that women should be economically independent, 81 per cent believed that they should receive higher education, and 53 per cent were of the strong opinion that facilities for this should be made available to them.[5] Every single one of the widows we spoke to in the Karnal Mahila Ashram and the Gandhi Vanita Ashram had ensured that her daughters were educated and earning. This itself constituted a definite break with the past, and was one of Partition's many ironies.

Bibi Inder Kaur whose story follows, was one of those whose life changed dramatically after Partition—in her view, for the better. As she said to us, "Personally I feel that Partition instigated many people into finding their own feet."

Bibi Inder Kaur: "I spread my wings."

How Partition affected men and women . . . . You see . . . men . . . either they were killed or they escaped. Both ways they were . . . spared. If they died the problems died with them; if they survived they were resettled, they earned their daily bread and carried on. [But the women] were either left behind and treated like outcastes, often raped and brutalised—I mean if she came, she came with a guilty conscience, with the stigma of having been "soiled". And even if they were kept back and sent on later, the younger ones were never the ones to be returned. When the Pakistanis did send some young girls back, they were never able to resettle here. Many were sent back forcibly, they didn't want to come, they had married there, they had children . . . Many young Muslim boys had married Hindu girls, very honourably. Then the government told them they had to return to their own country, but they didn't want to leave their husbands and children—there was no future for them here. Then the government arranged mass marriages for many of the women who did return—well, that's also like being raped, isn't it? After all, if they were happy there they should have been allowed to remain. So in every way, you see, women suffered much more. Then those whose children died there, they didn't stop crying their whole lives. A man adjusts more easily, emotionally; even if he loses his children he adjusts, if he loses his wife, he adjusts. A woman is more emotional, that's why she cannot forget it ever . . .

Even now, after 1984, we were in Punjab and we knew the women suffered terribly. They were raped, their daughters were carried off by the jhuggi dwellers, they were abandoned or killed . . . it was the women who suffered more. And only some of them can recover and stand on their own two feet. You know, we think we've done this for them, we've done that for them . . . even in Punjab they were given sewing machines thinking that, well, they can stay home and earn a few rupees by stitching a few clothes. But you can't call that being settled. A woman who has lived well, had a comfortable home . . . what can a sewing machine do for her? Give her five or seven rupees? One square meal? I grant you some of them were married, people took it upon themselves, thought it their duty to have them married without dowries . . . . They were the saints, they fed them and clothed them. But 50 or 100 got married? Maybe even a couple of hundred? Out of 13,000 families? That's no percentage at all. And that's why they were never resettled.

For me, when we came from Karachi to Bombay . . . you

see, I suffered no irreversible loss. It was like this: we were in a queue to get onto the ship; there were no tickets for berths, all we could hope for was deck space. There were separate queues for women and men. So my husband was in the men's queue and I was in the women's line with my three daughters. One was in my arms and the other two behind me. And there were two more, my cousin's widowed sister's children. More precious than my own because she wouldn't be able to have any more. So there were three of mine and these two, five children with me. My husband was on the men's side. And the crowds! The rush! Because everyone wanted to get onto the boat somehow. The coolies threw in our luggage. Now with all the pushing and jostling, my two young daughters got left behind. When I reached the deck I realized they were not with me. I thrust my youngest daughter into the arms of a Sindhi woman standing next to me and, wailing loudly, went to look for the other two. My god! What if someone had seized them and whisked them away? Pulled them to one side? I was so worried but at last I found them right at the end of the queue. How did you get left so far behind, I asked them. We don't know, they said, there were so many people pushing us . . . we had these children and we were being pushed around so we thought we would wait at the end of the line. How would they know what might happen to two young girls in such a situation? I thanked god that my girls were unharmed and that my honour was intact. I boarded the boat and thought now even if the boat sinks I don't care, I'm not worried.

. . . I now have my own house in Nizamuddin, I educated myself, I worked, everything sorted itself out in time . . . . I can't say I suffered as such, I can't say I suffered any real loss. But those who lost everything, whose daughters were left behind, whose children were killed . . . how can they ever forget?

You see, we had never really thought of leaving Karachi . . . but after '47 we saw that our neighbours were looking at us differently, looking askance at us. Where my husband's clinic was, that was the place where they started killing Sikhs. Their intentions took practical shape. But you can't blame them alone, people here also misbehaved. Now the way things happened in Rawalpindi, our original place. . . .the way the Muslims slaughtered children, women. . . in Pindi Muslims were in the majority, they started attacking. After a while things cooled down a bit. But as soon as Partition happened the "work" that had been started by the Muslims was picked up here . . . we were no less. We also raped women, we also murdered and burnt houses here. It was a question of action and reaction. That was bound to have an effect on Karachi, wasn't it? The second time I went to Karachi the Junagarh business had already taken place. Muslims suffered terribly there— they had to leave their homes. How could they let the Hindus rest in peace after that? You know, in this business of hating and killing—there was great affinity between Muslims and Sikhs . . . our culture was the same . . . our food, our dress, our language, everything was the same. As I told you, in Rawalpindi we had very good relations with the Muslims, with their pirs. When my nani passed away the pirs read from the Qoran Sharif, we had a paath of the Guru Granth Sahib, of the Gita . . . people lived together there because their culture was the same, their attitudes were similar . . .

I don't want to sound as though I'm praising my own community, but what I mean is . . . well, Sikhs are definitely a little more "broadminded"; they intermingle . . . . What I'm trying to say is that Hindus, Sikhs and Muslims were not divided then, they were not separate. They lived together even though their eating habits might have been different . . . Sikhs would not eat halal meat. So there were these differences. But we could have continued to live together . . . why would we have gone to Karachi otherwise? There was no ill-feeling in our hearts.

When Partition took place, what I think is, I may be wrong . . . we didn't want Partition on this side . . . our government didn't want that Pakistan should be a separate country. But then why did it come about? The root of this lies in the fact that, deep down, people did think the Muslims were different. In their hearts Hindus actually hated them. I remember we used to have *chics* in our house—they were old-fashioned houses—and I used to have an old woman come to massage me, she was Muslim. Now she would have to lift the *chic* aside to enter, wouldn't she? Well, my neighbours who were typical old-fashioned Hindus, they would say to us, you lift your *chics* and only then will we enter. Because they had been touched

by a Muslim! Hindu women wouldn't eat in train compart-
ments because of the presence of Muslims there. We Sikhs did
not do such things.

I don't know, during Mughal times, Hindus were very badly
treated . . . naturally, all that became part of our "inheritance"
somehow, a deep-seated dislike took root which began to show
itself in such actions. Our family, we had very close relations
with Muslims . . . my maternal grandfather had exchanged
turbans with the local elite Muslims to say that they were like
brothers. But we never ate in their homes, our daughters never
entered their houses, theirs didn't come to ours . . . but the
men were like brothers. We attended their weddings, they gave
us dry rations, *mishri* (crystallized sugar) . . . Now of course,
it's not like that at all, there's no difference any more. At that
time there was. And it rankled among the Muslims—because
they had ruled here, the Hindus had been their subjects and
slaves . . . they couldn't accept being ruled by Hindus.

Now about the immediate cause, my own feeling is that that
Jinnah was a very clever man and he had been part of the Congress and seen its attitudes. Now, I'm not being prejudiced
but my own thinking, from whatever I've heard and read, I'd
been hearing Mahatma Gandhi's lectures also . . . he was first
a Hindu. He was a great man, no doubt, but he was first a
Hindu. He had no real regard for the Sikhs even—"They eat
meat and fish, they dress well—." He was a good man, I'm not
saying he was not . . . but he disliked Muslims and Sikhs because they ate meat, etc. I am not denying that when the Hindus started harassing the Muslims he was the first person to
condemn it. When the incidents in Delhi took place he started
fasting, made conditions . . . but that Jinnah was very shrewd
. . . . He had realized that no Muslim could be secure or at
peace under Hindu rule—something the Sikhs didn't understand because they were so close to the Hindus, closer than
they were to the Muslims. Jinnah stuck to his demand for a
separate country because he had been in the Congress, he had
seen what all went on in it . . . we common people never knew,
but he was in it . . . he was close to Mahatma Gandhi, to
Jawaharlal, to Motilal Nehru, all of them. No matter how much
they tried to persuade him, with love, with friendship, he had
made up his mind.

And to some extent Jinnah was right. Muslims were a minority, they were economically backward and they were also conservative. So all these factors made them feel they could only prosper in a separate nation, they couldn't do so in undivided India where they would have been a minority and their share of power, facilities and resources would have been marginal. He was right, because in spite of all the inner conflicts within Pakistan Muslims are the rulers. India is a little afraid of Pakistan because it is a separate nation— it wouldn't have been afraid of Muslims if they were part of India. Those people who go to Pakistan now, like Sikh groups who visit Gurudwara Nankana Sahib, they say Pakistanis are very well off. Most Muslims who stayed on in India are not that well off. Now, Pakistan is a military dictatorship and we know the problems in such a rule, we know they cannot be very happy under such a rule, but at least they have a separate *identity*, a separate *existence*. We are afraid of that separate identity even though it is much smaller than ours and India is much larger, with vast resources. But we are afraid of their separate existence—and this is what Jinnah wanted.

I feel religion also played an important role. Jinnah might not have been a staunch Muslim himself but he went along with the Muslims. He couldn't have survived without their support. He wanted Pakistan to be a secular country like India, a free and democratic country. But other Muslims were old fashioned and conservative.

The economic reason was also an important reason. Hindus and Sikhs owned land, Muslims laboured on their land. In a way, they were exploited by us, they were under us. The close relationship which I spoke about was between us and a handful of well-off Muslims. But the majority were poor and they were exploited by us. For them Sikhs and Hindus were the same because they were close to each other. And the Sikhs also played dirty. They tore their flag, insulted it. Because of this the Muslims were more upset with the Sikhs and they would not have allowed the Sikhs to stay on. They took their revenge. Servants killed their masters. Those servants who could barely stand straight in front of their masters abducted the women of landlords and expressed their anger. It is these sections who turned into mobs. Jinnah was unable to control these elements.

Muslims were uneducated, not so enlightened and that contributed to their fanaticism. You see a similar tendency among the Sikhs, a kind of weakness. They also get easily agitated in the name of religion . . . it was this religious feeling which was used to mobilise Muslims.

. . . In Karachi I had only studied upto class VIII. My husband allowed me to learn sewing but not to study. Once he went out to war for a year and during that time I did Punjabi Honours. I began studying English also but couldn't finish because he came back, and I also had my third child. I wanted to study to stand on my own feet but was not allowed to. Since everyone did this to their daughters and women, I was not angry. So we came to Delhi. My husband who was a doctor, started his clinic. I used to see a young boy studying and I felt like studying too. I said to Doctor Sahib, let me do my Xth class, how will it matter? I won't start reaching for the stars. In Delhi a friend convinced my husband to let me continue. I was about 40 then, the mother of three girls. So I did my matric in two months! I became a little more confident.

I started teaching in a school, then I began teaching Punjabi at Miranda House. My husband agreed to my working but didn't want me to take any money for it. But the school insisted on paying me Rs. 50, and Rs. 30 for transport. I taught at Queen Mary's for two years. Then I was asked to do my F.A. and B.A. by the Principal of Miranda House—if I was teaching F.A. I should at least have a degree myself! My husband had to agree.

So I was earning but couldn't spend anything without his permission—I had to ask him to pay Rs. 150 for tuition from my own money. I used to study and teach—my students would give me a ride to college on their cycles.

I failed my F.A. and my failure became my husband's victory. *Meri har ona di jit ho gayi.* I said, okay, not this time, next time I'll pass. I took the exam again and passed — but failed my B.A.! I appeared again and this time I got 64 per cent. I was thrilled! I used to cycle 20 miles every day, work for 18 hours. When I said I wanted to do my M.A., my husband had a big fight with me. I felt, B.A. is a big achievement but I want to do an M.A. now. He was furious. He said, do a B.Ed. But I wasn't interested in teaching in schools only, I wanted more. This time I revolted and got admitted into a regular college against his wishes. My brother helped. I got a scholarship as a refugee and studied in Delhi University. Tolerance beyond a limit is wrong—after a point you must revolt.

Economically, of course, we were ruined. We had to struggle to educate our children, but for me there were also opportunities. Because I got out of the house my daughters benefited. They became confident, and flourished. We had bought a house in Nizamuddin which we rented out and lived in Khyber Pass which was close to the University. I taught at Miranda House in the mornings and studied in the evening. I stayed in the hostel for three months because my husband shifted to Khan Market.

We had our differences, my husband and I. He was angry with me because my daughter married a non-Sikh and I didn't put my foot down—he didn't speak to her for eight years. Blamed her for being my daughter, blamed me for having given birth to her! He was also proud of me, but only in my absence—he would never attend any programmes at Miranda House. I used to say, I'm not a sweepress there, you know!

Soon I got a lectureship in Punjabi M.A. classes at Khalsa College and started living in a Working Girls' Hostel. In the Working Women's Hostel I saw how women suffered—they couldn't get married because who would look after their parents? So many women had to support their families. Then they had to deal with their male bosses, men in the office . . . I taught at Khalsa College for nine years and then when Mata Sundari College for girls started, I went there as a Senior Lecturer. My confidence increased. Quite soon, I became Vice-Principal for nine months and then Principal. Then I came to Amritsar where I became the first Principal of a new college. I took no salary, only an honorarium and worked till I was 75. My two elder daughters and my brother helped me out financially—my husband never earned enough to help. Now I divide my time between Amritsar, Delhi and Dharamshala where I spend the summers. I'd be lost in Delhi—in Amritsar I have the Darbar Sahib, friends, my lectures on Guru Nanak . . .

. . . It was my husband who left me, really speaking, I always tried to keep some sort of relationship going with him. But I wasn't too unhappy because I had my job, a future. In a way I was glad that this obstacle had been removed. Partition provided me with the opportunity to get out of the four walls of my house. I had the will power, the intelligence, Partition gave me the chance. In Karachi I would have remained a housewife. Personally I feel Partition forced many people into taking the initiative and finding their own feet.

When we came we were bankrupt. Educating the children was difficult. But social values were changing, they had to. Early on, I made the connection between economic independence and education. Our relatives helped us but after all, how long could I be dependent on them? But where I benefited from this change, my husband lost. He felt a terrible loss upon Partition—his practice suffered, he was under great mental tension, he became more authoritative. I was happier, I was doing what I wanted. He wasn't. Then when we separated he no longer even had a stable family life.

There are millions of women like me who want to do something but cannot. I managed to because Partition gave me a chance. My husband feared that this would happen, that when I became independent I would be free—and he was right. I think he knew that if I got educated, became economically independent he would have no control over me, he would lose me. That is why he opposed the steps I took to get educated, to work. In a way he was right, because he did lose me. I gained much more than I lost. He only lost. I felt sorry for him but I never wanted to go back, back to that life.

I had spread my wings.

A Past Mourned

Whereas the dislocation of Partition enabled Bibi Inder Kaur to spread her wings, Somavanti felt she had been permanently grounded by it. Her world was one small room in the Karnal Mahila Ashram, and there she died in 1993. Not for her the freedom to roam a city, relocate of her own free will, live in places of her choice. For her freedom was in the past she had left behind. "There was peace—

sukh—at the time of the British, there was order. We could walk freely even when we lived in Muslim villages. There was no fear. Now there is no order, no just punishment."

Like Bibi Inder Kaur, Somavanti was the mother of three daughters, and one son; like her, she educated them all and the elder girls helped educate and support their younger siblings. Unlike Aiji (as Bibi Inder was called) Somavanti thought hers was a life made meagre and bereft in every respect. Loss of place, of property, of people, of peace.

Somavanti: "We belong nowhere."

My father had a wholesale cloth shop in Chhota Multan. We were three sisters and two brothers and the girls went to the gurudwara to learn how to read and write. There was also a widow whom we paid three annas a month for teaching us Gurumukhi. We did not go to any *sakool-shakool*. Bhaiji taught us some Japji Sahib. I studied only for a short while because at eleven I was married off. After a year I went to my in-laws for a visit (*phera*). I would spend six months here, six months there. I was married early because my husband was impatient, a pampered son who used to "go out". My father-in-law said get him married, he will settle down. My in-laws were sahukars, they had a lot of land. What can I tell you, how much? A lot. Our land had water and we could grow two crops. What fine and white wheat we used to get. *Halis* (labourers) used to work on our land. They were all Muslims.

Then they also had shops, my in-laws, cloth and general merchandise. My father-in-law was much better off than my father. He was called Shahji. He had so much money that every six or eight months there would be thefts. The thieves got tired of looting him. They said, "This chap has so much, it will never finish." So they set everything on fire. All his shops were burnt—the Muslims did it. My father-in-law did not report them to the police because he wanted no *vair* (animosity) with them. There were many well-to-do Hindus in our village—Narangs, Sethis, Kohlis, Anands, all high caste. They were all landed, all—maybe one or two were not, but all were landowners. My husband went to school for four or five years, no one studied more than that. They could read and write and do the accounts, that was all. From an early age he had started looking after the shop and other businesses.

I was 16 when my first daughter was born. I had two brothers-in-law and one sister-in-law. We all lived in a big haveli. My husband and I downstairs, and his two brothers, upstairs. There, we were all together but after Partition we got separated. My father-in-law died soon after our marriage. Although the shops and lands were divided the brothers were together, they looked after everything together. My husband, being the oldest, had more responsibilities and so did I. After my father-in-law died my husband became Shahji. There was so much well-being and so much comfort then.

. . . My husband found no work here. There was no peace, no rest, we were only glad that we were alive. I did not go to live with my father because everyone lived in small places. My mother was step, the real one had died. But my husband couldn't adjust. He would come back broken every evening, desperate. We couldn't help each other—we had to deal with our own fears. Our faces told our stories. He cried thinking of his past—there he was Shahji. He died two years later in 1950. We continued to live in the masjid. I stayed in Ambala for two more years after his death. My father used to come to sleep with us every night. Till today people are living in masjids.

I worked at home, did some stitching. We were too embarrassed to go and work outside in other people's homes. I used to stitch quilt covers, underwear for my brother's shop. We managed to survive. Around that time we heard about the Karnal Ashram through an acquaintance who was from the same village as us and who we used to help. We applied, and I got permission from Jullundar to go there. But I didn't want to go because of rumours that they separated children from their mothers and then married them off. My stepmother and I came here first to see and then I shifted. I had to come here because who would have fed me there? My father was old himself. In fact, after I came here he also went to an old people's home.

Here, I was given a room to live in and work in the Sewing Centre. I now had four children, three daughters and a son. My eldest daughter was eleven, in class V. They were all educated here, in the centre. I worked hard. There was no time to think. Worked the whole day, then shopped, cooked. Soon after eating, fell asleep. The next day the same routine. Women in the Ashram helped each other because they shared the same grief. But slowly everyone found their own ways . . . we were given work by the centre only. We used to get orders, the wages were low, we could make only between Rs. 30 and Rs. 100 a month, depending on the work. There was always enough work. We did beautiful work, good embroidery. I was the best in embroidery. The Ashram gave us rations for the children till they grew up and started earning. My daughter got training as a teacher and got a job. For five-six years she earned and helped with the younger children. My second daughter also got a job later, by then the first one was married. So, like this we managed somehow.

My son didn't study beyond class VII—he fell into bad "society". I sent him to Panchkula to study, he did not study. He wasted his time.

. . . Why this (Partition) happened—these are all big people's issues, what can I say? I really did not talk to many people. All we heard was that after the British left, Hindus and Muslims started fighting, they could not live together. Muslims felt they should have their own country, their own raj. But we always had good relations with Muslims. We did not eat with them, but everything else we did. We lent seeds to them which they returned with 25–50 per cent extra. We also had camels, Muslim servants looked after them. When my son was born the Muslim women came with *mishri* and one and a quarter rupees covered with a handkerchief. So many of them brought this gift. Muslim servants ate at our home, we visited them. We did not eat with them, but there was so much *pyar-mohabbat* (love and affection). Now what to tell you, how things changed and why? See what is happening between Hindus and Sikhs now. In the name of religion, all problems are created. We used to give and take daughters from Sikhs. But now, animosity is building up. We all learnt Gurmukhi, went to gurudwaras but now people are dying because of all this. I have been going to gurudwaras always—in this Ashram also there is a small gurudwara. I go there twice a day, for some peace, some good thoughts. I don't see any difference between Ram and Rahim,

between mandir and gurudwara. I have always found solace in religion. Whenever I am too upset, I think of god . . .
. . . I can't clean my own clothes, wash my own hair. I don't think I can live alone for too long—
Even today there is no peace. No peace outside, no peace inside. There is no peace even today. I don't sleep, there is a feeling of being unsettled. My daughters are also not at peace. There is no well-being.
My daughters did everything for me. My oldest daughter was my biggest support in my widowhood, without her help I could not have brought up the other children. We bought a fan, a radio. But you can't go and live with your daughters. My son-in-law is a very difficult man, gets angry for no reason. My daughter earns more than him but she has no say in anything. She just takes it all, with the result that she has developed T.B. All because of worries. I feel I cannot live with daughters. If I go and live with them I would feel a sense of obligation. There is no feeling of authority in a daughter's home. I would just suffer. My daughter also does not ask me.
. . . Oh, how much money we spent when our son was born. He came after two daughters so there were special celebrations. We went to Panja Sahib for thanksgiving. Every festival was celebrated with great *josh* (fervour). Now I sometimes wonder why we yearn so much for sons. But then there is no life without sons, girls belong to others, sons carry the line forward. There is no peace without sons. I know that sons can also be useless—that is bad luck. My daughters did everything for me, my son gave me nothing, he only took from me. Yet I cannot go and live with my daughters. Dependent people cannot be happy, my heart has never felt happy, never completely happy. He (her husband) couldn't tolerate it, he died of unhappiness. I felt I had to do whatever was written in my fate. I couldn't think of dying because my children would have become orphans. No one is happy—*Nanak, dukhiya sab sansar* . . .
Those who were happy there (in West Punjab) became unhappy here. Those who were poor were able to deal with things better, they were able to ask for things, get things, do any work. We were always too embarrassed. The poor ones now have big houses, gardens, malis. This is all luck. Sometimes the sun shines in one place, sometimes in another. It was our kismat to

see such bad times. We thank the government for whatever it did for us, we could live with dignity, we could look after our daughters. Our children got educated, they got stipends, admission. . . .

But I have no country now. This is not ours, that is no more ours. I still wish I could go back and see our homes. There were such nice paintings on our walls outside! Flowers, trains, the rooms were *rangeen*, beautifully made, it was like a mahal. I wish I could go back. People die for their country—we have nothing to die for. What could we women do?

. . . Now there is no country. Earlier we had a home , a country, because we belonged there. Now we belong nowhere. How can you have a country without a home, a job? How many different places we have lived in since Partition! The real country is the one we have left behind. That was our real home, the home we loved. Relationships were stronger, families looked after each other. All that has also gone, finished. Now no one cares. There is no hunger now for food, only a hunger for people.

Two Lives, Two Destinies

When Bibi Inder Kaur died in 1996 she owned three houses, one each in Delhi, Amritsar and Dharmashala. When Somavanti died in 1993, her belongings were packed in a neat bundle and handed over to her daughters. For her, as long as she lived, an amplitude of space could only be found in her past, in her home like a palace with beautifully painted rooms. This physical space found its emotional equivalent in the comfort and security of a caring and well-knit community—"There was so much *pyar-mohabat*. Now what to tell you, how things changed and why?" The young Somavanti was enveloped in warmth and well-being, psychologically at peace with her world. With Partition, order, freedom from fear and contentment were replaced with instability, death, permanent dislocation—emotional, physical and psychological—and ceaseless toil. "There was no time to think. Worked the whole day, then shopped, cooked. Soon after eating, fell asleep. The next day the same routine." Even dying was not an option. She cried often while speaking to us, when she recalled the happiness she had known; for her, the sun still shone most brightly in Multan and the broken rhythm of her life now only served to underline the undisturbed harmony of her past.

Somavanti was not unusual in feeling the way she did, although her story was more poignant than others we heard. The Dehra Dun study mentioned earlier (the only sex-differentiated one of Partition refugees that we know of) found that 67 per cent of both men and women believed that it would never be possible for them to regain their earlier status; of them, those in the above-50 age group were more pessimistic than the younger ones. When asked about the future, however, the study noted a most interesting difference: 33 per cent of men, but only 16 per cent of women agreed vehemently with the suggestion that they had "no hopes" for it; while 28 per cent of women but only 13 per cent of men disagreed strongly. Here again, those least optimistic belonged to the above-50 age group.[6]

When Bibi Inder Kaur joined Miranda House it was the first women's college in Delhi University to offer degrees to women. Aiji seized the opportunity that presented itself to her, welcoming the changed circumstances that now allowed her to pursue the studies she had had to interrupt in Karachi. She set about determinedly and single-mindedly creating a new life, gradually gaining her autonomy. With each new step she took she expanded the spaces she could occupy; even her move to the relative constriction of the Working Women's Hostel (a mirror, if you like, to the Karnal Mahila Ashram where Somavanti lived) was transitional, an anteroom to a more spacious environment. As her domestic space became freer, her professional stature grew from being head of department in a women's college to principal of a college in Amritsar, and an active career till the age of 75. Her home in Amritsar where we stayed with her, radiated calm and was filled with the peace that seemed to have eluded Somavanti all her life. Aiji's independence of spirit and thinking marked her conversations in a way that enabled her to see her past and her relationships in perspective, and to situate herself as a woman in a society undergoing enormous change. She recognized that change was beneficial for her, but that it meant persevering, not giving up—". . . not this time, next time I'll pass. I did, but failed my B.A.!"— and taking the risk of leaving her husband and living in a hostel with three young daughters. "We had to struggle," she said, "but for me there were opportunities. Because I got out of the house my daughters benefited. They became confident and flourished."

Somavanti's daughters, on the other hand, were their husbands' subordinates in the time-honoured tradition despite their education and earning capacity. Rigid gender roles and her own reinforcing of daughter–son stereotyping, kept Somavanti from making the break with convention that may have given her and her daughters more room for manoeuvre and opened up other spaces for them. For it was not that Bibi Inder Kaur met with no resistance: as she says, she needed her husband's permission even to pay her tuition fees from her own salary, but no false "sense of obligation" kept her from her pursuit. As she put it, "Tolerance beyond a limit is wrong—you must revolt." And although both their husbands lost out as a result of Partition and Somavanti's died "of unhappiness", Bibi Inder Kaur's husband's inability to rebuild his practice enabled her to become economically independent. Because she gained much more than she lost she "never wanted to go back to that life". And because Somavanti's kismat was "to see such bad times", she accepted that the sun would never again shine on her, that all was "gone, finished".

For women, the liberatory potential of the disruption caused by Partition has generally (and understandably) been obscured by the trauma of violence and dislocation.[7] That survival, and strategies for survival, can also be instrumental in women finding their feet is amply demonstrated by the experiences of Bibi Inder Kaur and Durga Rani Katyal. One struck out on her own, the other took advantage of facilities and training provided by the government for widows; both acquired economic self-reliance, of course, but also great self-respect, dignity and the immeasurable satisfaction of "asking no one for charity". Both bequeathed a legacy of confidence and self-worth to their daughters and both, spontaneously, preferred what they had made of their lives to what their lives may have made of them, had Partition not intervened.

Both agreed that it had given them the chance to forge their own destinies, to spread their wings.

Notes

[1] Government of India, Ministry of Relief & Rehabilitation, 1949
[2] Karuna Chanana, "Partition and Family Strategies: Gendei Educational Linkages among Punjabi Women in Delhi", *Economic and Political Weekly*, Vol. XXVIII No. 17, April 24, 1993.
[3] Ministry of Education, *Progressive Education Reports*, 1937–1947; 1950–51.

By January 1948, erstwhile Punjab University (Lahore) had made provisions for enabling its students to complete their studies by setting up a camp college on Mandir Marg; it was housed in the municipal corporation school which made its classrooms available in the evenings, to M.A. students only. Undergraduate and graduate degrees (from Punjab University) were offered in all the liberal arts subjects, political science, and pre-medical. The Camp College remained in existence till June 1959. For the first five years girls were admitted to all courses, and comprised about 25–30 per cent of the student body of approximately 4,500. Initially, the only condition for admissions was refugee status, but a few years later the college began enrolling those who were employed, as well. Hostel accommodation for girls was arranged in the YWCA (Constantia Hall), and in the YMCA for boys. (We are grateful to Prof. Randhir Singh and Shri Kundal Lal, both of whom taught at the Camp College, and Santosh Manmohan who was a student there, for this information.)

[4] Rachel Weber, "(Re)Creating the Home: Women's Role in the Development of Refugee Colonies in South Calcutta", unpublished paper, 1992. Weber's figures are from the Census of India, 1961, Vol. II, West Bengal, p. 64. She also notes that Jadavpur in South Calcutta, home to many refugees, has one of the highest female literacy rates in the city. She ascribes this to women entering various educational institutions in large numbers, post-Partition.
[5] R.N. Saksena, "Changing Attitudes and Culture Assimilation Among Refugees as a Result of Their Rehabilitation in Dehra Dun", Report (Agra: Institute of Social Sciences), n.d.
[6] Ibid., pp. 37–40.
[7] For an interesting discussion on women refugees' entry into political spaces see Rachel Weber, op. cit. Weber describes how the threat to their homes by landlords pressing for their evic-

tion, led women to participate in rallies and processions. They played a critical role in fending off land-grabbers and goondas (toughs) by, among other things, standing in front of a phalanx of refugees, holding their household weapons. In Weber's view, though, this did not signify a movement out into public space so much as an expansion of the domestic space to include participation in political, community and economic affairs.

tion, led women to participate in rallies and processions. They played a critical role in fending off land-grabbers and goondas (toughs) by among other things standing in front of a phalanx of refugees, holding their household weapons. In Weber's view though, this did not signify a movement out into public space so much as an expansion of the domestic space to include participation in political community, and economic affairs.

Belonging

Women and Their Nations

Own country? Of what feather is that bird? And tell me, good people, where does one find it? The place one is born in, that soil which has nurtured us, if that is not our country, can an abode of a few days hope to be it? And then, who knows, we could be pushed out of there, too, and told to find a new home, a new country. I'm at the end of my life. One last flutter and there'll be no more quarrelling about countries. And then, all this uprooting and resettling doesn't even amuse any more. Time was, the Mughals left their country and came to create a new one here. Now you want to pick up and start again. Is it a country or an uncomfortable shoe? If it pinches, exchange it for another!

—Ismat Chughtai, *Roots*

Dadi . . . was born in Meerut towards the end of the last century. She was married at sixteen and widowed in her thirties, and by her later decades could never exactly recall how many children she had borne. When India was partitioned . . . she moved her thin, pure Urdu into the Punjab of Pakistan and waited for the return of her eldest son, my father . . . . She had long since dispensed with any loyalties larger than the pitiless give-and-take of people who are forced to live together in the same place, and she resented independence for the distances it made. She was not among those who, on the fourteenth of August, unfurled flags and festivities against the backdrop of people running and cities burning. About that era she would only say, looking up sour and cryptic over the edge of her Qoran: "And I was also burned."

—Sara Suleri, *Meatless Days*

Displaced

Two nations were born on August 14 and 15, 1947, and it was thought that the issue of who belonged where had finally, though bloodily, been laid to rest. Fifty years later there are still 1,100 "displaced persons" in what are called "permanent liability homes" in India. Refugees from Bihar and Bangladesh are to be found not only in Sind and West Bengal but in Haryana and Madhya Pradesh as well. A steady stream of migration from East Pakistan continued right upto 1958, and again in 1964 after trouble in Kashmir led to riots in Dhaka and Khulna, and later in 1971, following the war of liberation for Bangladesh. A third new nation was born.

New nations, it seems, create their own refugees, or so it has been in the subcontinent. "For the last 50 years I have travelled from one place to another," says Ghafoor, a Bihari in Karachi, "from Bihar to Madras to Calcutta, then to Dhaka and now Karachi. I have been travelling all my life and at 75 I am still not settled."[1] In 1947 and again in 1971 there were those who gained a nation and those who lost a country—and, as one woman said to us, there were those who became "permanent refugees". For the vast majority, "country" was something they had always thought of as the place where they were born and where they would like to die. Now, suddenly, their place of birth was horribly at odds with their nationality; had nothing to do with it, in fact. And the place now called country, they felt little attachment to. Quite unexpectedly, and certainly unwillingly, they were violently uprooted and relocated in places and among communities they could not identify with, people they thought of as strangers. Own country? "Now there is no country," said Somavanti to us, "This is not ours, that is no more ours."

Partition made for a realignment of borders and of national and community identities, but not necessarily of loyalties. Thousands who opted for Pakistan returned a little later, an equal number, here and there, forsook allegiance to their families and never left at all. Some were unaware of Pakistan as a separate country till some years after its creation, even though they themselves had migrated to it. And any number failed to quite absorb the fact that there were borders now that couldn't be crossed. "My real home?" said one woman to us in Delhi, "the one at Sutar Mandi, Phullan Wali Gali, Lahore." Large numbers of people chose fidelity to place rather than to religious community: they converted and remained where they were. The choice may have been expedient or not—and, indeed, often there was little choice in the matter; what it suggests is that "country" is an elusive entity. Each time we asked the women we were speaking to whether they would die for their country, we got an eliptical response. Even Taran who said quite clearly, "We must fight back, we must oppose with violence if necessary," believed firmly that if women were to write history "men would realize how important it is to be peaceful".

The three stories that follow all deal with how these women came to terms (or not, as the case may be) with their relocation or dislocation—for as we realized, there can be dislocation without one's ever having been displaced. Whether the choice to go or stay was voluntary, they all speak about how they relearnt their roles in a "new" country. Kamila,* a Hindu, chose to rejoin her husband, a Muslim, and live in Pakistan as a convert; and the three Lucknow sisters† stayed back with their parents after all other members of their extended—and very political—family had left for Karachi. When, years later as adults they had to choose, they opted for Lucknow. Taran lived through 1947 and, as a Sikh, through the 1984 anti-Sikh riots in Kanpur. In '47 she had no choice, in '84 she said, she realized she had "no country".

---

* Not her real name.

† Names withheld at their request.

Kamila: "No going back."

. . . On August 14 Pakistan was duly declared an independent country, and the next day British rule in India formally came to an end. India was at last free from the stranglehold of a foreign yoke after a long, long struggle. It was an occasion for great joy, but it was being spoilt by widespread reports of looting and carnage from both parts of the subcontinent. Nevertheless, frantic preparations went on in New Delhi, the capital of India, to make August 15—India's day of Independence—an outstandingly festive occasion. No police was to be posted anywhere near the site of celebrations where an impressive rostrum was set up. Cars were parked for miles around the site, from where we had to walk to our seats.

There on the rostrum stood a beaming Jawaharlal Nehru, the hero of the Independence movement, now the new Prime Minister of the country, nodding and waving. Sitting around him were Sardar Patel and the other members of the Indian Congress hierarchy. There also sat Lord Mountbatten with his consort, the famous Lady Edwina. Everyone was smiling and seemed at ease. Speeches boomed on loudspeakers, while the audience laughed and clapped and laughed till all track of time seemed to be lost in the ensuing light-hearted banter and general friendliness. Suddenly a great cloud seemed to descend on me, till I was clutching my heart. Wildly I looked around, desperately trying to locate myself amongst all these carefree faces, and froze. Where in god's name was I? I shook myself with an effort and stood up in a panic. I felt my sister's hand pull me to her lovingly till I was drawn to her lap with my head hidden in her neck. Horses seemed to be racing inside me, thumping against my chest relentlessly. Somebody had forsaken someone, somewhere. Who, how, and why? Politicians seemed to have all the answers. Had I any? Was I an Indian, or had I ceased to be one by marrying a Muslim who had always lived in an area now acceded to Pakistan?

. . . I was in India when Pakistan was made, and I had a small child, he was three months old . . . so everyone was telling me, Hindus are being murdered there, this and that, don't go back, we've got good jobs for you here ! . . in the PIB, in AIR*, don't

*Press Information Bureau and All India Radio.

go . . . your husband had no business opting for Pakistan when you're here . . . he had left me in Delhi and returned to Lahore to attend a family wedding and there they asked him, do you want to opt for India or Pakistan, and he took Pakistan. Without consulting me. There was no way he could have consulted me—the telephone lines were jammed and the operators would start expostulating—they'd say "Jawaharlal Nehru, murdabad!" from there and the ones here would reply, "Jinnah, murdabad!" They'd be fighting among themselves and we'd be left saying, "Hello? Hello?" We just couldn't talk. We booked so many urgent calls, but nothing. So we couldn't consult each other. He thought, well, she's married to me so she should come here, his whole family was there . . . Now I had many friends who thought differently; I could understand that he hadn't been able to consult me, but still . . . I was slightly resentful. I thought, why wasn't I asked? Maybe I don't want to live in Pakistan, I want to be where my people are . . . he's secure, he has his people there, but I don't. Everyone said to me, all your links are in India except your child who is only three months old. You don't have to go back. Wait, he may come here, if he doesn't, doesn't matter.

So I was getting all this advice and then my father caught hold of me and said, "Look, you are so confused now but when you got married I said to you, you haven't had to make any sacrifices yet, they'll come when you start living according to the choice you've made, the life you've chosen. Now the time has come for that sacrifice and you're backing out because it doesn't suit you. What option did your husband have, after all? If he had opted for India, what job security would he have had as a Muslim? Maybe he will, maybe he won't. But now that you've chosen him, you'll have to face it. You've got to keep your vows."

I saw the truth of this. Then, I didn't know how to get back to Lahore. There was such heavy booking on trains and planes, and my husband kept sending me messages through Hindus who were coming from Lahore, asking me to return, to come home. I was in such conflict. I wanted to go, and yet not to go. Then, you'll be astonished, there were 14,000 people waiting to get onto flights to Pakistan, Muslims who were leaving India, and yet I got a booking, my father managed to get me on

somehow, he was so insistent that I go back to my husband.
He came with me to the airport. There—you won't believe me—
many Sikhs who knew us removed their turbans and placed
them at my feet, saying don't go, they are killing all the Hindus there . . . These were people my father knew, they made
me swear I wouldn't go . . . at the airport. Are you mad, they
said, that you're going . . . Now I hadn't really thought of it
like that, that I was a Hindu or a Sikh, I just thought, I am a
wife returning to her husband . . .
 . . . So I came to Pakistan. By then it was clear that there
would be no going back, there had been so much genocide,
there was no way it could be different. What had happened,
had happened. Now, when I reached the Lahore airport there
was a Hindu boy who'd studied with me in M.A., the police
had got hold of him . . . I·don't know what he had done but he
came and said, I want to talk to her for a minute. They were
confused . . . they didn't know who I was, a Hindu or a Muslim,
all they knew was that I had come from Delhi to live in Pakistan, that was good enough for them. So they allowed him to
talk to me. He came up and pressed some five hundred rupee
notes in my hand, "You take them, if I ever come to Pakistan
I'll take them from you, otherwise you keep them. I'd rather
you have them than the police." I didn't even remember him
properly, what happened to him, I have no means of knowing
. . .
 Then there was the pilot of a Pakistani plane who came up
to me, he was a friend of my husband's although I had never
met him. And he said, he's sent me to receive you. I didn't
believe him. I said, how could he know I'm coming today, I
didn't tell him. He said, no, he knows, he's taken the day off,
but there is no way you can get out of here because there is a
police cordon. But I am on duty, so you get into my car and I'll
take you. So there I was with this howling kid, minus a Muslim ayah who had stayed in India because she had married a
Hindu cook! She said, I'm not going back . . . He put me in his
car and dropped me at the gate of our house in Model Town,
this was my *jeth's* house, he was chief engineer, North-West-
ern Railways. He dropped me about a hundred yards from the
house and I had to carry this suitcase and my child . . . so I left
the suitcase on the road and walked the hundred yards to my

brother-in-law's bungalow. There my sister-in-law ran out, saying, "She's come, she's come!" They were overjoyed. My sister-in-law told me, "Your husband is in your father's house waiting for you, he's taken some servants and he's waiting." I said, "I can't believe this, this is nonsense, he's waiting for me . . . How does he know I am coming?" She said, "I don't know, he's taken leave, taken my mali and gone there." Now that mali was six foot five, tall and strapping, and my husband had handed him a staff to protect me with.

Between my brother-in-law's house and my father's house was a garden. That's all the distance there was. My husband had already started walking towards his brother's house to collect me, and we went home. The very next day in the house next to ours, two Hindus were murdered and then, every day, an army major would visit our house saying, "You hand over your wife to us . . . " Yes, he would come in his jeep and demand that I be handed over to the Pakistan army so that they could finish me off. My husband never told me this, he would just walk up and down with this major outside the house saying, why don't you kill me instead of my wife? By god, every day this happened.

One day, my chachaji—he was still in Lahore in Model Town, this must have been in early September—he came to see us, very worried. Really worried. He said, give me some water, the police are after me. They had forced him out of his house at gunpoint saying, get out and take everything with you. Well, we gave him full protection, kept him in the barsati upstairs. If we gave him water to drink he would put it down and look abstractedly at us . . . he was absolutely broken. Somehow, with great difficulty, we managed to get him out of Pakistan but he told me later that every few miles they would stop, point a gun at him and say, "Should we kill you? Leave you? Kill you?" They went on like this all the way . . . when he reached Amritsar, he was a wreck.

Meanwhile, my life was still in danger. That major kept coming for many days, I would see them through the window . . . I don't know how T. dealt with this problem. Now my husband had many relatives there who were well placed. Frankly, I don't know how it was sorted out, he never told me and I never asked.

I started to work in the Walton refugee camp. There I dis-
covered åll the missing quilts and blankets from our house
and many other articles like suitcases, etc., which the Bhavra
thieves must have spared. A few days later, Allah Jawai who
was the local maalish wali, appeared at our door and offered
her services. She told me she had a message for me. This is
what she told me. "The Bhavras say we are sorry we had to
rob you. As far as your Hindu property is concerned, we have
vowed to leave you not a scrap. But your life we will protect
with our own, have no doubt about that. It is not only because
you have chosen to live here with us in Pakistan, but because
you are the daughter of a father who saved many of our lives.
Out loyalty is at your command."

My god! What a country, what a people. My own now.

. . . I didn't know then how they would react to our marriage, after Partition. I mean, one has seen great loves dwindle
into enmities in no time—so I wasn't sure. It had been such a
catastrophic change . . .

But you see this is a great thing about Muslims, once they
accept you, they take you to their hearts. Nobody resented me,
treated me differently . . . my brother-in-law opened his house
to us, we stayed with him, we left my father's house. The family accepted me, never ostracised me, but then one day, my
mother-in-law said, "Why don't you have a nikaah anyway."
Now in a nikaah you have to say, "La Ilahi, Il Lillilah . . . " and
so on, so I said to my husband, she's worried that she won't be
able to marry off your sisters so I'm thinking, let's have a
nikaah. We had had a civil marriage earlier—and you know, in
those days, you had to renounce your religion for that, I had
to say I'm not a Hindu, he had to say I'm not a Muslim. But
now he said, no, you don't have to go through a nikaah, not
for my sake. Please don't. But I said, I've decided, I've made
up my mind, I'll do the nikaah . . .

But then one day, in a fit of anger, I tore up the nikaahnama
and my husband said, actually if you and I live together without a formal marriage it'll be much better! There'll be much
less confusion. That is why he said he had torn our civil marriage certificate too! After his death I found the certificate—he
had not torn it. But we never were meant to part so we never
bothered. For me nikaah was just symbolic. In any case, I'm

such a bad Hindu . . . I remember I quoted Galsworthy's "White Monkey" to him. An Englishman was surrounded by all these Muslims who said unless you say, "La Ilah . . . " we'll murder you. So he said, if it matters so much to you I'll say it, because it matters nothing to me . . .

So, it meant nothing to me but I thought it might be important for my children. I don't know. I wanted to belong, I shouldn't keep myself divided, half here, half there, I should be fully on one side . . . you know, this is a Hindu concept also, become one with where you are . . . I can't say his family were orthodox but, you know, there was this social pressure . . . I did it because I thought this will smoothen my path, I've to spend my lifetime here, why not belong to them. Once I'd made my decision I never regretted it, didn't think twice about it.

I did not feel my identity would have to change because my husband never pushed anything on me. People say Muslim society is very intolerant but I think in certain ways it is more tolerant than Hindus. Those Sanatani Hindus who are orthodox, who have so many restrictions, are terrible to live with. Arya Samajis who were converting Muslims called this ceremony, *shuddhi*. Now *shuddhi* is a terrible word because it implies they were *napaak, ashuddh* and they became *paak* through conversion. These were unbearable words and acts for most Muslims. I myself found them unbearable. It is because of this attitude that Pakistan was created. You treat them like *achut*. Friends are visiting you at home and people are saying, keep their plates separate. Is this the way to treat people? Is this human? I couldn't tolerate this. Luckily my own family never did this, but if they had I would not have liked it one bit. There were many more factors which played a role, but Hindu orthodoxy *ne maar daala*. It has made a division even inside India.

I swear to you that at an individual level I did not feel any deprivation. I have said what I wanted to say, I have done what I wanted to do. In the family they just said she has different views. . . But the cultural deprivation was something else. Things were not accessible to me, dance, music . . . all the singers had left, the only ones who remained to sing were the prostitutes and their singing was so vulgar. I had brought my sitar, my tanpura, but my husband said you'd better hide them, people will say I've married a courtesan. Very reluctantly I put them away. I was so fond of music but I was aware of the distinctions that were being made . . . Suddenly, Muslims thought of singing as a bad thing . . . Life-styles also changed, but not so much because our families were of the same social and professional standing and there had been so much interaction before Partition. But I was a student of literature, wrote poetry, these things I felt much more. But you know, those days if I said I want to go to India to see some dance, I went. Sometimes I think I had the best of both worlds.

. . . There is resentment among Hindus and Muslims because of Partition, loss of property and so on, otherwise where is the resentment? When Hindus and Muslims meet each other abroad, in England or America, they instantly become the best of friends, even today. It is the politicians who are responsible for the divisions, for the hatred.

The British only took advantage of these inherent divisions, they harped on these. There must have been reasons also for Jinnah's feelings going sour. It could, of course, have been his ego, his desire to become a big leader, I don't know. Jinnah was no great Muslim, he married a Parsi woman.

. . . Even now many Indians have not accepted Pakistan. There is a friend of mine in India whom I have been inviting to visit Pakistan but she says she will visit Pakistan only when the two countries have become one, which of course means never. This is the meanest kind of possessiveness. We have to move on, we can't go back to the past.

You see, with Partition everybody lost. Pakistan lost in many. ways, their faith was shaken in a way. They were a big minority, an important part of the cultural life of India. But because Pakistan was created as a Muslim country, religious fanaticism was bound to take place. They started saying don't sing, don't dance. Those Muslims who uprooted themselves physically from U.P. and places had to uproot themselves culturally as well. It was more difficult for them, I think. I still had my roots in India.

But it can never go back to what it was. It can never be the same again.

The Lucknow Sisters: "Insecure, yes. Unsettled, no."

After Partition we felt an aloneness—some obstruction somewhere, in our work, lives, and there was difficulty. Our father was left here alone. Earlier all the brothers would look after the mango orchards, we had an income from there . . . then we didn't feel it so much. But after Partition when there was no work, no jobs, then we felt it.

Earlier, more people from here would go to visit Pakistan, one-way traffic, but now people come and go from both sides. The ones who come from there they are surprised to see that we worship so freely here, observe our religious duties, can say the azaan loudly. Nobody minds. Our Hindu neighbour, she always says when she hears the azaan in the morning, then she wakes up. So many people say how much they like the sound of voices in prayer from the masjid. . . .

If Maulana Azad's plan had been accepted by the Cabinet Mission the trauma of Partition could have been avoided . . . all the bloodshed and destruction . . . from Hyderabad to Punjab, the whole country was engulfed. We were fortunate in Lucknow because nothing happened here, people were extremely cultured. Hindus had economic power, nothing happened. Relations between Hindus and Muslims here were so good. Oh, don't ask . . . from the time of Wajid Ali Shah the relations were very close. Our grandfather's mazhar is here, he was a favourite of Akbar's— he gave him Lucknow and the neighbouring areas as an award. Since then the friendships have been strong. . . .

Women were all kept indoors, in parda, whether Hindu or Muslim, it was the same. The men had the same bad habits, good habits, whether they were the Rai Sahib or Khan Bahadur. Same love of good things . . . This was a society where the bonds were so strong, feelings ran so deep, outsiders can never be a part of it.

. . . Our uncle (Khaliquzzuman) left in 1947. It was winter, we were sitting outside when the trucks came. He came to say goodbye to Mian Jaan. We knew they were going—they didn't discuss anything with us, they might have talked to our father. A chartered plane was going to take them all and Apa would also have gone—she was older, 14, our parents wanted her to go because it was not safe, Ammi cried and cried—but there were too few seats. There was a cross on our house, too. Yes, we were afraid, our family was political, our Chacha was in the League. Nothing much happened but we were afraid, there was danger. Lakhs of Muslims went from Lucknow. . . Even if we had been able to go we would never have adjusted there. We were so attached to our parents and Abba Jaan absolutely refused to go. Ammi, too. It's very difficult to leave one's place—my uncles and others just left in the commotion, almost without thinking what are we doing . . . He was wealthy, Chacha, he thought there was danger . . .

Our home was a centre for the freedom struggle in the 1930s. All the big leaders came to our Chacha's house—Nehru, Patel, Sarojini Naidu, they used to come and stay during British raj, no one else would have taken such a risk. But slowly, they began to drift apart and Chacha left to join the Muslim League. And there he became a senior officer—he must have weighed everything before deciding . . . Our Phupa also left. Jinnah told him he had to go, there were very few people of his calibre in Pakistan. He was made the first advocate general, he felt he was required there. Our father could not have gone, he had very young children, he was 57–58, he was an artist, a zamindar . . . And he had a strong conviction, he did not want to leave even though his family was leaving. Chacha tried his best to take him, he called him many times afterwards, but our father did not once say he wanted to go. He would pace up and down, go out, come in, go out, come in. But he didn't hesitate, even for a minute. The *sukoon* (peace of mind) you get in your own place . . . Our Dadi and one Chachi were all that was left . . . It took Abba Jaan so long to recover from it. He didn't speak for such a long time. He never spoke about it. He went once to Pakistan, in '52–'53, his uncle had passed away and he stayed for three months. But he never wanted to live there—everything was all right, there were no problems, but return he had to. All his relatives were there but to move at his age—it wasn't possible.

He was silent for so many months. He used to go to a bookshop in Aminabad and sit there for hours, reading, reciting Hindi dohas. People loved to listen to him, dohas and Urdu poetry and stories . . . But he was very disturbed.

We went, too, we thought we might stay back, our two brothers were there, they were working, had good jobs . . . here there was no question of their getting any work. We went to settle them into their home, we rented a place in Karachi—but we couldn't adjust. *Dil nahin laga* otherwise maybe we would have stayed on. We didn't like people's attitude, it was showy, loud. We couldn't understand them—they had money, everything, but they seemed rootless. *Pair nahin tike.* We couldn't live away from Lucknow.

If Muslims had not gone to Pakistan they would have done the sensible thing. But all the top families left—if they hadn't they would not have got as much as they did in Pakistan. They could never even have imagined such property here. So many unemployed young men have gone from here—they didn't want to go but what chances did they have here? Now they go to the Middle East. For twenty years after Partition they kept going but they never settled down. One woman was told that now pigs roam the streets of Lucknow—she said, please give my love to those pigs!

We never wanted to go because this is our country. Our roots are here. We were homesick in Pakistan. People say Muslims belong in Pakistan but this is the greatest insult, a terrible accusation. What have we to do with Pakistan? It's like any other neighbouring country but that we should be loyal to it, that is unthinkable. We belong here, this is our nationality. To suspect us, to doubt us is a grave offence. When there are riots and the government does nothing then we do feel desperate, but that passes in a little while, it's over. And people have learnt to live with riots. Those who went away have never felt settled. This didn't happen to us, we have never had the feeling of being unsettled. Insecure, yes, unsettled, no. We're in our own place. When there's danger, we may feel insecure, but we're in our own home. Still, Partition cast a shroud of silence on our entire family. . . Why? We're all scattered, nothing remains—no Ids, no marriages, no celebrations, no happiness.

. . . By calling it an Islamic republic will Pakistan become Islamic? The day Muslims become Muslim you will automatically have an Islamic republic. Just by saying so, you can't make it one. *Yeh kehte kehte, Zia Saheb chale gaye.* (Zia ul Huq died trying to make it happen.) And you don't need an Islamic republic to observe Shariat. Nor is India secular—read forty years of our history and you won't find secularism anywhere. Every religion should be equal but this is not the case. Sometimes it seems the government is secular, at others, not.

In our history Hindu and Muslim rulers always fought—there were Hindus in the Muslim king's army and Muslims in the Hindu raja's army. The fight was between the rulers not the people. Today everyone is fighting each other, provoking the man on the street in the name of religion. The so-called custodians of religion don't know its first tenet, they cannot even read the *qalma* but they instigate fights in its name. Hinduism in danger! Islam in danger! It's all nonsense. Hindu-Muslim unity is a very old thing—they were one in 1857, two arms of the same body. But now Muslims are told, you don't belong here, you should go to Pakistan . . . Why Pakistan was made was because there, they thought, there will be one place where Muslims will belong, find jobs . . . So Partition happened because of religion . . . but there were other reasons, too.

. . . When we came back from Karachi because Abba Jaan had passed away we didn't realize our Chacha had made Pakistani passports for us, he thought we would stay there. We had to get a visa to come back. Then they wouldn't give us our Indian passports again. We said, it's a mistake, we live here, we don't live in Pakistan, we're Indians. They said, no, you are Pakistanis, you have Pakistani passports, you'll have to get visas. For 19 years we had to keep getting visas because they said you're not Indian. *Ab beta, hum na Hindustan ki taraf, na Pakistan ki—hum kehte hain, aap is garib aadmin ka masla tai karen, to hum aapko jaanen.* (So, we belong neither to India nor to Pakistan. We will be reconciled only when our peculiar problem is resolved.)

Taran: "Where is my country?"

Of course we were all emotionally affected by Partition—one of my masis (aunts) went mad in the camp at Wah—even though we never really suffered in a terrible way, we didn't lose any of our family members, we survived on what we had. We had some money and gold that we had brought with us. We managed, but for years we felt we had come to a foreign land.

I was born in 1931 in Nankana Sahib where my father used to teach untouchables. He had an M.Sc. and a B.T. at that time. My grandfather had instructed my father never to work for the British. We were five brothers and five sisters. I went to school at Atari and Preet Nagar. When Partition took place I had studied upto class IX and had to stop for a couple of years because of all the moving—we were in a camp for a year. I finished my matriculation later, but around this time I started writing poetry, love poetry!

. . . We saw it all. We started packing everything in huge trunks, all our trousseaus—utensils, clothes, everything—we packed the furniture and put it aside for our return. We took along just a few clothes and beddings for a month or two, after which we thought we would be back. So what if Pakistan is made? We'll stay on, anyway.

My father was a contractor; he was in Ranchi those days (August '47) on work. When he heard about all the violence he came to take us away, and we travelled for four days before reaching Ranchi. Two of my sisters who were in Pindi and Lyallpur were evacuated by the army later. After staying with our brother for a month we moved to a camp in Ranchi because we were assured of rations. There were more than 1,000 people in this camp, from all over — Sind, Gujrat, Bahawalpur. We stayed there for a year after which we bought a house, quite a big one for Rs. 5,000, but for years we felt we had come to a foreign land.

In Ranchi we all fell sick. There was no wheat, all we got to eat was rice and we weren't used to it. But I was still in the pink of health and looked after everyone. And we longed to meet some Punjabis—there wasn't a single one around. But, really speaking, we didn't mind all the hardship because we felt everything would be solved with independence. All the difficulties—no food, no medicines—were minor, we just waited for independence for our beloved country. How many songs of liberation I used to sing! I remember once when I was a little girl we had gone to Lahore and took part in a *jalsa*, singing these songs. One of them had a line in it which said: "Throw out the invaders, throw out the foreigners!" and the police arrested us for anti-government sentiments! We were schoolchildren! On August 14 I couldn't sleep! I just couldn't imagine what the dawn of freedom would feel like. At midnight we heard the gun salute—and for a moment I thought there was going to be trouble again. But it was the sound of celebration! Our joy was so much greater than our suffering. We were unhappy about Partition, of course, but we thought it was inevitable, unavoidable because of the attitude of Jinnah and Gandhi. Yes, even Gandhiji. If he had really been against it, it would never have taken place. The way he handled things, it led to Partition. Maybe he didn't want it but he accepted it. They used to sing songs, saying Gandhi had won freedom without blood, without swords—didn't they see how much blood was spilt? How many people died? How many women were killed, burnt alive?

In 1948 itself we realized that there was no going back to Pakistan. We lost everything we had left behind but now we were in our own country, safe and free. Of course we missed our homes, our old country—I still miss it, I still roam the streets of Punjab in my mind, I loved it—but it's like bidding farewell to your daughter when she gets married. We felt we had come home.

. . . A woman has no religion—her only religion is womanhood. She gives birth, she is a creator, she is god, she is mother. Mothers have no religion, their religion is motherhood. It makes no difference what they are, whether they are Hindus, Sikhs, Muslims or Christians.

We girls would often talk about death—some were afraid, others thought of it as a glorious death—dying for an end, for freedom, for our honour. For me everything was related to freedom, I was dying for freedom.

But 1984 was different—it shocked me.* We went to sleep on the night of (October) 31st, worried about what would happen the next day. We had started receiving phone calls from friends in other parts of the city informing us about arson and looting. The next morning when I looked out of the window I saw little children making off with shoes, TVs and other small things which they had looted. I was alone at home with my

---

*For about one week after Indira Gandhi's assassination in 1984, Sikhs in many north Indian cities were deliberately targeted for arson, looting and killing. More than 2,000 were killed in Delhi alone.

(deaf and dumb) daughter. I heard that they had set fire to rickshaws owned by Sikhs behind our house, near Khalsa College. In our neighbourhood a bookshop and a scooter shop were burnt—we wondered whether they had burnt the gurudwara.

Our neighbours upstairs asked me to move in with them because I was alone. I didn't know what to take along, what I might need. I didn't know what might happen. The killings had already begun. In the end I put whatever I could into a small plastic basket—one underwear, a sanitary napkin, one shawl, a sweater for my daughter and our toothbrushes.

The memory of '47 came flooding back, except that I feared this might be much worse. Even our neighbours had started looting—I just couldn't believe it. Our Hindu friends kept calling and informing us of what was happening elsewhere, warning us to stay indoors. I called the police station, only to be told, "You're still alive, aren't you? We'll come when something happens."

In the evening I told my neighbours we couldn't just sit around waiting for someone to come and kill us, we should do something to defend ourselves. But they were scared stiff and had virtually bolted themselves into their homes. My neighbour with whom we were staying said I would get them into trouble. There was another family on the top floor of our house and I went to them saying we should do something—but they didn't want to take any action.

I suggested to the family we were with that we connect the doorbell to an electric wire which could be activated if a mob arrived. Other friends said they were arming themselves with petrol bombs. I rushed down to my flat to get as much kerosene as I could. All the while my neighbour kept telling me that I would get them into trouble. But I told her I wasn't going to die like a mouse, trapped—I would die fighting.

In '47 I was too young to resist, to fight for my life. Our elders did the thinking for us. It's not that they gave up without a fight, they also defended themselves as well as they could. One of my relatives fought till he was completely overcome, and then killed his whole family himself. He survived then, but later went quite insane and died.

And here were all these people sitting with bowed heads

and folded hands, waiting to die! That's why I was so upset. Why shouldn't we fight for our right to live? Should we crawl on bended knees, begging for mercy? I refused to do that. Then, in '47, I might have been willing to die for freedom, but now I was fighting for my survival.

My neighbours said, "But who will fight? Where are the men?" I said, "I will—I'm a man." Another young woman said, "I am, too" and then a third. There were three of us now— although the husbands of the other two said, "Look, don't provoke anything, just ask for mercy." I refused. How can you succumb to criminals? But they weren't prepared to fight.

On the evening of November 2 my son's young friend rang and said he was coming around with some colleagues from the army to take me to safety. I couldn't take my neighbours' cowardice any more—one Hindu family in the neighbourhood said they would eliminate the "troublesome" Sikhs but spare the rest. Can you believe that some of the other Sikhs agreed to this criminal bargain? "Why meddle in other people's affairs?" they said.

I absolutely refused to go along. I told them that if anyone touched that family I personally would throw a petrol bomb at them from my house. Then they said, if they hear you talking like this they'll kill you too. "Go and tell them what I'm saying," I said, "this is how they will kill us, one by one, till none of us is left." When my son's friend arrived with the army truck I offered to take the other families along, but they were afraid that if they left their homes the neighbours would walk in. We had heard them saying drunkenly, "I'll take flat number 3, you go for the other one."

I felt I had lost everything. I was afraid my husband and son were both dead. They were both going to be travelling on trains and we knew what was happening on them. My neighbours begged me not to go, you're the one who's kept us together, they said. I felt I had nothing more to live for, but still I would die fighting. I said I would stay back on one condition, and that was if we all resisted together, put up a brave fight. They agreed, and I decided not to go. I told my son's friend that I would not leave.

That night we all kept vigil, made plans for the next few days. For five days we kept watch together, but I was so disheartened by their timidity, their fear. They feared for their lives, their property. They feared 1947.

But what happened in 1984 in Kanpur was very different—it happened in our own homes, our own country. 1984 was such a big shock. It was only then that I asked, "Is this the freedom we gave up everything for?" When the Hindu mobs shouted, "Traitors, get out!" I asked myself, "Traitors? Is this what I sang songs of independence for? Was handcuffed at the age of six for? Which is our home now?" I tell you, I felt a great sense of detachment from everything. Nothing mattered any more—home, possessions, people, had no meaning. 1947 was no shock, the shock is now. They have branded us by calling us traitors. I tell you truly, now even the Indian flag does not seem to belong to me. Nothing is mine any more, not even my own home. I'm not for Khalistan — I could never live in a country where they force religion down your throat, force you to pray, to wear a particular dress, certain colours, I can't stand the music that blares out of our gurudwaras. Why should I settle for one Khalistan when the whole country is ours? We fought for freedom for India, not for Khalistan. If we wanted a separate country we would have asked for it in 1947. Khalistan has been thrust upon us. But we want an open house, a big house with the breeze blowing through, not a small hut. I want the freedom to think as I like, to go where I please, to keep long hair, live like a Sikh, carry a kirpan if I want to. But I won't be forced by anyone.

Muslims had their reasons for demanding Pakistan; they had been dominated by Sikhs and Hindus for a long time. They were the working class, we were the exploiters. Hindus and Sikhs were traders, shopkeepers . . . economic reasons were important. And they knew they could never get the better of Hindus on the bargaining table, they were just too clever. And the Sikhs were with the Hindus.

We treated them badly—practiced untouchability, considered them lowly. We wouldn't eat with them—on stations there was Hindu water and Muslim water, Hindu food and Muslim food. People sold tea shouting, "Hindu chai, Mussalmani chai!" Everything was separate. When my grandmother travelled, if a Muslim happened to touch her food she would consider it polluted. At school, if a Muslim girl worked the hand-pump

Hindu girls wouldn't touch the water. This was normal. They would first clean the pump with mud (mud was cleaner than their hands!) and we used to do this to our own classmates, our friends. I never practised this, nor did my father, but he could do nothing about my Dadi. I went to Muslim homes, ate there but never told her about it. Untouchability was the main reason for Partition—the Muslims hated us for it. They were so frustrated and it was this frustration which took the form of massacres at Partition, of the ruthlessness with which they forced Hindus to eat beef . . .

I want to tell you about Barkat. My brother had a friend called Barkat. He was like a brother to us, we tied rakhi on him because he had no sisters. He had recently got married and the Sikhs abducted his wife . . . But I'll tell you about when I was about 12 and he was 16, 17. He was always at our place and he was very fond of me. We were very, very close—but we could never share the same plate with them. My Dadi just wouldn't allow it. She loved Barkat but couldn't tolerate his touching our water or food. If he used water in the bathroom and she, without knowing it, used it too, she would curse him and tell him he had polluted her, violated her religion. Barkat didn't stop coming to our house but he knew exactly what Dadi thought of him.

We are still in touch with Barkat—he lives in Lahore. Some years ago I went to Atari from Amritsar and saw my old home-town. I ran around like a child, totally uninhibited, went into our old home, saw where we had played . . . The people who lived in that house were very friendly; I went to meet our old neighbours and they recognized me. They told me Barkat had been there just the day before—he had gone to Jalandhar to see the cricket match—and my brother went all the way to Atari to meet him. They saw each other on opposite sides of the border and shouted across, telling the army to hurry up with the formalities, "Can't you see, my friend has come to meet me? Remove these barriers, quick, let us embrace each other." They wept when they finally met, it was so wonderful to see. They were together for four days.

I've never been able to visit Pakistan again but my older sister visited Lahore. Because Barkat is there, for us Pakistan is inhabited. In 1947 when my brother got married his baraat went to Lyallpur and Barkat went along. Rioting had begun so there was curfew in the city. We had to have passes to go through and tell everyone that Barkat was Barkat Ram! He was a League member, a big supporter of Jinnah's. We knew that, of course. When he came over my father would joke, "You'll only get a paratha if you curse Jinnah!" So he would say, "Pakistan, murdabad! Jinnah, murdabad! Now give me my paratha!"

. . . Those were beautiful days, and it was a beautiful relationship. Now, after Partition, after 1984, where is my country? In a way, my country is where I was born, which is Pakistan. Country is where you feel at home, where you are accepted, where you know the smell of the land, the culture, where you can breathe freely, think freely. But as a woman, if I cannot call a home my own, if my home is not mine, how can a country be mine?

Between Community and State

The question of where people "belong" when countries are divided along religious or ethnic lines has bedevilled this century more than any other. Siege, strife, civil wars that simmer or rage for protracted periods are such a present feature in so many countries that, in some ways, they seem almost to define them. But today's wars are fought by non-combatants. In every disturbed area of the world civilians are in conflict with each other over religion, ethnicity, resources, livelihood, life itself. Five per cent of World War I's casualties were non-combatants; in contemporary wars, 95 per cent are. As a result there are millions of refugees, political fugitives, voluntary exiles, asylum-seekers, those on the run; they are to be found mostly in the developing world, and a very large proportion of them are women and children.

The designation "stateless" is now so commonplace that it excites little comment, even as governments grapple with another category of people called "permanent liabilities". The repatriated Tamils of Jaffna and the Eastern Provinces, for instance, have no place to call their own in either India or Sri Lanka; "displaced persons" of erstwhile East Pakistan are still in a kind of limbo in India and live under the threat of being declared "infiltrators" or "illegal immigrants" any time. Any number of second-class citizens are to be found in every country of South Asia and, everywhere, those in a minority whether linguistic, ethnic or religious, are vulnerable.

Kamila's anguished cry, "Was I an Indian or had I ceased to be one by marrying a Muslim?" finds a heartbreaking echo in the Lucknow sisters' lament—"So we belong neither to India nor to Pakistan. We will be reconciled only when our peculiar problem is resolved." Their indeterminate status is mirrored in Taran's shocked yet poignant realization: "Traitor?" I asked myself, "Is this what I sang songs of independence for? Was handcuffed at the age of six for? Which is our home now?"

All the women were acutely conscious of their place and their identity as Hindu, Muslim or Sikh in either country, and communicated a highly developed sense of self in relation to both. Although Kamila and the Lucknow sisters seem to have reconciled their lives with their choices, their accounts nevertheless reverberate with things unsaid. Kamila, for instance, was extremely reluctant to speak about her status as a convert in a rapidly Islamising Pakistan; she kept reiterating her good fortune in being part of a cosmopolitan family and social community, both of which allowed her to gloss over the obvious tensions in her life. Any choice entails adjustment and some compromise, she said; but of course she was perfectly aware that, in her case, her choice acquired much greater significance because of Partition. Now, she had to choose one country over another, one religion over another, even though they might mean little to her, personally. Her children all have Muslim names (and she herself changed hers) because, she said, she didn't want them to be "confused" about who they were.

In conversation, the Lucknow sisters admitted that none of them married because all the "suitable" candidates had migrated to Pakistan. This particular condition was consequent upon, first, their father's decision to stay back and, second, their own decision to return to India from Pakistan where things might have turned out differently. The poignancy of this was not lost on them. Nor was the fact that materially they had suffered a double loss: losing their land as a result of the abolition of zamindari, and losing out by not accepting the offer of plenty in Pakistan. Accepting, instead, the insecurity of belonging neither here nor there.

Taran's predicament is the most explicitly stated of all, and the least ambiguous. Superficially, her situation was probably more stable than the others, but after 1984 she felt she could never be completely at ease again, anywhere. Her insight about her status went much beyond community and country, however—as a woman, she said, she now understood that she could not even call her home her own, so how could a country ever be hers? With blinding clarity she realized that she had no part to play in determining either.

Hindu, Muslim, Sikh; India, Pakistan, Khalistan, Bangladesh—redrawn borders, newfound countries and old communities forming and reforming each other through bitter contest. The play of identity politics in South Asia has become so volatile over the last few decades (almost since independence, in fact) that it begs the question: is there a stable national or regional identity in the subcontinent today? The definition of nationality has seen so many changes during this period that it defies any "lowest common denominator" basis.[2] In the post-Independence period, for example, India and Pakistan both proclaimed secular national identities, even though the national movement itself was made up of two competing "nationalisms" which eventually made for the division of India. Twenty-five years later a nationalism born of linguistic difference resulted in an earlier religion-based nationalism being replaced by a linguistic one: Bangladesh came into being. Since then, we have seen many nascent regional identities challenging the notion of a homogenous national identity as Sind, Baluchistan and the North West Frontier Province in Pakistan, and Punjab, Assam and Kashmir in India have come to the fore. In Sri Lanka, a Sinhala "nationalism" has resulted in a ten-year civil war and a demand for a separate Tamil eelam (state), and a syndicated Hinduism in India is threatening to "re-unite" the country around "culture" and "civilization". Meanwhile, both the Pakistani and Bangladeshi states have moved towards consolidating their Islamic character, Pakistan now as a highly militarized Islamic state, Bangladesh as an Islamic republic. The identity of the nation-state itself is thus continually redefined.

How and when women enter this redefinition is, of course, a question of religious, ethnic or linguistic affiliation but, as we have seen, it is also contingent on their status within religious and ethnic communities and their relationship with national processes. "Belonging" for women is also—and uniquely—linked to sexuality, honour, chastity; family, community and country must agree on both their acceptability and legitimacy, and their membership within the fold.[3]

The question: do women have a country? is often followed by: are they full-fledged citizens of their countries? Recent feminist research[4] has demonstrated how "citizen" and "state subject" are gendered categories, by examining how men and women are treated unequally by most states—but especially post-colonial states—despite constitutional guarantees of equality.[5] "The integration of women into modern 'nationhood'," says Deniz Kandiyoti, "epitomised by citizenship in a sovereign nation-state somehow follows a different trajectory from that of men."[6] The sources of this difference, she continues, are various and may have to do with the representation of nation-as-woman or nation-as-mother (Bharat Mata, for example) to be protected by her male citizens; they may have to do with the separation of the public-civil sphere (usually male) from the private-conjugal one (usually female); or with women as symbols of community/ male honour and upholders of "cultural values"; and most crucially, with their role as biological reproducers of religious and ethnic groups. Nira Yuval-Davis and Floya Anthias identify three other ways in which women's relationship to state and ethnicity can be seen as different from men's: as reproducers of the boundaries of ethnic or national groups; as participating in the ideological reproduction of the community; and as signifiers of ethnic or national difference. They point out that while feminist literature on reproduction has dealt extensively with biological reproduction and the reproduction of labour, it has "generally failed to consider the reproduction of national, ethnic and racial categories".[7]

State policies with regard to population, for instance, are a clear example of its active intervention in the reproduction of race or community. Yuval-Davis and Anthias demonstrate how fears of a "demographic holocaust" have influenced population policies in Israel, through extending maternal and child benefits to those Jewish women who bear more children. Similarly, the Malaysian government offers attractive incentives to Muslim women graduates, urging them to play their part in maintaining ethnic superiority in multiracial Malaysia.[8] Periodic calls to women to produce more sons as warriors and defenders of the nation also form part of this scenario. Our discussion on the recovery of Hindu and Muslim women, post-Partition, and the role of the Indian state in both reinforcing ethnic difference and reaffirming the necessity of regulating women's sexuality in the interests of national honour, underlined the significance of women as reproducers of ethnic and national boundaries. It also indicated how the state participates in maintaining patriarchal control in the private and conjugal domain, and demonstrated how its anxiety regarding sexual trespass mirrors that of the male brotherhood, whether familial or communitarian. Thus is Anderson's "deep comradeship of men" reaffirmed, and patriarchal privilege reinforced.

The intense preoccupation of the Indian state with women's appropriate sexual conduct finds legal articulation in the form of personal laws—Hindu, Muslim, Sikh, Christian, Parsi—which govern marriage, divorce, inheritance, custody and guardianship of children and adoption.[9] The simultaneous and parallel operation of civil, criminal and religious laws is in paradoxical relationship to the secular nationalism of the Indian state, and it brings us back to the question of women's equality, as citizens, before the laws of a secular country. Legal intimation of how women's individual rights as citizens can be abrogated *in the interests of national honour*, was found in the Abducted Persons (Recovery and Restoration) Act of 1949. The passing of the Bill without modification, despite legislators' reservations, proves that such an interest takes precedence over the fundamental rights of (female) citizens. (The suspension of the civil and democratic rights of citizens in the interests of national *security* is a familiar case, but here the issue is different.) Thirty-seven years later, in 1986, the state once again acted to demonstrate how women's rights could be suspended *in the interests of the community* when it enacted the Muslim Women's (Protection of Rights in Divorce) Bill. This Act specifically excluded Muslim women from the purview of Section 125 of the Criminal Procedure Code, a provision that enables a person to claim maintenance on grounds of indigence.[10] The law is secular and available to all citizens of India regardless of caste, creed, sex or race. Orthodox sections of the Muslim community claimed immunity from the law in question, saying it violated the Shariat or Muslim Personal Law under which a divorced Muslim man has no obligation to provide for his ex-wife. Pressure from this section, as well as a fair amount of political calculation resulted in the enactment of the Muslim Women's Bill, and the right of Muslim women to social and economic security was thus subordinated to the community's right to freedom of religious practice. Two constitutional guarantees—the equality of all citizens, and the freedom to practice and propagate one's religion—were in contest, and the latter prevailed.

Women, then, simultaneously but oppositionally, "belong" to community and country: to the former as far as the regulation of the personal domain is concerned; to the latter in all other civil and criminal matters. The state's willingness to "enter" the private domain in order to demonstrate its sensitivity to the question of community identity and rights is in direct contrast to its reluctance to "interfere" with the same domain by legislating in favour of women's equality within it. It does not require much analysis to see that, in effect, both responses are the same. So, all attempts by the women's and democratic rights' movements to gain gender justice in personal matters from a secular state have come to nought.[11] Stiff opposition from religious conservatives in all communities, as well as vociferous campaigning for a uniform civil code by extremist right wing Hindu political parties have ensured that women's status as citizens in India's secular national polity is fundamentally unequal. As Deniz Kandiyoti puts it:

> The regulation of gender is central to the articulation of cultural identity and difference. The identification of women as privileged bearers of identity and boundary markers of their communities has had a deleterious effect on their emergence as full-fledged citizens. . . evidenced by the fact that women's hard-won civil rights become the most immediate casualty of the break-down of secular projects.[12]

The rise of religious or cultural nationalism in all the countries of South Asia is cause for concern, in general, but especially for women because of its tendency to impose an idealised notion of womanhood on them. Such ideals are usually derived from an uncorrupted, mythical past or from religious prescriptions, and almost always circumscribe women's rights and mobility. When the question of ethnic or communal identity comes to the fore women are often the first to be targetted; the regulation of their sexuality is critical to establishing difference and claiming distinction on that basis.Then the question of where women "belong", of whether they emerge as full-fledged citizens or remain "wards of their immediate communities"[13] is contingent upon how the politics of identity are played out, and how their resolution takes place between community and state.

The preceding discussions and life-stories are an attempt at a gendered reading of Partition through the experiences of

women. In their recall, the predominant memory is of confusion, of the severing of roots as they were forced to reckon
with the twin aspect of freedom—the bewildering loss of
place and property, of settled community, of a network of
more or less stable relationships, and of a coherent identity.
Overriding all these was a violence that was horrifying in
its intensity, one which knew no boundaries; for many
women it was not only miscreants, outsiders or marauding
mobs they needed to fear—husbands, fathers, brothers and
even sons could turn killers. That terrible stunning violence
and the silencing pall that descended like a shroud over it
have always just hovered at the edges of history; breaking
the silence has exposed not only the cracks in family mythologies about honour and sacrifice, but the implicit consensus that prevails around permissible violence against
women during periods of highly charged communal conflict.

Family, community and state emerge as the three mediating and interlocking forces determining women's individual
and collective destinies; and religious identity and sexuality as determining factors in their realization of citizenship
and experience of secularism. Partition caused such a
major upheaval that it disrupted all normal relationships
on a huge scale and placed women in a relationship with
the state that was as definitive as that with family and community, and as patriarchal. It once again recast them as keepers of national honour and markers of boundaries: between
communities, and between communities and countries. The
dispute over abducted women and who their rightful claim-
ants were so compromised their status as to deny them every fundamental right as adult citizens. Each of their multiple identities—as women, as wives and mothers, as members of families and communities, and as citizens—was set
up against the other making any honourable resolution of
their predicament, impossible. Only an arbitrary and basi-
cally communalised response won the day; this, in turn,
made for women's quite different experience of citizenship,

for their identity was defined primarily as that of members of religious communities, rather than as subjects of a secular state.

Yet significantly, and linked to survival, the fact of Partition also paved the way for women's abrupt entry into the economic life of the country—as social workers, wage earners, breadwinners, farmers, teachers, professionals or students of one sort or another—in numbers that may otherwise have been spread over many years. The uncertainty of their circumstances and the break-up of the extended family pushed women and girls into the workplace and educational establishments, thus expanding their social space even as dislocation often entailed a drastically shrunk, or even completely alien, physical space. Such social mobility would no doubt have come sooner or later; Partition hastened the process. The incidence of mass widowhood, moreover, compelled the state to step in as social rehabilitator with far-reaching consequences both, for the women, and for the process of social reconstruction itself.

Neither India nor Pakistan has escaped the aftermath of Partition: their separate yet linked histories have played out the consequences of communal politics in full ingloriousness. 1947, 1964, 1967, 1971, 1984, 1992 are milestones not just for one country or two, but for the entire subcontinent. In between, and continuously, are the protracted battles fought over identity, national as well as sub-national. Those values and principles we took for granted in the first flush of freedom, democracy, social justice, secularism, pluralism—are besieged, bruised and battered. Ambiguity and equivocation mark the discourse of the state on these issues in India; strident obscurantism and belligerence in Pakistan.

In either case, the predictable outcome for women is: resurgent patriarchy. The endeavour has to be not for less "secularism" or the retreat of the state, but for a proactive secularism and a genuinely neutral state apparatus. A return to self-regulating communities has very regressive consequences for women; the importance of having the choice to exit the community cannot be over-emphasized, nor can the desirability of equality as citizens of a secular state be seriously challenged. The alternative, as demonstrated most violently and soberingly by Partition, is the eternal subordination of all other identities—gender, class, caste, region—to an exclusive and confining religious or ethnic community.

Notes

[1] Azhar Abbas, "The Twice Displaced", *Outlook*, Special Issue on Partition. May 28, 1997.

[2] Amrita Chhachhi, "Identity Politics", in Kamla Bhasin, Nighat Said Khan & Ritu Menon (eds.), *Against All Odds: Essays on Women, Religion & Development from India and Pakistan* (Delhi: Kali for Women, 1994), p. 2. See also Nighat Said Khan, Rubina Saigol & Afiya S. Zia, "Introduction" in Khan et al (eds.), *Locating the Self*: op. cit., pp. 5, 7. and Nighat Said Khan, "Reflections on the Question of Islam and Modernity", in Khan, et al, op. cit., pp. 77–95.

Feminist activists and academics have written extensively on the issue of the state, cultural identity and gender in South Asia, and the last twenty years have seen widespread mobilisation by the women's movements in all the countries of the region against religious fundamentalism and cultural chauvinism. It is not possible here to summarise the many debates and positions on the issue except to say that, generally speaking, their critiques have been sharp, and their analysis of the intersection of nationalism and gender, insightful. For a further elaboration of all the above, see also Kumari Jayawardena & Malathi de Alwis (eds.), *Embodied Violence: Communalising Women's Sexuality in South Asia* (Delhi: Kali for Women, 1996); Zoya Hasan (ed.), *Forging Identities: Gender, Communities and the State in India* (Delhi: Kali for Women, 1994); Tanika Sarkar and Urvashi Butalia (eds.), *Women and the Hindu Right: A Collection of Essays* (Delhi: Kali for Women, 1995); and Deniz Kandiyoti (ed.), *Women, Islam and the State* (Philadelphia: Temple University Press, 1991.)

[3] Recent writing and analysis by Indian feminists on the issue of the dalit (low caste) woman's unequal relationship to caste-community and citizenship has introduced the critical dimension of caste into the discussion, in important ways. In our view, their experience of inequality, as dalits and as women, underlines (rather than undermines) the case for gender just secular laws. See V. Geetha and T.V. Jayanthi, "Women, Hindutva and the Politics of Caste in Tamil Nadu," in Sarkar and Butalia (eds.), *Women and the Hindu Right*, op. cit.; pp. 245–69; Anveshi, "Is Gender Justice only a Legal Issue?" in *Economic and Political Weekly*, March 8, 1997; and V. Geetha, "Periyar, Women and an Ethic of Citizenship", unpublished paper, n.d.

[4] See especially, Nira Yuval-Davis and Floya Anthias (eds.), *Woman–Nation–State* (London: Macmillan, 1989); Marilyn Lake, "Personality, Individuality, Nationality: Feminist Conceptions of Citizenship 1902–40" in *Australian Feminist Studies* 19, Autumn 1994, pp. 25–38; Marie Leech, "Women, the State and Citizenship: Are Women in the Building or in a Separate Annex?" op. cit., in *AFS* 19, pp. 79–91; Deniz Kandiyoti, "Identity and Its Discontents: Women and the Nation" in *Millenium*, op. cit., pp. 429–443; Rian Voet, "Women as Citizens: A Feminist Debate" in *AFS*, op.cit; pp. 61–77.

[5] Yuval-Davis & Anthias, "Introduction" in *Woman–Nation–State*, op. cit., p. 6

[6] Deniz Kandiyoti, "Identity and Its Discontents", op. cit., p. 429.

[7] Yuval-Davis & Anthias, op.cit., p. 7.

[8] Chee Heng Leng, "Babies to Order: Recent Population Policies in Malaysia" in Bina Agarwal (ed.), *Structures of Patriarchy: State, Community and Household in Modernising Asia* (Delhi: Kali for Women, 1988); Deborah Gaitskell and Elaine Unterhalter, "Mothers of the Nation: A Comparative Analysis of Nation, Race and Motherhood in Afikaner Nationalism and the African National Congress", in Yuval-Davis & Anthias (eds.), op.cit., pp. 58–76.

[9] The Pakistani state's preoccupation with it led to the promulgation of the Hudood and Zina Ordinances in 1979, the most dramatic examples of state intervention in the personal domain in the subcontinent. For discussions on women/gender and Islamisation, generally, and the Shariat, in particular, see Shahla Zia, "Women, Islamisation and Justice", and Fauzia Gardezi, "Islam, Feminism and the Women's Movement in Pakistan" in Bhasin, Khan & Menon (eds.), *Against All Odds*, op. cit., pp. 70–81; 51–58. Also, Hina Jilani, "Law as an Instrument of Social Control" in Khan, Saigol & Zia (eds.), *Locating the Self*, op. cit., pp. 96–107.

[10] The Bill was enacted after the Supreme Court of India upheld a high court judgement that awarded Shah Bano, a poor 68 year old Muslim woman who had been divorced by her husband, maintenance of Rs. 500 a month. Her husband appealed the judgement on the grounds that it violated Muslim Personal Law, by which he and his ex-wife were governed. The case became a cause celèbre in many ways and was taken up by the Muslim clergy and religious fundamentalists under the rallying cry of "Islam in danger". The then Congress-I government knuckled under and passed the Bill in 1986.

11 There is a vast body of writing available on this subject and the debate has once more come to the fore with the Bharatiya Janta Party pressurizing the United Front government at the centre to fulfil the promise of the Constitution by enacting a uniform civil code. Women's organizations and political parties have participated in the debate and presented their views which are by no means unanimous. For a fuller discussion see, among others, Anveshi "Is Gender Justice only a Legal Issue? Political Stakes in UCC Debate", op. cit., Kumkum Sangari, "Politics of Diversity: Religions, Communities and Multiple Patriarchies", in *Economic and Political Weekly*, December 23 and December 30, 1995); Working Group on Women's Rights, "Reversing the Option: Civil Codes and Personal Laws", in *Economic and Political Weekly*, May 18, 1996; Draft Resolution of the All India Democratic Women's Association, "Equal Rights, Equal Laws", Delhi, December, 1995; "Visions of Gender Justice", Report of the Women's Groups Meeting, Bombay, December 1995.

12 Deniz Kandiyoti, "Identity and Its Discontents", op. cit., p. 443.

13 Ibid.

Appendix I

Abducted Persons (Recovery and Restoration) Act, 1949
(Act No. LXV of 1949)

An Act to provide, in pursuance of an agreement with Pakistan, for the recovery and restoration of abducted persons

WHEREAS an agreement has been reached between the Government of India and the Government of Pakistan for the recovery and restoration of abducted persons;

AND WHEREAS it is expedient to provide, in pursuance of the said agreement, for the recovery of abducted persons and for their temporary detention in camps pending restoration to their relatives;

AND WHEREAS the Governors of the United Provinces and East Punjab and the Rajpramukhs of Patiala and the East Punjab States Union and United States of Rajasthan have, under the provisions of sub-section (1) of section 106 of the Government of India Act ,1935 (26 Geo. 5, c. 2), accorded their previous consent to the making of this law;

It is hereby enacted as follows:

1. *Short title and extent.* (1) This Act may be called the Abducted Persons (Recovery and Restoration) Act, 1949.

(2) It extends to the United Provinces, the Provinces of East Punjab and Delhi, the Patiala and East Punjab States Union and the United States of Rajasthan and shall remain in force up to 31st October 1951.

2. *Interpretation.* (1) In this Act, unless there is anything repugnant in the subject or context,

(a) 'abducted person' means a male child under the age of sixteen years or a female of whatever age who is, or immediately before the 1st day of March, 1947, was a Muslim and who, on or after that day and before the first day of January, 1949, has become separated from his or her family and is found to be living with or under the control of any other individual or family, and in the latter case includes a child born to any such female after the said date;

(b) 'camp' means any place established, or deemed to be established, under section 3 for the reception and detention of abducted persons.

(2) In the application of this Act to any Acceding State, references to the Province and the Provincial Government shall be construed as references to that Acceding State or the Government of that State, as the case may be, and references to official Gazette shall be construed as references to the corresponding official publication of that State.

3. *Establishment of camps and notification thereof and of officers in charge.*

(1) The Provincial Government may establish as many camps in the Province as it may consider necessary for the reception and detention

of abducted persons, and any place established in the Province before the commencement of this Act for the reception and detention of abducted persons shall be deemed to be a camp established by the Provincial Government within the meaning of this section.

(2) The Provincial Government shall, as soon after the commencement of this Act as may be practicable, notify in the official Gazette all camps in the Province and the names of officers in charge thereof.

4. *Powers of police officers to recover abducted persons.*

(1) If any police officer, not below the rank of an Assistant Sub-inspector or any other police officer specially authorised by the Provincial Government in this behalf, has reason to believe that an abducted person resides or is to be found in any place, he may, after recording the reasons for his belief, without warrant, enter and search the place and take into custody any person found therein who, in his opinion, is an abducted person, and deliver or cause such person to be delivered to the custody of the officer in charge of the nearest camp with the least possible delay.

(2) In exercising any powers conferred by sub-section (1) any such police officer may take such steps and may require the assistance of such female persons as may, in his opinion, be necessary for the effective exercise of such power.

5. *Maintenance of discipline in camp.* (1) The Provincial Government may make regulations for the transfer of abducted persons from one camp to another and for the maintenance of health and good order in the camp and of harmonious relations among the abducted persons detained therein.

(2) In making any regulations under this section, the Provincial Government may provide that a breach thereof shall be tried and punished by the officer in charge of the camp in such manner as may be prescribed in the regulations:

Provided that no abducted person shall be liable to be tried in a criminal Court in respect of any offence made punishable by any regulations made under this section.

6. *Determination of question whether any person detained is an abducted person.* (1) If any question arises whether a person detained in a camp is or is not an abducted person or whether such person should be restored to his or her relatives or handed over to any other person or conveyed out of India or allowed to leave the camp, it shall be referred to, and decided by, a tribunal constituted for the purpose by the Central Government.

(2) The decision of the tribunal constituted under sub-section (1) shall be final;

Provided that the Central Government may, either of its own motion or on the application of any party interested in the matter, review or revise any such decision.

7. *Handing over of abducted persons to persons authorised.* (1) Any officer in charge of a camp may deliver any abducted person detained in the camp to the custody of such officer or authority as the Provincial Government may, by general or special order, specify in this behalf.

(2) Any officer or authority to whom the custody of any abducted person has been delivered under the provisions of sub-section (1) shall be entitled to receive and hold the person in custody and either restore such person to his or her relatives or convey such person out of India.

8. *Detention in camp not to be questioned by Court.* Notwithstanding anything contained in any other law for the time being in force, the detention of any abducted person in a camp in accordance with the provisions of this Act shall be lawful and shall not be called in question in any Court.

9. *Protection of action taken under Act.* No suit, prosecution or other legal proceeding whatsoever shall lie against the Central Government, the Provincial Government or any officer or authority for, or in respect of, any act which is in good faith done or intended to be done in pursuance of this Act.

10. *Power to make rules.* (1) The Central Government may, by notification in the official Gazette make rules to carry out the purposes of this Act.

(2) In particular, and without prejudice to the generality of the foregoing power, such rules may provide for—

(*a*) the constitution and procedure of any tribunal appointed under section 6;

(*b*) the manner in which any application to review or revise any decision of the tribunal may be made under section 6;

(*c*) the manner in which any abducted person may be delivered to the custody of any officer or authority under section 7 or restored to his or her relatives or conveyed out of India by any such officer or authority.

11. *Repeal of Ordinance XVIII of 1949.* (1) The Abducted Persons (Recovery and Restoration) Ordinance, 1949 (XVIII of 1949), is hereby repealed.

(2) Notwithstanding such repeal, anything done or any action taken in the exercise of any powers conferred by or under the said Ordinance shall be deemed to have been done or taken in the exercise of the powers conferred by this Act as if this Act were in force on the day on which such thing was done or action was taken.

Gazette, 28 December 1949.

Appendix II
Number of women and children recovered from Pakistan (December 1947–August 1955)

Punjab Pakistan	6.12.47 to 31.12.49	1.1.50 to 31.12.50	1.1.51 to 31.12.51	1.1.52 to 31.12.52	1.1.53 to 31.12.53	1.1.54 to 31.12.54	1.1.55 to 31.7.55	1.8.55 to 31.8.55	Total
Campbellpur Dera	12	24	39	13	1	:	:	:	89
Ismail Khan	15	3	4	:	2	:	:	:	24
Gujranwala	364	4	6	4	:	3	2	:	387
Gujrat	320	41	38	8	15	18	12	1	453
From Gujrat State	487	:	:	:	:	:	:	:	487
Kunja Camp (Gujrat)	950	:	:	:	:	:	:	:	950
Jhang	86	3	4	2	1	:	2	:	98
Jhelum	163	19	29	17	8	5	1	:	242
Lahore	181	11	15	9	7	3	9	:	235
Lyallpur	148	24	12	8	4	4	2	:	302
Mianwali	209	9	6	1	1	2	1	:	229
Montgomery	202	10	6	3	4	6	1	:	232
Multan	296	10	5	6	6	2	1	:	326
Muzaffarpur	95	5	12	1	:	:	3	:	116
Rawalpindi	180	51	21	16	5	7	6	:	286
Sargodha	104	3	5	2	5	2	2	:	123

									Total
Sheikhupura	229	5	8	7	1	:	3	:	253
Sialkot	615	55	24	19	10	8	6	1	818
Others	145	6	:	:	:	:	:	:	151
Total	4981	287	234	116	70	60	51	2	5801
Northeast Frontier	16	:	:	:	:	:	:	:	16
Dera ismail Khan Kohat	5	:	:	:	:	:	:	:	5
Other departments	392	23	8	16	25	3	5	:	472
Total	413	23	8	16	25	3	5	:	492
Baluchistan	10	:	:	:	:	:	:	:	10
Sind	30	12	9	5	16	4	8	:	84
Desi Rajya Bahawalpur	579	1	10	4	2	4	1	:	601
Others	:	:	:	:	:	:	:	:	:
Total	579	1	10	4	2	4	1	:	601
Jammu & Kashmir after 21.1.49	259	548	482	333	211	89	95	26	2043
Total no. of women & children recovered	6272	871	743	474	324	160	160	28	9032

Appendix II (contd.)

Number of women and children recovered from India (December 1947–August 1955)

Indian Punjab	6.12.47 to 31.12.49	1.1.50 to 31.12.50	1.1.51 to 31.12.51	1.1.52 to 31.12.52	1.1.53 to 31.12.53	1.1.54 to 31.12.54	1.1.55 to 31.7.55	1.8.55 to 31.8.55	Total
Ambala	660	63	174	74	96	37	20	1	1125
Amritsar	1095	125	207	52	133	98	50	2	1762
Ferozepur	1383	169	284	117	270	138	59	6	2426
Gurdaspur	987	59	115	53	73	22	5	...	1314
Gurgaon	54	8	9	13	16	...	...	1	101
Hissar	242	29	55	33	38	21	10	...	428
Hoshiarpur	413	35	47	33	46	19	6	...	599
Jalandhar	539	32	47	33	45	36	13	2	747
Kangra	218	9	43	7	...	11	3	...	292
Karnal	390	45	43	39	34	14	6	...	571
Ludhiana	744	92	133	65	152	58	16	1	1261
Rohtak	110	7	40	19	9	5	1	...	191
Simla	2	...	...	...	...	...	...	...	2
Others	1887	25	43	33	72	32	8	3	2103
Total	8724	678	1240	571	984	491	297	16	12921

Other Delhi areas	62	2	...	...	...	...	...	...	64
Patiala East Punjab									
Faridkot	230	27	30	21	35	26	9	...	378
Jind	288	22	8	12	30	7	2	...	369
Kapurthala	329	14	38	18	45	8	12	...	464
Nabha	609	96	93	84	111	71	17	...	1081
Patiala	1348	375	526	338	697	497	158	19	3924
Other States	476	...	...	7	...	...	8	...	491
Total	3280	534	695	480	918	575	206	19	6707
Rajasthan Alwar	163	13	9	3	6	2	...	1	197
Bharatpur	107	4	2	...	2	...	...	...	115
Other Departments	5	...	4	...	2	3	7	2	23
Total	275	17	15	3	10	5	7	3	335
Jammu & Kashmir after 21.1.49	211	162	24	108	128	43	24	1	701
Total no. of women & children recovered	12552	1413	1974	1162	2040	1114	434	39	20728

Source: Kamla Patel, *Mool Suta Ukhadela.*

Index

Robinson, Francis 6

Sachar, Lala Bhimsen 36
Sangari, Kumkum 199, 202
Sarabhai, Mridula 49, 69–70, 74–
    75, 78–79, 83, 85, 91, 97, 99,
    101–03, 107, 127, 152, 185,
    190–91, 193–95, 197, 199, 202
Scott, Joan 11, 25, 199, 202
secularism 107; and nationalism
    4; and the state 122–126, 159
Sedgwick, Eva 109
sexuality *See Women's sexuality*
Shah Bano 259
shame *See Honour*
Sheikh, Farzana 5, 22
Sheikhupura Tragedy 49 *See also*
    Refugees
Singh, Giani Kartar 36
Singh, Tara 36
social reform movement 108
social relations between religious
    communities, affection/amity
    3, 12; *See also Communal;*
    prejudices/taboos 12
Somavanti 216–23, 229
state, the (Indian) 11, 97; and its
    Recovery Operation 107, 159,
    252 *See also Abducted Persons*
    Bill and Recovery; and the role
    of women 109; as abductor
    125; as parent-protector *(mai-*
    baap) 123–24, 148, 153, 159,
    161–62, 252; as rehabilitator
    20, 256; equality in the nation-
    state 109; ideology of 110; role
    vis-à-vis female citizens 21;
    role vis-à-vis Hindu and
    Muslim communities 21;
    modernity and 108; secularity,
    sexuality and 122–26, 160, 252,
    254
Stree Shakti Sanghatana 14, 25–26

stories *See Life stories*
suicide 42, 45–46, 51–54, 77;
    celebration of 56; threat of 98
Sunder Rajan, Rajeshwari 200,
    202

Taran 46, 56, 230, 250
Thapar, Krishna 91–93, 170, 193,
    199, 200
Thapar, Premvati 169–70
trains, out of Pakistan 142–43;
    violence on 37, 177, 188;
tribunal 105–06
two-nation theory 4, 5, 6, 12
Tyagi, Mahavir 105

Uniform Civil Code 254, 260
United Council for Relief and
    Welfare/Rehabilitation 151,
    188–89

violence, against minority
    communities 33, 35, 49, as
    reprisal 39, 76; **against**
    women 11, 19, 20, 31–64,
    amputation of breasts 43–44,
    as a means of desexualising a
    woman 44, burning 32,
    communal 3, 9, 12, 54, 58, 63,
    255, disfigurement 32, ethnic
    8, gendered telling of 54,
    mutilation 43–44, patriarchal
    consensus on 60, Partition 11,
    229–31, 255, permissible 31,
    255, rape *See Rape*, sexual 41,
    42, 195, tattooing bodies 43;
    and death 37; and exchange of
    popula-tions 123; arson 35, 49,
    196, 210, 216; brutality 38, 39,
    42–43, 57, 174, 196, 208;
    forcible recovery as an act of
    40, 57, 105; looting 35, 49, 196,
    231; mob violence 39; murder